W9-BWD-399

THE RISE OF MODERN RELIGIOUS IDEAS IN AMERICA

— Editorial Director —

SYDNEY E. AHLSTROM, American Studies Program, Yale University

GEORGE S. MORRIS

Philosophy and Christianity

*A Series of Lectures Delivered
in New York, in 1883, on the
Ely Foundation of The Union
Theological Seminary*

BR
100
.M67
1975

Reprint Edition
with a New Introduction

BR100.M67 1975 ST. JOSEPH'S UNIVERSITY
Philosophy and Christianity : STX

3 9353 00153 9897

THE REGINA PRESS

154763

Reprint Edition 1975

THE REGINA PRESS
7 Midland Avenue
Hicksville, New York 11801

New Introduction © 1975 by The Regina Press

Library of Congress Catalog Number: 74-78279
International Standard Book Number: 0-88271-016-8

This volume is reprinted from an original in the Yale
University Library according to the standards established in 1972 by the Rare Book Libraries' Conference
on Facsimiles.

Manufactured in the United States of America.

INTRODUCTION TO THE REPRINT EDITION
by Sydney E. Ahlstrom,
American Studies Program,
Yale University

NO SPECIAL PLEADING or complex argumentation is required to establish the importance of George Sylvester Morris (1840-1889) as a major figure in the history of American philosophy. He was the effective founder of a strong philosophic tradition at the University of Michigan and a leading proponent of the academic professionalization of philosophy in the United States. He was an early proponent of idealism and perhaps the first American thinker to develop, in his own distinctive way, a dynamic and organicistic Neo-Hegelian point of view. He was a powerful influence, both directly and indirectly, on the philosophic development of several other major thinkers, most notably John Dewey, whom he enlisted as a colleague at Michigan. And finally, he made a major contribution to what he called the intellectualization of Christianity, and thus gave considerable impetus to the process by which philosophical idealism became a major element in the liberal theologies of the later nineteenth century.

Morris was born in the town of Norwich, Vermont, and grew up in a family where Puritan nurture was a lively reality. His training in this tradition was continued at Dartmouth College across the Connecticut River in Hanover, New Hampshire, where he was the most outstanding student in his class. After a stint in school-teaching and nine months in the Union Army he entered Union Theological Seminary (New York) in 1864. Here he came under the strong influence of Professor Henry Boynton Smith, a leading intellectual voice in the "New School" Presbyterian Church whose own personal theological outlook had been transformed by studies in Germany. Under such tutelage Morris's thinking shifted away from the Scottish Realism taught at Dartmouth and toward the historical and idealistic tendencies then so prominent in the German universities. Encouraged by Smith, he changed his vocational aims from the ministry to university teaching and during 1866-67 studied languages, philosophy, and theology in Europe. The most direct influences on his thought during this period came from Smith's friend at the University of Halle, Hermann Ulrici and from Friedrich A. Trendelenburg of Berlin, who was then at the height of his influence as a critic of Hegel and a critical champion of Aristotle. In 1874 Morris published an article on Trendelenburg that significantly enlarged that philosopher's American reputation. In it one finds the crucial quotation that "the organic conception of the world, founded in Plato and Aristotle is the principle that must animate the philosophy of the future." This conviction remained central to Morris's development, though it gradually led him to a greater appreciation of Hegel than Trendelenburg might have approved.

On returning to America Morris was forced, as Hegel and Trendelenburg had been, to become a private tutor for a time; but like both of them as well, he devoted his spare time to a work that established his reputation: a translation of Ueberweg's famous history of philosophy, which was published in two volumes (1871-73). In 1871 he was appointed to the faculty at Michigan as a professor of modern languages. In 1878 he began teaching philosophy at The John Hopkins University in Baltimore, and in 1880 became a professor there, in which year he also published his *British Thought and Thinkers*. Then finally, in 1881 when circumstances were propitious, he was offered the chairmanship of the philosophy department at Michigan, a position which he held until his death.

The long and steady process by which Morris moved to his mature philosophical outlook has been described in detail by M. E. Jones in his biography. But probably his most important observation for present purposes is that the Ely Lectures, delivered at his *alma mater* are, according to the same authority, "the most important single expression as well as climactic exposition by Morris of his own positive views." Here in a context that was both Christian and academic he expounded two of his fundamental philosophic positions. *First*, an organic view of the universe in which religion is seen as subsisting in the form of a relation between God as a spirit and man as a spirit (a view which according to Morris's earlier biographer places him on the "Hegelian Extreme Right"). *Second*, a view of philosophy's place in institutions of the higher learning as a theory of knowledge and a theory of being, the science of sciences itself. This book, therefore is of considerable consequence not only in the history of American religion and philosophical speculation but in the history of education.

Biographical Suggestions:
Herbert W. Schneider, *History of American Philosophy* (1946) and Henry A. Pochmann, *German Culture in America 1600-1900* (1957) place Morris's life and thought in the larger context of the late 19th century flowering of philosophical idealism. R. M. Wenley, *The Life and Work of George Sylvester Morris* (1917) is a basic biographical source. Marc Edmund Jones, *George Sylvester Morris: His Philosophical Career and Theistic Idealism* (1948) provides a meticulous and subtle developmental exposition.

PHILOSOPHY AND CHRISTIANITY.

PHILOSOPHY AND CHRISTIANITY

A Series of Lectures

Delivered in New York, in 1883, on

THE ELY FOUNDATION OF THE UNION THEOLOGICAL SEMINARY

BY

GEO. S. MORRIS, Ph.D.

PROFESSOR OF ETHICS, HISTORY OF PHILOSOPHY, AND LOGIC, IN THE UNIVERSITY
OF MICHIGAN, AND LECTURER ON ETHICS, AND THE HISTORY OF PHI-
LOSOPHY, IN THE JOHNS HOPKINS UNIVERSITY, BALTIMORE

NEW YORK
ROBERT CARTER & BROTHERS
530 BROADWAY
1883

Copyright, 1883,
BY ROBERT CARTER & BROTHERS.

St. Johnland
Stereotype Foundry,
Suffolk Co., N. Y.

Cambridge:
Press of
John Wilson & Son.

PREFACE.

——o——

THIS series of lectures was delivered, by appointment, as
the fifth course on the foundation established in the Union
Theological Seminary by MR. ZEBULON STILES ELY, in the
following terms:—

"The undersigned gives the sum of ten thousand dollars to
the Union Theological Seminary of the city of New York,
to found a lectureship in the same, the title of which shall
be 'THE ELIAS P. ELY LECTURES ON THE EVIDENCES OF
CHRISTIANITY.'

"The course of lectures given on this foundation is to com-
prise any topics that serve to establish the proposition that
Christianity is a religion from God, or that it is the perfect
and final form of religion for man.

"Among the subjects discussed may be,—

"The Nature and Need of a Revelation;

"The Character and Influence of Christ and his Apostles;

"The Authenticity and Credibility of the Scriptures, Miracles, and Prophecy;

"The Diffusion and Benefits of Christianity; and

"The Philosophy of Religion in its Relation to the Christian
System.

"Upon one or more of such subjects a course of ten public
Lectures shall be given at least once in two or three years.
The appointment of the Lecturer is to be by the concurrent

action of the directors and faculty of said Seminary and the undersigned; and it shall ordinarily be made two years in advance.

" The interest of the fund is to be devoted to the payment of the Lecturers, and the publication of the Lectures within a year after the delivery of the same. The copyright of the volumes thus published is to be vested in the Seminary.

" In case it should seem more advisable, the directors have it at their discretion at times to use the proceeds of this fund in providing special courses of lectures or instruction, in place of the aforesaid public lectures, on the above-named subjects.

" Should there at any time be a surplus of the fund, the directors are authorized to employ it in the way of prizes for dissertations by the students of the Seminary upon any of the above topics, or of prizes for essays thereon, open to public competition.

"ZEBULON STILES ELY.

"NEW YORK, MAY 8th, 1865."

With the consent of Mr. Ely, and of the Faculty of the Union Theological Seminary, the following lectures were repeated, in the first month of the present year, at the Johns Hopkins University, in Baltimore.

The Table of Contents is a reproduction, almost without change, of a "Syllabus" of the course, which was distributed among the auditors.

Figures, embodied in the text, refer to notes contained in the Appendix.

JUNE 11, 1883.

TABLE OF CONTENTS.

——o——

LECTURE I.

RELIGION AND INTELLIGENCE.

LECTURE II.

THE PHILOSOPHIC THEORY OF KNOWLEDGE.

LECTURE III.

THE ABSOLUTE OBJECT OF INTELLIGENCE; OR, THE PHILOSOPHIC THEORY OF REALITY.

LECTURE IV.

THE BIBLICAL THEORY OF KNOWLEDGE.

LECTURE V.

BIBLICAL ONTOLOGY:—THE ABSOLUTE.

LECTURE VI.

BIBLICAL ONTOLOGY:—THE WORLD.

LECTURE VII.

BIBLICAL ONTOLOGY:—MAN.

LECTURE VIII.

COMPARATIVE PHILOSOPHIC CONTENT OF CHRISTIANITY.

PHILOSOPHY AND CHRISTIANITY.

—oo;o;oo—

LECTURE I.

RELIGION AND INTELLIGENCE.

I PRIZE highly the privilege of addressing you on
the theme chosen for the subject of this course
of lectures. At the same time I appreciate rever-
ently the responsibility resting upon one who under-
takes to deal with such a theme. We are about to
lay inquiring hands upon the foundations of the most
sacred and the purest interests of humanity—the
interests of religion and intelligence. Deeper and
more impregnable foundations than these, we may
be sure, there are none. Whatever we may do, we
cannot shake them. They constitute the rock of
ages, which can never be moved. May we only be
permitted, in our way and measure, to demonstrate
—that means simply to point out, to show, to bring
into clear and evident sight—anew what that rock
is, and how religion and intelligence both rest upon
it in harmonious union and to the complete satis-
faction of man's highest, spiritual and intellectual
needs.

To-night we are, by way of introduction, to enter
upon a more general, preliminary consideration of

the relations which, from the nature of the case, may or must exist between religion and intelligence.

And first we note that religion, even if it should be held to involve, in itself, no function of intelligence—nay, even though it were regarded as involving the complete subjection or abrogation of intelligence in the religious subject—cannot withdraw itself from the liability of being made an object of intelligence, *i.e.*, of what is called intelligent or scientific inquiry and examination. To this liability it is subject in common with every other conceivable phase, phenomenon, or incident of the world of reality in which we are placed. Intelligence, thought, knowledge, consciousness, must have its object. This object may be intelligence itself, or anything whatever that enters within the realm of man's conscious knowledge or experience. Its relation to intelligence may be purely, or, at all events, predominantly mechanical, external, accidental. Objects in such relation are, for example, stocks and stones, in which, as first perceived, intelligence does not, in any especial degree, find itself reflected, or through the mere taking cognizance of which it does not find itself specially strengthened or built up. They are *there*, the intelligent subject is *here*—mechanically separate from and independent of them. They are viewed as casual, not necessary objects of his intelligence. He takes note of them and observes that they "are there," that they exist; perhaps, if he belong to a learned society or, for any other reason, be disposed to cultivate the scientific

habit of mind, he enters into a more minute examination of them; he subjects them to the test of fire
and of hammer, and, after taking copious notes of all
that he observes, is ready to inform the world respecting the phenomena of stocks and stones. He
has met the first requirement of intelligence respecting stocks and stones. He has ascertained and knows
the immediate, sensibly demonstrable facts about
them. But, I repeat, his relation to them is, so far,
relatively and characteristically mechanical and accidental. Certain " objects," " facts," or " phenomena" are brought—it may be either wholly fortui-
tously, or in consequence of a systematic intention
on the part of the inquirer—within the range of
his observation, and he simply observes and records
the first and direct result of his observation.

Now anything whatever that comes within the
range of conscious intelligence may and in the first
instance must be made an *object* of intelligence, in
the foregoing sense. The first and lowest, but, also,
indispensable condition of knowledge, is, to be aware
of the objects of knowledge; to take note that they
are there, "before the mind"—as men say—or within
the range of conscious experience, and then to observe how, or with what phenomena they exist,
under what guise and in what relations they immediately appear. Now, religion "is there," exists in history and among men, nations, and tribes at
the present day Nay, what are called "religions"
exist, with characteristic, visible marks of agreement
or of disagreement among themselves. Upon them,

as objects in purely mechanical relation to intelligence, the latter may fix its attention. It may do
this in the same unbiased way, or with the same
absolute freedom from presuppositions, with which
it addresses itself to the analytic observation and
description of rocks and trees. Looking at religion
in its manifestations as one among the many different objects *presented to* intelligence, its first work
will be to take accurate note of all these manifestations, whatever they may be, whether existing in the
form of myth or fable, of sacred legend or story,
of dogma or of practice, of rites, ceremonies, etc.
The result of all this praiseworthy and indispensable industry will be what is called the "Science of
Religions." From such mechanical relation to intelligence, religion—or, rather, religion viewed with
reference to its visible or historic phenomena—cannot withdraw itself.

But the forementioned industry—an industry like
that of the ant, being devoted to the amassing and
orderly arranging of multitudinous items of information respecting particular facts or classes of facts—is
only the beginning of, or, better, the mere scaffold-
ing for, the true and complete work of intelligence.
It is the first step leading to complete or absolute
intelligence, or *comprehension;* but it is only that.
I may, for example, know the names of all the classes,
orders, families, genera, species, or what not, of living existences; I may be familiar with their habitats,
their modes of life, their peculiarities of form, color,
etc., and yet I may not know what life is.   What I

know is precisely the special *modes*, the phenomena, of life, these alone—but not *what* it is to *live*. The *essence* of life may still be to me a profound mystery. I may still be wholly unaware that, in Aristotle's just and pregnant phrase, "life is energy of mind." And so, too, with regard to stocks and stones, I am far from having absolute intelligence respecting them, when I am simply able to describe their immediate, phenomenal properties. In addition to their possession of these properties, these objects have this distinction, viz., that they *exist*, that they *are*, that they in some way possess *being*. In what way or sense do they *exist*? Wherein does their *being* consist? They are, by common repute, material objects. But *what* is it to be material? Is material existence absolute and independent existence? Is there such a thing as absolute matter, wholly independent of and unrelated to spirit? Or is what we call material existence only a dependent function of Absolute Mind —a part, for example, (speaking in Berkeleian fashion) of the Logos, the word or language, through which the Absolute Spirit, God, expresses himself to his finite children? These are questions to which intelligence must find an answer, before its work can be called ideally complete. They are questions which are imposed upon intelligence, by virtue of its own nature. And questions such as these, relating to absolute *essence* and *cause*, are precisely those which form the special subject-matter of *philosophy*.

Now just as little as religion can withdraw itself from the liability of being made the object of scien-

tific observation and thus of being brought into at
least a mechanical relation to intelligence, just so
little can it evade the liability, nay, the necessity,
of being brought into that nearer relation to intelligence which philosophic inquiry involves. The
science of *religions* must be followed by the philosophy of *religion.* After learning what are the phenomena of religion, intelligent man must ask, *What
is religion?* Is it an hallucination, or a well-founded
reality? Is it a mirage, or do those who breathe
its atmosphere constitute the true city of God on
earth? The question must and will be asked. Nay,
it is asked, and has again and again been asked.
Religion has been and is sure, over and over again,
to be placed in the crucible of philosophic intelligence, and its votaries cannot with indifference look
upon the result of this test. Shall this result be,
in the language of a recent foreign writer,[1] that
religion "is nothing more nor less than a belief in
conflict with experience, and resting on the most exaggerated fancies," or that—in the words of him who
may be regarded as the profoundest and most deeply
experimental philosopher of modern times[2]—religion,
in the territory of human consciousness, is "that region, in which all riddles of the world are solved, all
the contradictions of speculative thought are reconciled, all agonies of the feeling heart are allayed,—
the region of eternal truth, of eternal rest, of eternal
peace?" If any doubt exists as to the answer which
real philosophy, real intelligence, real and complete
experimental inquiry, gives and must give to this

question, this state of things cannot but be looked upon by religion with the greatest concern.

There is indeed a "knowledge that puffeth up," or, rather, that is itself puffed up, being like a bubble, without real or absolute content and substance, and from which religion has, in the long run, nothing to fear. It is a "wisdom of this world" and of "the princes of this world, that come to nought." That is to say, it is a wisdom, a knowledge, all of whose categories or conceptions are derived purely from analytic observation of "this world" on the side of its absolute relativity, as sensibly presented in the conditioning forms of space and time; in short, as a world of relations which are purely and only finite. It boasts of being in the highest degree concrete, while in reality it is in the highest degree abstract. For while it makes the foregoing boast, it declares with equal boastfulness—or else with mock-humility—that it considers only phenomena, and not absolute causes and essences. It abstracts—looks directly away from—the infinite and absolute, which the finite as well reveals as conceals, and by and through whose power and essence the finite *is* and has its nature. It abstracts, therefore, from the essential, from the absolute content and substance, in order to fix its attention exclusively upon the phenomenal sign or symbol. It reads the *language* of the absolute—for this is what we may call "this world" of sensibly finite relations—and ignores its meaning. And this is indeed nothing other than the legitimate work and method of pure mathemat-

ical and physical science, whose true and intelligent
votaries, being aware of the special ontological limitations of their peculiar work and method, are also,
and consequently, aware that these limitations prove
nothing, *pro* or *con*, respecting the absolute limitations or range of intelligence. But there are those
who seek—by usurpation, as it were—to make themselves "princes of this world"; *i. e.*, who adopt this
realm of knowledge as their kingdom of intelligence;
nay, who proclaim this to be the only and absolute
kingdom of intelligence for man; and who, consequently—and very naturally—in the matter of absolute and final knowledge respecting essential truth
and reality, "come to nought." Their last word is
not a proclamation and demonstrative exhibition
of that truth of everlasting and essential reality
and power and life—that truth of Eternal Mind and
Love—the knowledge of which is, for religion, "eternal life," and for philosophy the consummation of
all labor of intelligence. Not this is their last word,
but—Agnosticism! Assuming to speak not simply
for themselves, but for all mankind, in the past, the
present, and the future, they pronounce the verdict,
Ignoramus et ignorabimus. The absolute, they say,
is the unknowable. Now this doctrine has surely
nothing but the form of knowledge without its substance; and this, I repeat, because in the very choice
and adoption of its peculiar data, presuppositions,
and method, it abstracts from the substance. It
finds, naturally, in its conclusions no more than
its premises contained. This *formal* knowledge,

then, with reference to religion, finds its only positive labor in collecting, classifying, and generaliz-
ing the phenomena of *religions*. It thus attains, at
most, only to a so-called science of *religions*, but not
to science of *religion*. It can exhibit great stores
of information in discussing the former, but is dumb
with reference to the latter; or, confessing that in "religious ideas" there is a "vital element,"[3] finds this
element in man's invincible and enslaving ignorance,
rather than in his practical and theoretical possession, through intelligence, of that truth, which, since
it makes man spiritually free, can have no other truth
superior to it, *i. e.*, is absolute.

From such abstract, negative wisdom, religion,
if it be indeed a concrete reality, has nothing to fear.
Agnosticism, as a cloud formed from the mists of
dogmatic ignorance, may temporarily—and perhaps
will always, in scattered, shifting places—cast a
chilling and confusing shadow. But like all that is
purely negative, it will be chased away by the sun-
light of positive, experimental reality. The concrete always thus triumphs over, persists in spite of,
and refutes, the abstract. So it was, in the case of
the issue between the Christian Church and English
Deism. The implicit and in itself thoroughly justifiable, though ill-defined, aim of the latter was to compass a philosophy of religion. But the theoretic or
philosophic bases, on which it went to work, were extremely abstract, dogmatic, narrow, being mainly derived from Locke, and being in kind the same on
which, too, nowadays the substanceless, spectral

structure of Agnosticism is reared. It was no wonder, therefore, that Deism ended, not in real comprehension of religion, but in conceptions, the adoption
of which cuts the nerve of all religion,—the conceptions, namely, of God either as a purely tran-
scendent and mechanical First Cause, or else (as in
the case of Hume) of God as a being whose existence
is wholly indemonstrable. Against such negative
results as these the Church triumphed—not so much
because the theoretic or quasi-philosophic principles
which its defenders at that time nominally accepted
as a basis of argument were superior to those of their
adversaries; on the contrary, many of the leading
Apologists swore by the same philosophic (*i. e.*,
Lockeian) tenets as the Deists;—it triumphed because there was in it something living and concrete, an element of vital, self-evidencing and self-
propagating reality.

I may add that, even if religion were pure illusion,
it would not necessarily have anything to fear from
the philosophy of Agnosticism. An illusion has, at
all events, this dignity, viz., that it is a phenomenon;
and an illusion which, like religion, is as widespread
as the human race, can scarcely dread detection
from a philosophy which professes to know *nothing
but phenomena*, and which, therefore, making this
profession, has no right to single out a particular
phenomenon and assert, or attempt to prove, that
it is unfounded in—has no true correspondence with,
or relation to—absolute reality.[4]

With reference, then, to any attack upon religion

which may come, or appear to come, from Agnostic quarters, religion may consider herself essentially safe. She may do this, because history has demonstrated that she is, with reference to such attack, invulnerable, and also because, in the matter of resistance to it, the cause of religion is, from the very nature of the case, identical with the cause of philosophy; and philosophy is, among other things, and first of all, the demonstrative, experimental refutation of Agnosticism.

For philosophy, let me remind you, has an historic and indeed, like religion, a perennial existence. It exists as demonstrative and in the highest and most pre-eminent degree experimental science. Indeed, philosophy may well be defined, in distinction from all other sciences, as the science of experience as such. It determines—finds out and declares—what is the absolute nature of experience, and what is that nature of being, of reality, which is given in and is organically one with experience. Twice, in the history of occidental thought, has philosophic science reached its flood-tide, first in the classic philosophy of Greece, with Plato and Aristotle, and again in the now classic philosophy of Germany. *Results* were reached in both cases—not disparate and opposed, but confirming and complementing each other. How should this be otherwise?—since the subject-matter of inquiry, viz., the world of man's conscious experience, or what we call the world of reality, and the agent of inquiry, viz., human intelligence, were in both cases the same. So modern mathematics does not overturn, it only supplements and extends, ancient mathematics.

The results of philosophic inquiry exist, then, and are embodied in literary monuments accessible to the world. These results, too, have been wrought or assimilated into the intellectual life-blood of the western world to a remarkable degree and with most influential effect. The classic philosophy of Greece was the intellectual rudder of a score of centuries. With its aid Christianity itself, in the persons of its earliest apologists, first took its bearings in the world of intelligence, found and further made itself at home in this world, and so was the better able to commend itself successfully to a pagan world, waiting to receive its light. Nay, more than one Christian apostle found in the armory of Greek philosophy the words and conceptions best adapted to convey, in epistles now universally accepted as canonical, "the truth as"—to their divinely illuminated minds—it was and everlastingly "is in Jesus." Nor has the positive substance of the classic philosophy of Greece, essentially, been displaced to-day—any more than Homer and Sophocles and Phidias have been displaced. Men no longer write Homeric epics, or Sophoclean dramas, nor do they longer seek to honor "the gods" through new statues, of Phidian conception and execution. Yet the truth of artistic conception, which is handed down to us in the immortal works of these artists, is a possession, a positive instruction, an inspiration for all time. The "relativity," if we may so term it, of ancient art is rather superficial and accidental, than essential. The like is true respecting the fundamental philosophical conceptions of the Greek masters in philosophy, their conceptions respecting intelligence and respecting that nature of Being which alone intelligence can, must, and does recognize. The final result of that modern philosophic movement, beginning immediately with Kant, which has now become classic, was an essential reaffirmation of the best Greek conceptions respecting the universal, necessary, and eternal nature and content of human experience. But it was not mere reaffirmation, not mere verbal repetition. It was a new demonstration, the outcome of the labor of the modern mind through centuries of struggle. It was therefore peculiarly relative to the needs, the difficulties, and the peculiar lights of the modern world. And we must say that it was, correspondingly, more complete than the ancient one; and it must further be added that the new light of experimental fact— and philosophy neither is, nor ever pretends to be, anything but the comprehension of such fact—the new light of experimental fact, I say, owing to its possession of which modern philosophy was able, on the one hand, to correct and, on the other, to render more complete the demonstration begun in Greek philosophy, was, notably and especially, the light shed by the fundamental facts of Christianity.

The object of this parenthesis in my present argument is to insist upon the fact that philosophy has an historic existence; that this existence is not

confined to the past, but continues through its
results—often most powerful where least observed
—in the present; and that philosophy has demonstrated many things. But I wish no less strenuously
to insist that philosophy also exists in another fashion than this purely historic and general one. It
exists universally—at least in an ideal way, as the
object of the most deep-seated and radical impulse
of human intelligence. It is still and always will
be cultivated, with more or less of industry, energy,
and success. And I say, as speaking for those who
now seek intelligently to cultivate it, or may here-
after do so, that they recognize, and must ever
recognize—so far as they truly recognize anything
whatsoever about the matter—that, while philosophic intelligence does not consist in repeating
the words of others who have gone before, it is
fatally and foolishly recreant to its own professed
purpose, when it ignores the past. The past is not
to be ignored, but to be known, comprehended, and
valued at its precise worth. All worth is not in the
past, but it is just as true that the past is not without worth. Some things have been demonstrated.
This is to be recognized. Some things have been
incorrectly, it may be altogether falsely, conceived
and demonstrated; (in what science is the reverse
true? yet the existence and worth of the science
are not therefore denied;) and these are to be examined anew. The work of philosophy is absolutely
free, presuppositionless inquiry. But it is equally
catholic and comprehensive. It is concerned only,

like religion, to know the truth. " The love of the truth" is, in Platonic phrase, its only inspiration. And experimental fact, in the true and complete sense of this term, is, I repeat, philosophy's only guide.[5]

Returning now, to the point in our argument, from which the foregoing digression proceeded, I repeat that, as the first and, as it were, negative, part of her own peculiar task, philosophy herself has overthrown, and stands ever ready to overthrow, the slender ground of false theory on which Agnosticism rests, and this by the only means appropriate to such work, namely, the evidence of experimental fact. If, therefore, religion may seem to have anything to fear from Agnosticism, philosophy herself will, if need be, aid her in routing this enemy.

But it is a question of far different concern for religion to ask, What then, is the verdict that philosophy pronounces upon religion, when, having accomplished the preliminary task of demolishing its natural adversary, sensational Agnosticism, it proceeds to its positive work of sounding to its lowest depths the sea of our conscious experience; or, what amounts to the same thing, examining the deepest foundations of the world of reality as it exists for man ? Does it find there a secure and everlasting home for religion, or does the logic of fact compel it to pronounce religion a parasitic excrescence upon human life, not to be carefully and energetically fostered, but to be cut off and consumed in

the flame of truth ?   Is religion in its essence—not
in its changing garb of story, image, rite, and practice—true or false ?   Has it an imperishable substance of reality, or is its edifice only held up by
sand-ropes of illusion, prejudice, and ignorance ?
The essence of religion is contained, for intelligence,
in certain presuppositions respecting the absolute
nature and relations of things, with the truth or
falsehood of which religion, as an object of intelligence, stands or falls.   It presupposes that absolute
being is Spiritual, and that Divine Spirit is the
source and king and goal of all dependent being.
It assumes that the world is not merely a vast,
fate-directed mechanism, but that it is suffused, up-
held, nay, everlastingly created by the power and
wisdom of Divine Spirit.   It implies that man is, in
his true nature and intention, a spirit, and that he
is able, required, and above all, privileged to enter
into living relations to the Divine Spirit,—in which
relations, more especially, religion directly consists
or has its immediate life.   Does philosophy confirm
or overthrow these presuppositions and implications ?   Religion shares with natural science the
larger part of the honor of being the historic mother
or matrix of philosophy.   Is she devoured by her
own offspring ?   And if not, what nature, what
justification, what reality, does philosophy recognize in or for religion ?

   These questions, which indicate in broadest outline the general scope of the discussions upon which
we propose to enter, are not so novel and striking

as they would be if there had never been such a
thing as religious philosophy cultivated among men.
But they are fundamental, and each new generation
must meet and answer them anew and independently, as a condition of the maintenance of a
robust and self-sustaining—not to say self-propa-
gating and world-saving—religious intelligence.
No science is preserved and maintained by mere
tradition. On the contrary each generation and
each individual student, while accepting the old
as a datum, must redemonstrate it in order really
to have masterly possession of it. And most of all
is this true concerning that science which religion
presupposes,—the science of God in his relations to
man and the world, and of man and the world in
their relations to God.

I have thus far spoken of the relation of religion
to intelligence only as a relation into which religion may and must perforce be brought, whether she
will or not. But a higher and deeper truth is that
religion—and, above all, Christianity—both presupposes and invites the searching and illuminating light
of true intelligence and finds in it the immediate subjective source of her best strength. Religion, according to the Christian ideal, is freedom—absolute
freedom—not only for feeling and willing, but also
for thinking, man, through the truth. " The truth
shall make you," without any qualification added,
i. e., absolutely and most truly, " free." Christianity's promise is " eternal life," through the knowledge of the Spiritual Father, who as such is declared

to be "the only true God," and of him whom God
has sent and who expressly declared of himself
that, in order to be rightly known, he must disappear from the physical presence of his disciples and
reappear to their spiritual and only true sight, in
his true and everlasting spiritual nature, by revelation in and through the eternal "Spirit of truth."
Religion is thus, from the point of view of Christianity, a partaking of the Holy Ghost, which "guides
into all truth." Its pastors, so far as they are "after" Jehovah's own "heart," "feed his people with
wisdom and understanding." Religion presupposes,
and has, for one of its immediate aims, the promotion
of absolute intelligence—intelligence, that is to say,
respecting the nature of absolute being, or God, and
respecting the absolute nature and relations of man,
and of the finite universe which immediately surrounds man and first seems to claim him exclusively
for its own. To its ministers, more than to any
other class of men, is given the indirect protection,
and, even, largely the direct promotion of the absolute or universal intelligence of communities and
individuals. Hence, as I scarcely need to add, the
obvious and universally recognized necessity that
these ministers should be men of the most highly
trained intelligence and of substantial knowledge.

In view of this nature of religion it may even be
said that in religious philosophy it is not so much
intelligence, or philosophy, that judges religion, as
religion that, through intelligence, takes cognizance
of and judges its own self.

Religion, as presupposing and requiring knowledge of the Absolute, and philosophy, as the pure, unbiased search for and demonstration of it, occupy like ground. Each implies (1) a process, way, or means of intelligence, by which (2) the Absolute Object of intelligence is reached. Our purpose and method will require us, accordingly, first succinctly to indicate the general nature and results of the philosophic theory of knowledge and of the absolute or final object of knowledge; and then to seek to state, in part with greater fulness, the conceptions respecting the same topics, which are presupposed or proclaimed by Christianity; with a view to showing that the Christian conceptions are not repugnant to the conceptions of philosophy, that the former are, rather, the fulfilment and enrichment of the latter, and, in general, that in positive, substantial, concrete and historic philosophy—in distinction from the negative, abstract, and substanceless empiricism, which is often, though falsely, supposed to represent the last result of philosophic inquiry— "true religion" finds itself, not disgraced, but justified,—and not eviscerated, or reduced, as regards its content for intelligence to a spectral *caput mortuum*, but left rich in positive, living, deeply experimental, and all-significant substance.

LECTURE II.

THE PHILOSOPHIC THEORY OF KNOWLEDGE.

'Αρχὴ δὲ ἡ νόησις.—Arist. Met. 12, 7, 4.

THE philosophic theory of knowledge, or the
theory of philosophic knowledge, is nothing
but the completed science of knowledge, intelligence, or experience. Philosophic knowledge is
nothing but intelligence completely fulfilling in
kind, if not in degree, its own ideal, or realizing
its full *specific* nature and function. In one respect
such knowledge is something *sui generis;* in another
it is not. Intelligence in its fundamental nature is
an organic process. The complete nature of intelligence may in all strictness be likened to an organism; nay, it *is* an organism. If a whole organism is,
with reference to or in comparison with its separate
members, something *sui generis*, then this description applies to philosophic intelligence. And this
is the case. A whole organism is something more
than any of its particular members, or than the mere
mechanical aggregate of all its members. It is, or
represents, the common life or animating and uniting principle of all its parts. It is, I say, the *common* life of *all* its parts, and is not the exclusive

(20)

property of any one part, nor obtained by mere summation of the peculiar properties of all the parts taken severally. And so it is *sui generis*. And yet, in its fulness and completeness, it is not without any of its parts. As it, the unifying and vivifying principle, permeates them all, so it presupposes them all, as the condition of its own reality and perfection. The life and reality of the whole are in and through the life and reality of its parts or members. The whole has thus, in a sense, all its parts both ideally and really in common with itself; and, thus considered, it is not *sui generis*. Least of all does the living whole contradict its members! Complete, philosophic, or, as it is often equivocally called, absolute intelligence, does not contradict or overthrow, nor can it dispense with, the minor, particular functions of intelligence and their achievements. If historic information and mathematico-physical science, for example, represent the fruits of special functions or directions of intelligence, philosophy, as, in Platonic phrase, objectively the "science of wholes," or subjectively the result of the functioning of complete or "absolute" intelligence, neither overturns, nor can afford to affect indifference to, the methods and results of such special sciences. To suppose the contrary is simply absurd.

Philosophic intelligence, or philosophy, is therefore not separated from all other intelligence, or science, as the purely *a priori* from the purely *a posteriori* (as these terms are often, and, indeed, too generally used). It does not differ from the latter

as the inexperimental, magical, miraculous, differs
from the experimental, simple, and immediately obvious. No such chasm separates it from all other
works of intelligence. If it were thus separated, it
would contradict its own nature. The inexperimental and inexplicable is no subject, object, or field
of intelligence, but only, at most, of unintelligent
superstition. Intelligence is nothing but the full,
self-manifesting and self-recognizing light of experience. In "absolute intelligence," or philosophy,
experience simply takes, or seeks to take, complete
account of herself—not to contradict or to look away
from any part of herself.

To have experience, to know—not to have or do
which were for man the same thing as not to be—
wherein does this consist ?

It is obvious, to begin with, that intelligence, or
knowledge, is, so to speak, bi-polar, or implies 'of
necessity a double reference (1) to a subject or agent
that knows, and (2) to an object, which is known.
These two, subject and object, are so closely corre-
lated, are bound to each other in such inseparable
organic unity, that neither can be regarded exclusively by itself, except through a process of abstraction, which like all abstraction, mutilates the
living whole and changes the very nature of that
which is abstracted. The question, which lies immediately before us, obviously requires us to consider
the process or nature of intelligence more especially
on its subjective side. What—we wish to know—is
the true and complete description of intelligence

as a process whose seat is in a knowing agent? The form of the question makes apparent abstraction from the objective side of intelligence. We must therefore see to it that our abstraction is only relative and is not carried so far as to pervert the essential nature of the subject of our inquiry. The more express and explicit examination of intelligence on its objective side will follow in the next lecture.

In answer, then, to our present inquiry, we remark, first, that that science of intelligence, that knowledge respecting the fundamental nature and process of knowledge itself, which we seek, is not contained or furnished in Formal Logic. Formal Logic only teaches us how to handle given data of intelligence or knowledge, so that, under manipulation, or employed as terms in a process called reasoning, they may suffer no detriment, or may reappear in a so-called "conclusion" with nature and value unchanged. Or else, given a conclusion, formal logic teaches us the art of finding admitted data—"premises"—that will, as it is said, substantiate or "prove" it, *i. e.*, in reality, be identical with it, only in another and more familiar form. The fundamental principle of such logic is thus the so-called Principle of Identity, whose formula is $A=A$; together with the obverse of this principle, the Principle of Contradiction (A is not non-A), and the Principle of Excluded Middle (A must be either B or non-B; a third alternative is impossible). These principles logic presupposes as axiomatic, self-evident. It does not demonstrate or deduce them. It adopts them as immediately or intuitively given, and simply teaches how, in correct thinking, they are to be applied to data which, themselves also, are assumed as already supplied. Since formal logic does not inquire after the ultimate warrant of its principles, as contained in the nature and process of intelligence itself, and since it raises no question as to what it means for something to be a datum of intelligence, or as to what are the conditions, contained in the nature and process of intelligence, upon the fulfilment of which alone anything can become a datum for intelligence, this science can in no proper sense be styled the science of intelligence or of knowledge *per se.* It is only a partial, analytical science of the *mode* of intelligence, and not of its *nature* or *essence.*

Still less, secondly, is the science, which we seek, to be looked for in what has been known as Empirical Psychology. Here it is that a long and conspicuous list of British inquirers, represented by such names as Locke, Hume, the two Mills, Spencer, and others have more or less blindly sought for it, but with final results, over which as an inscription the one word "Vanity" can alone be appropriately written. The true motive for the existence of the Scotch Common Sense, or Intuitional School, as represented by Reid and Hamilton, lay precisely in the sense, which these men and their supporters had, of the essential vanity, the pure negativism, of that sensational empiricism, which their rivals had ostensibly deduced from empirical psychology. The

result of all this alleged examination and explanation of intelligence, on the part of the empirical
school, was not philosophic *science*, but *nescience*,—
not the illumination of intelligence, but only the en-
veloping of it in new and thicker clouds of apparently
baffling mystery. The conclusions reached were in
flagrant contradiction of the universal practical postulates of intelligence, and the merit of the Scotch
School consisted in the energy with which it reaffirmed some of the more obvious of these postulates
under the guise of "necessary beliefs," "native notions," or "intuitions." To comprehension of these
postulates the leaders of the Scotch School themselves did not indeed come. As to the origin or
absolute justification of the "beliefs" in question,
the How, the Whence, the Why of them, its members had scarcely one reasonable word to offer.
Reid's "explanation" of them was the precise opposite of explanation. It consisted in ascribing
them to the "*magic*" of our "constitution." They
were he said, "as it were, *conjured* up by nature;"
how, or with what absolute sense or justification,
one could not tell. And with Hamilton the case
stands substantially not at all better. It is true
that he, rather feebly echoing the phraseology of
Kant, talks of "the spontaneity of reason," as ac-
counting for primary beliefs. And in the same tone
it happened to Reid to speak of the province of
"common sense"—otherwise conceived as the faculty of necessary beliefs—as identical with that of
"reason," viz., "to judge of things self-evident."

But this only amounted, in Reid's case, to giving to
beliefs that were confessedly unaccountable, though
necessary, the euphemistic description of "things
self-evident," and making "reason" identical with
a faculty of "magic." Reason, the fundamental
faculty and the very root of all intelligence and
all experience, was in effect made to be a faculty
of the unintelligible, inexplicable, and inexperimental! And so with Hamilton. The fact is, that
the method of the Scotch School was essentially
identical with that of their ostensible adversaries.
Their whole wisdom was, after all, in kind nothing
but the wisdom of descriptive empirical psychology.
It consisted in pointing out the *immediate content* of
intelligence or experience, but not in demonstrating the science of intelligence or experience as such
or as a living process, and still less of the absolute
object of intelligence. It may be added, for the
sake of completeness, that the only work which,
under the circumstances, the Scotch School could be
expected by its polemics to accomplish, it seems
effectually to have accomplished. The later sensational empiricists, *e. g.*, J. S. Mill and H. Spencer,
admit as necessary, though indeed quite inexplicable and scientifically unjustifiable, certain of the
beliefs, which it was the merit and the peculiarity
of the Scotch School to insist upon, such, for example, as the belief in self.[1] This marks a substantial
advance upon the position of Hume, who represents
in completest and most consistent form the purely
negative results of epistemological inquiry pro-

ceeding from the postulates and by the method of
a narrowly sensational psychology. Hume, too, recognized the beliefs in question, but not as inherently
necessary, nor as inexplicable. He found an ostensible explanation for them, an explanation by which
they were *in substance* explained away. All belief,
namely, was for Hume but a peculiar phenomenon
of consciousness. It was a case of unusual strength
and vividness in our ideas, due to customary, but
inherently contingent, association; and it was
nothing else. It signified or proved nothing beyond itself as a contingent mental phenomenon.[2]

In brief, then, empirical psychology is incompetent
to furnish us the science of which we are in quest,
because its work is wholly restricted to the analytic
recognition of conscious phenomena—of thoughts,
feelings, ideas, fancies, wishes, and the like—which
we are said involuntarily to " *have,*" or which, in the
peculiar language of psychology, are simply *given
for*, or *presented to*, intelligence. Its work, I say,
is wholly restricted to the recognition of these phenomena as they are *given*, or as they immediately
appear, and of the rules of co-existence and sequence which obtain among them. It has to do,
then, with finished *products* or furnished *materials*
of intelligence, and not with that organic *process* of
intelligence or experience, without which the products would never exist and the materials would be
given in vain.[3] It deals only with pure effects, and
it is no wonder that it then sees in the effects at
most only the *evidence* of some cause, or causal

process, but not *what* that cause or process is. The same is fully true even with reference to that latest form of empirical psychology called physiological psychology. Here, the steps of a mechanical process are traced, in the phenomena of the nervous system, which run parallel with and immediately condition certain other phenomena called states of consciousness, feelings, or sensations. But this process is not itself the process of intelligence. For intelligence it is only relatively a process; absolutely considered, it is for intelligence a product, an effect, a final result or object of intelligence. So true is this, that Mr. Spencer, as English spokesman of those who seek in psychology the science of intelligence, says expressly that his belief that he possesses a nervous system, is inferential; it is a "conclusion" of intelligence. That is to say, in the language just above employed, it is a product of intelligence. How shall then the process, which is believed to be observed in the object of this inferential belief (the nervous system), be that process of intelligence whereby the belief itself is created? Mr. Spencer goes on further to assert that there is no "perceptible or conceivable community of nature" between the facts of physiology and those of psychology. Self-evidently true as this assertion is, from Mr. Spencer's point of view, it is, if taken without any qualification whatsoever, thoroughly arbitrary and dogmatic. From the spiritualistic point of view of philosophy, the two classes of facts in question, in spite of their absolute specific difference, are demonstràbly one through their inclusion in, or functional dependence on, a genus of reality that at onçe transcends and is immanent in them both.[4] Reserving, therefore, our right to protest against the unqualified form and tone of Mr. Spencer's assertion, it is enough for us now to note that so far as the denial of any community of nature between physical and psychical facts is justified in fact, just so far is the inference strengthened that the physical process is not identical with the process of intelligence. Analytico-descriptive, introspective, empirical psychology is a science, and physiological psychology is a science—each of them devoted to the legitimate work of exploring a portion of the field of phenomena which are at once given for and also dependent for their existence on intelligence. But neither of them is the science *of science* or of intelligence. Neither of them can ask after that nature of intelligence, which is itself the condition of the existence and of the observableness of the field of phenomena in the exploration of which each is engaged.

Such are among the reasons why we cannot apply with hope of success to the formal logician or to the empirical psychologist for information respecting the science of intelligence, knowledge, or experience, as such. Where, then, does this science exist, if indeed it have existence? It exists *in philosophy*, which is quite another thing than either formal logic or psychology. It exists, historically, in philosophy, so far as philosophy itself has a well-founded historic existence. For philosophy exists only by grace of and through the science of knowledge. Nay, no denial of the possibility of positive results for philosophy, no philosophical scepticism, and no materialistic and anti-philosophical dogmatism, ever existed or can exist, except on the express or implied ground of results flowing from some alleged science of knowledge. We are accustomed, correctly, to think and speak of philosophy as the science of being as such, the science of absolute reality, or of the absolute nature of things, etc. But what is reality or being but *object or subject of knowledge?* It belongs to "reality," in the definition of philosophy, to be *known*, just as necessarily as it belongs to water (for example) to be wet. Just as there can be no science of any but wet water, so there can be no science of any but known or knowable reality. No greater absurdity or injustice was ever committed than through the attribution to the great philosophers of a disposition, wish, tendency, or even, in any just sense, the *attempt* to demonstrate anything about a sphere of reality which transcends intelligence. This injustice is nevertheless not uncommonly committed, and the view which leads to it has had its most influential modern supporter in Immanuel Kant, whose argument, nevertheless, rests only on the essentially dogmatic basis of an incomplete theory of knowledge, in which "sensible affection" is uncritically, and in the face of the tendency of Kant's own discoveries and demonstrations, held to be the only touchstone of reality. Whenever, and so far as, intelligence absurdly identifies itself with its instrument, viz., sensation, its conception of reality is sensible, and only sensible; and then the lurking and indestructible feeling that the sensible is not the all of reality finds expression and seeks to justify itself in the doctrine of a realm which is held to transcend intelligence, because it transcends sense — a realm of unknowable "things-in-themselves."[5] This sense-begotten and altogether dogmatic prejudice is the whole explanation of the charge, so current in modern times, that philosophy in its search for the absolute reality, seeks or pretends to go beyond and demonstrate something independent of experience. But whenever intelligence comes to know *itself in* its instrument (sensation), and hence also in its distinction from and superiority to the same, its conception of reality is corrected accordingly, and becomes that which is set forth in the great philosophies—the philosophies of Aristotle, Leibnitz, Hegel, etc.,—and which, as we shall see, Christianity at once presupposes and proclaims. I repeat then, that intelligence and reality, like father and son, or like subject and object in consciousness, are strict correlates. There is no science of the one, without science of the other. In this sense Parmenides spoke truly, "Thought and Being are one." The science of being *per se* is but the demonstrative interpretation of intelligence, or experience, *per se*. Wherever, therefore, philosophy has a positive existence, there you may look for more or less complete developments of the science of knowledge. I need scarcely add that in modern philosophy these are found in greater extent than in ancient philosophy. The difference, however, is only one of completeness and extent, but not of kind.

What, then, has the philosophic science of knowledge to tell us?

First, it is obvious that intelligence is comparable to a light. Such comparison is very commonly made. The expressions, "light of intelligence, of knowledge, of consciousness, of experience," have passed into common speech. The same metaphor, which they express, is implied in the employment, for the purpose of expressing purely intellectual functions, and relations, of such words as to *see* and *perceive.* For instance, one will or may say, on the ground of a purely rational persuasion, "I *see* that perfect virtue is perfect humanity." "*Was man weiss sieht man erst,*" says Goethe, carrying the metaphor to the apparent verge of paradox, and yet remaining strictly within the realm of experimental truth. Physical *light*, we may say, is but a part of, and is conditioned by mental light. What, in the view of physics, exists "objectively" in the case of light is only molecular motions. These are not seen, nor do they of themselves constitute light: the latter in its peculiar nature exists for us only in and through our *conscious sensations* of sight. The light of intelligence is the light of our own existence and, for us, of all other existence.

But the notion of light is that of a purely simple quality—a somewhat that is diffusive and all-comprehensive, but contains in itself no element of difference. Pure light, while it renders all objects visible, is, taken by itself alone, invisible. Light cannot be perceived without the presence of illuminated objects. So it is with the light of conscious intelligence, which is—or would be—a perfect blank, without objects of intelligence. Physical light must have, we may say,—repeating our previous statement in another form,—a content, in order to be known. The same is true of conscious intelligence. Suppose, now, one were to attempt to explain light by an analytical examination of that which I have termed the "content" of light (viz., the sum total, the universe, of illuminated objects or of things visible), and were finally to declare that the universal *law of this content*—say, the physical law of gravitation or of evolution—was a law to explain the whole or specific nature of light. Should we not call this arrant nonsense? Yet such procedure would be quite of a piece with the method of the empirical psychologist, so far as he supposes, that by analyzing the *content* of conscious intelligence, and ascertaining the laws of co-existence and sequence which obtain therein—laws of association, for example—he has found the key of explanation for the nature of intelligence itself. No. Just as physical light, as a thing *sui generis*, has an objective explanation that is pe-

culiar to itself, so is it with intelligence and its light.
Physical light is objectively and physically explained
as a peculiar mode of motion. Subjectively, or consciously, it is a mental phenomenon not to be confounded with any other. Further, it is not known
without visible objects, but is not to be identified
with any or all of them. Analogously, the light of
intelligence is objectively explained as a complex
process, whose law and factors are subsequently to
be named. Subjectively, it is a thing, which we
must for the present, at least, term unique and inde-
finable, and yet is immediately known as the life of
all knowing. It is not known without intelligible
or conscious objects, but is not to be identified with
any or all of them.

Intelligence, I said, is a process. As such, it is
an *activity*, and that, too, not a quasi-activity, or
phenomenon of activity, such as is pure motion in
time and space, but a genuine and substantial one,
such as Aristotle terms an *energy*. In short, it is an
organic and spontaneous, self-realizing and self-ful-
filling activity. Of these, points, now, in their order.

And first I mention that the facts which demonstrate that intelligence is such an *activity* as has
been described, are overlooked by the empirical philosopher, who admits no results or methods but those
of mechanico-physical science and empirical psychology. He, the rather, forsakes fact and betakes himself to metaphor—to a metaphor, by which it is made
the nature of intelligence, or " mind," to have no
nature, but to be, in Locke's phrase, only " like a

piece of white paper, upon which nothing has ever been written." Objects, then, whose right and power to exist independently of all intelligence it never occurs to the empiricist to question, are supposed— still in the language of metaphor—to produce "impressions" or to imprint legible "characters" on the passive paper-like mind, and the result is—knowledge! Here knowledge is taken in the abstract or abbreviated sense of mere information, a so-called intellectual *possession*, acquired, not by an *active industry* of intelligence,—for intelligence is regarded as originally nothing positive, "having no nature," no real being, and consequently no power to *do* anything,— but by *gift* from a "world" of unintelligent and, strictly speaking, unintelligible objects, in which alone true *reality*, *unqualified being*, is held to reside, and which mechanically strike upon the mind and so produce their "impressions." Knowledge, intelligence, mind, is thus nothing real *per se;* it does not by its intrinsic nature share in essential reality; it is only the simulacrum, the fancied transcript, or insubstantial image of reality. It is the manifestation, the appearance, the *phenomenon* of reality.

This is the traditional basis of the theory of knowledge which is styled "sensational," since it derives its whole strength from an analysis of one of the characteristic aspects of sensible knowledge. This theory, which ends by essentially abolishing the distinction of subject and object *in* knowledge, (*i. e.*, by rendering subject and object unknowable and hence indistinguishable), begins by assuming the distinction in

name, but interpreting and applying it as purely
mechanical in fact. A mechanical relation is one
that holds, and is possible, only within space and
time. Objects in mechanical relation are separated
in space or time, or both. They are wholly distinct
from each other. They are inherently, or as to their
natures, unrelated, or have nothing in common. At
least, it is not essential to mechanical relation that
such community of nature should exist. Such objects merely co-exist or follow each other. They
constitute only a loose aggregate, not an organic
whole. If held together, this is by a power external
and superior to themselves, that is to say, by a power
whose relation to them is (again) conceived as only
mechanical. Thus simply co-existing or following
each other, the nearest relationship into which they
can enter with reference to each other is that of external contact, as the result of local motion So, in
the sensational theory of knowledge, object is originally conceived as moving up into contact with subject and leaving its mark upon it, which mark then
remains as the all of knowledge, taking the impossible place of subject and object at one and the same
time.[6] In other words, the originally supposed subject and object disappear in—or remain outside of—
the final product, and as the analysis of this product is supposed to constitute or discover the whole
of our actual knowledge, it remains impossible to
furnish a rational explanation of the ground upon
which the original supposition was made. The logical result is Hume's scepticism—or abstinence from

all opinion—respecting the real existence of object and subject ("external world" and "mind"). Less consistent is the modern doctrine of Agnosticism, which persistently holds to the reality of subject and object, though acknowledging and loudly proclaiming their complete ultimate unknowableness.

There is indeed a mechanical aspect of knowledge—more especially of sensible knowledge—but this aspect is superficial or, at best, only conditional, not essentially constitutive. The best proof of this is found in the fact that the attempt to found a science of knowledge on the supposition that the fundamental and exclusive relation of subject and object is mechanical ends not in *science* of subject and object, but in nescience with regard to them; not in explaining intelligence to itself, but in rendering the very possibility of intelligence inexplicable.

The deficiencies of the sensational theory of knowledge, and the true relation of mechanical sense to organic intelligence, were well understood and powerfully set forth in ancient times by Plato and Aristotle and in modern times, before Kant, by Leibnitz—but in each case, from a peculiar point of view, or with reference to the peculiar form in which the problem of sensible knowledge was presented to the philosophers by the sensationalists among their contemporaries. The views of Leibnitz, in particular, were developed [1] with special reference to the modification of sensational theory set forth in Locke's Essay. But after Locke came Hume, who reduced to final and most consistent expression, that which with

Locke existed rather in the form of germinant ideas or first rude beginnings. And the deficiency of the sensational theory, as delivered to the world by Hume, was first clearly perceived and declared by Kant. It was this that awoke Kant from his "dogmatic slumbers," and led him to begin—only to begin, not to complete—a new demonstration of the true whole science of knowledge, which is of peculiar interest and importance for us, not only because we live in an intellectual age that still rings with the echo of Kant's achievement, but also, in particular, because Kant pointed out in the sensational theory its fatal failure to recognize the element of mental or *intelligent activity*, and showed how, and in what sense, this element, in order to the erection of a truly experimental science of knowledge, (and more immediately of sensible knowledge itself,) is to be, and must be, restored.

The state of the case, as presented (in part, explicitly, and in part, as will be noted, only implicitly) by Hume, is briefly this. All knowledge is held to be either immediately or derivatively sensational. Sensation is mechanical impression. Impressions have no breadth—they are not complex. They are atomically simple. These statements do not correspond to the first appearances. "Impressions" seem to be complex, to have definite extent and character. But analysis, the only instrument of method which pure sensationalism admits, must resolve all complexity into mere insubstantial appearance—just as, in the hands of the physical philosopher, it resolves all appearance of complex material existence into the (supposed) essential simplicity of independent atoms, standing in purely mechanical relations to each other. So, for Hume, the real truth about our sensible consciousness is, that it is made up of a series of independent and (in the last resort) atomically simple sensations, impressions, or "perceptions," which follow each other with an inconceivable rapidity, but between which no real or necessary connection—*i. e.*, no other relation, essentially, than the purely superficial and accidental mechanical relation of matter-of-fact contiguity or remoteness in time and space—is perceivable. In truth, the premises of the theory do not even admit the admission that even such mechanical relation is perceivable. Strictly interpreted, they would restrict consciousness, and by consequence knowledge and intelligence, to the immediate instantaneous present, to the entire exclusion of the past and the future, and a man's "knowledge" at any instant would consist only in the simple impression which happened to constitute his "mind" at any instant;—*i. e.*, his knowledge, for well-known psychological reasons, would be no knowledge. Hume's theory, as Kant perceives, ends logically in this way, and Kant's way of expressing its deficiency consists in saying that it excludes the idea, the possibility, and, above all, contradicts the fact, of *combination* or *synthesis* among the elements of our (sensible) knowledge. For, as matter of fact, such combination or synthesis exists, and that not in purely casual, accidental forms, but in forms of rule or law, which are necessary and universal.[8]

The casual, or "habitual," synthesis Hume admitted, positing, to account for it, the faculty of memory and certain principles of association. The necessary and universal he denied. Kant takes issue with Hume on this point, declaring that the necessary and universal—necessary and universal truths—having the form of necessary and universal syntheses of elements of knowledge, are, as matter of fact contained in those sciences (pure mathematics and pure physical science,) which have to do, the one with the formal, the other with the material, side of sensible knowledge. The *fact* is established. The only question is, What nature of intelligence, or of the process of knowledge, does the fact at once imply and reveal? The fact, I said, of the existence of the necessary and universal syntheses in knowledge is established. But even if it were not, yet Hume himself admits the existence of fortuitous and even habitual syntheses and this in opposition to the strict requirements of the purely analytic method of the theory of knowledge founded on the presuppositions of sensational psychology.[9] That which needs to be explained, but for which the purely mechanico-sensible theory of knowledge has no sufficient explanation, is the existence of any synthesis whatsoever, whether fortuitous or necessary, and hence of any actual sensible knowledge whatsoever; for there is no such knowledge, whether in the form of perception or of conception, which does not involve and exist in the form of a synthesis or combination of those elementary materials of knowledge, for which alone analytic sensationalism has an eye. And so ˉKant's answer to the above-mentioned question consists in showing that, and how, *all* synthesis in sensible knowledge involves the immediate, characteristic and exclusive *work*—the *active work* —of organic and organizing mind. All synthesis is the immediate and continued work of a synthetic, *i. e.*, combining, activity, which, *if* the materials of knowledge, that it unites or combines, are conceived as provided by the mechanical operation of foreign *objects* upon the subject,[10] must, on its own part, be recognized as having its seat exclusively in the *subject*.

But, now, it is synthesis alone which makes knowledge to be knowledge; or, at all events, without synthesis knowledge is not. And as synthesis is primarily an activity—the synthesizing or combining *act* of intelligence conditions the resulting, observable *fact* or *state* of synthesis in the finished product or content of intelligence—so is it with knowledge. Knowledge, intelligence, consciousness, these words are primarily to be considered as active, transitive substantives. They denote something which does not consist in the mere *passive* "receiving" or "having" of informing "impressions" or of "contents." In this purely mechanical way the white paper "has" the characters imprinted upon it, and the tea-kettle "has" its liquid "contents"; but neither paper nor kettle is any wiser or more intel-

ligent on this account. No, knowledge is strictly
in the first instance, or fundamentally considered,
an ideal or mental *activity*, the most characteristic
and universal form of which, as far as we now see, is
synthesis,—combining, unifying, joining the manifold
in one.

But in what way is this synthesis effected, or what
is its relation to the elements combined? Is this relation wholly mechanical, and hence indifferent?
For instance, a bushel basket may be termed a
form of synthesis with reference to the potatoes
which fill the basket. It combines or holds them
together, but only mechanically. It belongs in no
sense necessarily to the nature of potatoes, that they
be put into a basket, nor to the nature of the basket
that it should contain, or be a means of mechanical
synthesis for, potatoes. The relation of basket and
potatoes is fortuitous and mechanical.

The most universal forms of synthesis in sensible
knowledge are—to follow, a little longer, in the
track of Kant—space and time, and the categories
of quantity, quality, relation (notably, the relation
of substance and accident, and of cause and effect,
or law of order), and modality. Are space and
time, now, ideal baskets, as it were, into which, for
lack of any other receptacle prepared to receive
them, intelligence arbitrarily puts foreign " objects," which are in themselves indifferent to space
and time? Are the objects of sensible consciousness as indifferent to space and time, as the potatoes
to the basket? And in employing the categories,

those master-forms of intellectual *conception* (another name for *synthesis*), under which alone—to speak with Kant—the material of knowledge furnished through sensible impressions can acquire for us objective form and character,—in employing, I say, these categories for the purpose of effectuating more definite synthetic union among the perceptional elements of knowledge, are we forcing the latter, as it were, into a strait-jacket, to which, they, through their very nature, stand, if not in an attitude of positive rebellion, yet of complete indifference?

To these questions, the science of knowledge, considered as the simple, honest, and complete demonstration of that which lies within the range of and constitutes experience, and prosecuted without regard to gratuitously imagined and absolutely supposititious conditions of knowledge and of existence which are alleged to transcend experience,[11] gives and can give but one answer. The relation of so-called subjective, mind-generated, synthetic *form*, to so-called objective, sense-generated, discrete *matter* of sensible consciousness, is not merely mechanical. Only in a superficial sense can it be thus styled. In essence it is organic.. It is, in kind, not a dead, but a living relation.[12] Space and time are not merely receivers or containers of physical objects, such that the former and the latter might and would still remain all the same—and wholly unchanged, even though separated from each other. Nor are the categories merely a dress, which, sensi-

ble objects may—but need not necessarily—put on,
and which serves, like all dress, rather to conceal
than to reveal the immediate, true, and characteristic nature of its wearers. Time and space without
sensible objects, and sensible objects without time
and space, are purely mechanical, forced, and unreal
abstractions. The like must be said respecting the
categories, as forms, when considered apart from
their content, and of their content—the so-called
"raw material" supplied in sensuous consciousness
—when viewed in separation from the categories.
If the object were in purely mechanical relation to
the subject and hence to be conceived as essentially
separate or absolutely and only different from, and
opposed to the latter, then the reverse of what has
just been said would be true. But then, too, it
would also be true that the "subject form" or
container would never attain to, be placed upon,
or receive the "object matter" or content of knowledge. Thus it is that, maintaining the foregoing
supposition, the theoretical sensationalist (as Locke,
Hume, *et al.*,) and the critical idealist (Kant), who
start with the express or implicit assumption of the
mechanical relation as the fundamental one between
subject and object, come quickly to the conclusion
that the true object is an unknown and unknowable
substrate or thing-in-itself, which the subject-forms
of intelligence never reach. This conclusion is a
reductio ad absurdum of the premise on which it
rests. The science of knowledge has nothing to
do with unknowable objects. It has no ground on

which to posit their existence. It has positive ground for absolutely denying their existence, for *knowing* that they do not exist, since the very conception of them is a pseudo-conception, *i. e.*, a false and impossible one, like that of a square circle or a piece of wooden iron.[13] The science of knowledge is the science of experience, and not of that which contradicts the very nature of experience; of reason, and not of unreason; of intelligence and consciousness, and not of that—viz., abstractions, creatures of a self-deceiving imagination—which gives the lie to intelligence and makes of consciousness a nightmare. The object of *sensible* consciousness is within and not without consciousness; and be it that there are good reasons for terming *this* object—*i. e.*, the object in its characteristically sensible aspect—phenomenal, yet the noumenon, the absolute reality, which, as men say, "corresponds" to it, is not concealed by it. The phenomenal object is not a vail or screen effectually to shut out from us the sight of the noumenal object. Nor is the former separated from the latter by an impassable interval. On the contrary, to thought it instrumentally reveals the true object—as we shall have occasion more expressly to see in a subsequent lecture. At present it suffices for us to note that in the phenomenal object, which alone sensationalism and critical idealism permit us to know, we have not an object standing in merely mechanical relation to the forms of our knowledge. Its fundamental relation to them is, the rather, wholly

organic. To begin with, the so-called material of
sensible knowledge—the "matter of sensation"—
enters, in knowledge, into an active, synthetic, organizing process of knowledge, just as the raw
materials, upon which the plant subsists, are taken
up by the organic forces of the plant into the process of its own life. And then the "forms" of
knowledge themselves—time, space, and the categories—are as the members—hand, foot, etc., or
root, branches, and the like—of a living organism.
All of them are easily demonstrated to have no
absolute independence of each other, just as root
and branch can have no such independence. Though
different, they yet have something in common. That
which is the source of their *common* life, activity, and
nature, is reflected in each of them, but adequately
represented *in concreto* by none of them. What this
source is, we must presently inquire.

But first let us gather up the results of what has
thus far been said.

1. Within the realm of experience or of real knowledge, or more especially of sensible experience—for
it is this alone that we have thus far been considering—the forms of the subject are the forms of the
object, and *vice versa*. What is of the subject, is
not, for that reason, not of the object, and *vice versa*.
On the contrary, the subjective is *eo ipso*, and *mutatis
mutandis*, objective, and the objective in like manner
subjective. In this consists their organic unity. And
so, in the realm of sensible knowledge, knowledge
consists just as much in finding the subjective re-

flected in the objective as, *vice versa*, in finding the object reflected or imaged in the subject.

2. Knowledge consists in a unifying process. For it is synthesis, and synthesis is nothing but the combination of the manifold in one. Knowledge, then, is the reduction of multiplicity to unity, and of the manifold particular to the single universal. Or, just as truly, it is *finding* unity in multiplicity or the universal in the particular. But by this process the manifold and particular are manifestly not abolished. On the contrary, they are reaffirmed. Indeed, it is only in this way that they can be at all, even in the first instance, affirmed. The manifold and the particular are gathered up into the universal—they are not cast away—and it is only in this way, as the science of knowledge has shown us, that any knowledge of them is possible. We understand, then, what the ancients meant, and what the moderns re-echo, by the saying that *science*—ἐπιστήμη, *knowledge as such*—is only of the universal. But not, I repeat, of an abstract universal—an universal abstracted or separated from the particular. Such an universal intelligence cannot think. In pretending to think or assert it, it pretends to think or assert absolute unreason and absolute unreality, or the absolutely absurd. The most perfect illustration of the abstract universal is the sensationalist's unknowable substrate, or thing-in-itself, or "force," which is at once supposed to contain all *absolute* reality and yet to be exclusive of all *known* reality.[14] It is the abstract (Eleatic) one, which is separated from all

plurality and has consequently no power to explain
the latter. It can enter as a term into no science.
It is not only unthinkable, contradicting intelligence;
it is also useless. It has nothing to do with science.
It is no "result" of science.

Knowledge, then, is of the concrete universal.
The true universal alone is concrete. The particular, to which only this name (" concrete ") is so
often given, is, as such, indeed abstract. It is separated, abstracted—or looked at in separation and
abstraction from—the universal to which it belongs.
As such, it is termed a mere " brute fact," which is
not known, *comprehended*, rendered intelligible or an
object of *science*, because viewed in abstraction from
all but its immediate *individual* self. It is like the
accidentally discovered member of an unknown organism, which cannot be truly known until the idea
of the whole organism is seen reflected in it and is
read in or from it. The whole organism involves,
includes, or *comprehends* it. The law of the whole
is its law, and it is only through our knowledge of
this law that we in turn *comprehend* the isolated fact
or part. In purely physical science, of sensible phenomena, the reflected image or counterpart of the
concrete, organic universal is law of co-existence or
sequence,—scientific law. And a sensible phenomenon is approximately *known* and comprehended,
only when some such law has been discovered for it.

The forms of knowledge or intelligence, now, were
said above to be as members of one common organism, sharing in a common life. And, indeed, it is

obvious that they could not be forms or denote processes of intelligence if the reverse were true. They denote, as we have seen, activities, synthetic activities, and an activity denotes an agent. Now if we were to suppose each activity to denote a separate agent, it is obvious that we should be introducing into the subject of intelligence just that unconnected diversity, which we had to escape from in the immediate sensible object of intelligence, in order to render the latter in any way possible or conceivable.[15] And we should also be flying in the face of obvious fact. Each subject of intelligence is immediately aware that all the forms and products of his intelligence are his, that they belong to him, as one individual self, and not to another. The particular acts of synthesis, which follow the forms of the fundamental "categories" of intelligence, are themselves again combined in the all-inclusive active synthesis of self-consciousness. In every act of conscious intelligence self-consciousness finds itself reflected—or, rather, realized. Self-consciousness is that "light" of intelligence, which we mentioned near the beginning of our inquiry. And if the special forms of intelligence are the *members* of an organism, self-consciousness represents this organism in its wholeness and entirety. *It* is the source of the common life and the common nature of all the members. And it is a pure, ideal activity. It is a "*pure*" activity, having no substrate; that is to say, it is not a mode of motion, which, as such, cannot be conceived and does not exist without something—some sort of "matter," whether ponder-

able or imponderable—which is moved and which
presupposes—or is relative to and, as men say, conditioned by—time and space; which latter are, the
rather, demonstrably dependent functions, rather
than independent conditions, of self-consciousness.
It is an "*ideal*" activity, for none other can be organic, diffusing itself through many members and
yet always remaining the same—the one in and
through the many. The activity of self-consciousness is also spontaneous; not that it is independent
of its conditions, terms or factors, but that it is their
mistress. It *uses* them—not, *is used* by them. It
is not simply—it, as such, is not in any sense—their
mechanical *resultante*. But its material or objective
content, so far as it is purely given in sense-conditioned consciousness, does result from the fore-
mentioned conditions in a way that, in its first form
and appearance, is for self-consciousness contingent
and mechanical, or independent of its choice.[16] Yet
sensible consciousness, as we have seen, does not become real consciousness until it is enfolded in the
embrace of self-consciousness, or—more accurately
expressed—until it is wrought, as a term, into the
organic process of self-consciousness. This then is
the state of the case, as regards the relation of "objective" consciousness to self-consciousness in man.
Objective consciousness becomes real, only when it
becomes subjective, or a part and function of self-
consciousness. And, on the other hand, self-consciousness becomes real, only when it finds an object
and finds and realizes itself in that object. So far as

the object is *given* in apparent independence of self-consciousness, we have just as much right to say that the subject finds its forms in the object as that the subject puts its forms on the object. The one is just as true as the other. The individual, therefore, as a knowing agent, finds himself set in the midst of an intelligible world, of which he is a part, or to which he is akin, and not placed as a knowing machine, over against a world, which is wholly unrelated to him and refuses to have anything to do with the forms of his intelligence. The forms of his intelligence are the forms of the world's existence as a given object of intelligence, and *vice versa.* We can understand thus what Aristotle meant by terming the soul the "place of forms" and declaring that it knows by becoming in some sense its object or one with its object. The form of the (particular) object becomes for the time being—in the act of knowledge—the (particular) form of the subject. The subject knows, recognizes, itself in and through this form and in and through the same form *has—possesses* and knows—its object. The important inferences, which this state of the case authorizes and enforces respecting the real nature of both subject and object may even now be foreseen, but their development must be reserved for our next lecture.

But the "forms," the universal, are recognized only in the *light* of self-consciousness. Their recognition is the work of a self-conscious activity. We must never forget that the forms in question are according to the experimental science of knowl-

edge, nothing, or at best only dead abstractions,
when viewed independently of the self-conscious
activity of which they are in their very nature organic members. But the organic activity of self-
consciousness is a spiritual one. It is personal. It
is the radiating or expansive centre of a process
which extends over the whole world of intelligence
without ever losing itself. Wherever it goes, it is
still "at home."[17] And yet, as we have seen, in
man it is not an absolutely independent centre.
On the contrary, it is dependent. It is only *conditionally*, relatively, quasi-mechanically dependent
on so-called objective conditions. These are, for the
rest, as we have already seen, nought but its other
self. Or rather, they are organically, ideally one
with the dependent forms of itself. But self-consciousness in man is *intrinsically* dependent upon
an absolute self-consciousness. Man is, indeed, like
the Leibnitzian monad, potentially a mirror of the
whole universe. The latter is all potentially contained in his intelligence. But only potentially.
The realization of intelligence implies a patient and
long-continued labor, and the end is still always
incomplete. Man finds himself, after all, only as an
organic part of an intelligible world, in knowing
which he assumes, with reference to it, the attitude
of its organic head. This *rôle*, however, he only
assumes; he does not *fill* it. Not only is it true
that he never completely fills it; it is also impossible for him not to suppose that before he assumed
it and while he still fragmentarily or incompletely

fills it, it was and is eternally and absolutely filled by an absolute subject, an absolute self-consciousness, that neither waxes nor wanes, and is "without variableness or shadow of turning." The light of his own self-consciousness reveals itself as a borrowed light. It is organically dependent upon the light of an absolute self-consciousness, and, being organically dependent, the life and law of absolute self-consciousness are read in it. And again, being thus organically dependent on and hence dependently *one* with the absolute self-consciousness, the essential truth, in kind, of its own forms and of the normal results of its own labor, is guaranteed to it.

Let us see how the case stands. The forms of sensibly objective knowledge, the forms of that knowledge whereby the world exists for us, are forms of intelligence; they are forms of the *subject's* intelligence. They are at once form and conditional result of a synthetic activity of intelligence subject to, or in organic dependence on and union with, the spiritual, personal process of self-consciousness. Of this much we may assure ourselves by following the track of Kant's demonstrations. But, on the other hand, they are not the peculiar forms of the *individual* subject. Not even Kant, with all his theoretical subjectivism, would go so far as to admit that his "Critique of Pure Reason" was, after all, only a critique of his own—viz., of Immanuel Kant's and of no other person's—reason. On the contrary, the scientific nature and value of the results reached by him depended on their being demonstrably valid, not for one man, but for all men. Human intelligences are many; human intelligence is one.[18] But now, the world is not created by our intelligence. Nor does it exist as many separate times as it is known. It exists independently of our individual intelligence and independently of the intelligence of the whole aggregate of finite and knowing individuals in the universe. It only remains, therefore, to suppose that the individual subject's synthetic activity in intelligence is not simply or primarily creative, but the rather recreative, not productive, but reproductive. The forms of synthesis, of intelligence, of universality, of law, nay, of spirit, are somehow there in objective existence, before we know them. Not being there by virtue of their dependence on and organic involution in the personal self-consciousness of any finite individual, and yet being demonstrably inconceivable, except in such relation to some self-consciousness, it only remains possible—and the facts render it absolutely necessary—to see in them indices of a self-consciousness which is not subject to the limitations of finitude, but is infinite, not relative and dependent, but absolute and independent, not dependently particular, but universal. And so the organic unity of object and subject—of the world of objective form and of subjective, *individual* intelligence—on which the possibility of knowledge was seen to depend, will itself be possible only because both object and subject, world and finite mind, are alike in living, organic dependence on absolute intelligence. The "light" of individual intelligence will be seen to exist only by reflection from, or through participation in, the light of absolute intelligence, and we shall see with what perfect reason Aristotle could declare that the "active reason" of man, the true organon or agent of *science*, the faculty of the universal, was "something divine," belonging not to the *individual*, *as such*, but entering into him "as by a door." And so we shall perhaps perceive that St. Paul was not speaking anything, but literal truth, when he denied "that we are sufficient of ourselves to think any thing as of our (*individual*) selves; but our sufficiency is of God"—who is the Universal and Absolute Self, and whose consciousness is the condition of all *true* consciousness, or of all consciousness of *truth*.

We may conclude, then, by way of recapitulation, that the philosophic science of knowledge demonstrates—

1. That knowledge is inexplicable on the sensational theory of subject and object, in knowledge, as only different, or mechanically distinct, from each other; knowledge is therefore not a purely mechanical, sensible, or physical process;

2. That subject and object, in spite of their numerical difference, must be organically one, and that they are indeed thus one in a spiritual process of self-consciousness which conditions, rather than is conditioned by time and space and their relations;

3. That finite self-consciousness involves and reveals its dependence on an absolute self-consciousness, which, provisionally, we can only call, in agreement with philosophy and religion, the self-consciousness of an absolute and divine Spirit.

LECTURE III.

THE ABSOLUTE OBJECT OF INTELLIGENCE;—OR, THE PHILOSOPHIC THEORY OF REALITY.

A GERMAN historian, of philosophic mind, expresses a truth, that, in our first lecture, we have already briefly encountered, by saying that "the end of philosophy is the absolute, and the absolute is the beginning of theology."[1] In other words, theology and religion presuppose, or, rather, claim livingly to possess and exhibit, that truth which philosophy conquers only after a laborious siege against the strongholds of error and a prolonged and systematic approach to the citadel, where truth herself sits enthroned. Or, in still other words, the presupposition of religion is the highest fruit, or, at all events, the highest ideal, of intelligence. Religion always claims to be a practical expression of the truth, of *the* truth *par excellence*, of the highest and last truth for man. Philosophy is, or aims to be, the reflective and systematic analysis and demonstration of absolute truths,—of truths which command and comprehend all other truths, and of realities which bear a like relation to all other realities. It is only because of this relation of religion and

philosophy to the same object, that the temporary
or occasional appearance of conflict between them
is possible. And it is only because of this same
relation that in true philosophy—*i. e.*, in the fruits
of comprehensive, catholic, thorough, and genuinely
experimental inquiry respecting the universal nature
and object of intelligence—true religion necessarily
finds her own lineaments prefigured and the security
of her own foundations demonstrated. That such
is the relation of Christianity to the demonstrable
results of philosophic inquiry—this is the main thesis
of the present course of lectures. The two main
subjects of philosophic investigation are—as has
been previously indicated—the Science of Knowledge
and the Science of Being or of Reality. From the
result of our discussion of the former of these topics,
one may, I imagine, already feel somewhat the close
connection between philosophic inquiry and religion,
and the immediate bearing of the former on the foundations of the latter. But before going on to contemplate this connection and bearing more explicitly,
and in special relation to Christianity, it will be necessary, in the present lecture, first to indicate in
outline what conception philosophy establishes respecting the absolute nature of reality. We have
seen in brief what is the nature, and what are the
ideal presuppositions of intelligence, as a "subjective"
process. We have now to see what philosophy's
impartial and complete examination of man's actual,
living experience shows respecting the absolute nature of the object, or objects, of intelligence.

Mr. Matthew Arnold in one place refers to the question as to "what being really is," as a "tyro's question."[2] To the tyro it is, no doubt, a tyro's question, and, in the tyro's superficial way of conceiving and answering questions, is at once trivial and easily answered. But science and philosophy are not the affair of tyros, and in the view of science and philosophy the question referred to is the most fundamental and comprehensive of all conceivable questions. On the answer given to it depends logically and fundamentally the complete enlightenment or the total confusion of intelligence, and the everlasting quickening or the deadening paralysis of all the springs of man's most characteristic life—his life in love, and joy, and hope, in free society, in art, in religion. Intelligence may indeed exist and be cultivated in narrower spheres, without any express reference to the ontological question. But in this case it is not complete. It does not wholly know itself, and its own implications, nor all that is really implied and given in its immediate objects. And since, after all, the ontological question is sure in some way to be raised and answered by every man—if not consciously and "theoretically," then unconsciously and "practically," no assurance is furnished, in the case supposed, that the answer may not fall out to the practical confusion of intelligence. The highest question of intelligence cannot be answered at haphazard, or, if thus answered, is almost sure to be answered wrong; and the wrong answer is, in this case, like the cloud that permanently obscures the sun and makes men finally to be perversely in love with darkness, rather than light, and even to mistake the former for the latter. It leads them, for example, expressly or practically to see in mechanical sense the standard and limit of organic intelligence, and in "sensible objects" the type of absolute reality—and a greater "confusion of intelligence" than this was never known. And so, again, practical life, in individuals, and in societies and nations, may be, and often is, covered with the fairest blossoms and fruitage of a noble, ideally determined civil polity, of genuinely inspired art, of morality and religion, while yet "the tyro's question" as to "what being really is" is never expressly raised and consequently never expressly answered. But the fact is that such life really contains the true answer to the question. The answer is given, not in the abstract terms of a mere definition, but in concrete illustration, in living fact and act. True life *is* true being. But let, now, one who is born into the atmosphere of such life, have doubts and queries raised in his mind as to "what being really is." Let him, further, see no way to avoid admitting the conception, ever more or less prevalent among scientific men, of the world as pure mechanism, whose roots are in blind force. Then, since what is thus true of the world as a whole is true of all its parts, and since man, the individual, must regard himself as part and parcel of the world, the individual is forced to regard all the apparently spontaneous play and earnest purpose of his life as themselves pure mechanism; freedom is then necessarily viewed as an illusion, responsibility as a phantom, and existence is robbed of all its dignity and privilege. Is it not obvious that the practical bearings of ontology are of tremendous consequence? One point has just been indirectly alluded to, which here, at the beginning of our discussion, needs to be more expressly emphasized. It is what is called the *unity of being*. The practical consequences of ontology, on which we have just been touching, flow, as is seen, from the assumed unity of existence. When we determine the fundamental and universal nature of all existence, we determine, by necessary inclusion, the fundamental and universal nature of human, and of all other particular, existence. Of what nature the unity of being is, and how it is to be conceived, has already been partly indicated or prefigured, in our examination of the theory of knowledge, and will subsequently be more concretely illustrated. At present I remark only that the notion of the unity of being —in some sense—is fundamental and essential to all science. It is the express or implicit presupposition of all science. And everything depends, in ontology and theology, on the way in which this unity is understood.

In the largest generalizations of physical science, no attempt is made to reach an absolute unity, but only a relative one—the unity, namely, of the sensibly phenomenal or material universe. Thus the earliest Greek inquirers, turning their attention only to questions of speculative physics, only

presupposed and attempted to demonstrate the unity
of the physical universe in its proximate or sensible
essence, as consisting of water, air, fire, or the like.
Of precisely similar nature, or scientific quality, is
our modern nebular hypothesis, with its accompany-
ing theory of cosmical evolution. The unity which
is sought in such theories is, we may say, not the
unity of essential being, but of its sensible form or
appearance. Attention is directed upon one sphere
or aspect of existence, the so-called physical or sensible one, and search is directed for the one phenomenal mode of such existence, which underlies all
others and is the " unity " of all. Thales said that this
mode was water, Anaximenes called it air, Heracli-
tus fire, and Anaximander τὸ ἄπειρον—the indefinite.
Precisely so, modern science terms it unqualified,
undifferentiated matter, in the " indefinite " form of
a nebula. And it then seeks to trace the *modal*,
but by no means the *causal* process, whereby from
the originally homogeneous and indefinite condition
the present heterogeneous and highly differentiated
state of things came into existence. It constructs,
as well as it can, the phenomenal history of the physical universe. But *what* is the original nebula?
What is matter? Wherein and by what power does
it consist? What is the nature of that force whereby
" matter " evolves—or, under material forms there
is evolved—the varied and wonderful universe? Physical science, as such, does not answer these questions—its highest and last generalization, which
transcends and includes even such theories as those

just referred to, being that all that is *physically* knowable, in the absolute and final sense of the term, is figured space and motion. Note it well: not *matter*, as absolute substance, but *figured space* —a purely ideal form; and not *force*, but only the phenomenon of force, viz., *motion.* Matter, or absolute being in any form, is, for pure mathematical and physical science, confessedly "unknowable," and force is "inscrutable." [3]

Thus physical science finds, and, in truth, seeks, no absolute, but only a relative, unity of being, and that, too, not in the undivided realm of absolute or universal, but only of sensible or phenomenal existence, and this, again, not in respect of real substance, but only in respect of phenomenal or apparent form or mode. And yet, as is seen, within its peculiar and limited sphere, and in its peculiar way, physical science illustrates the truth that being is one, and that the unity of being is the presupposition upon which alone any science is possible. This state of things, it will be remembered, was prefigured in our last lecture, where it was shown that all real *science*, all real *knowledge*, consists in a reduction of the particular to the universal or in a comprehension of the many in the one. Or, otherwise, expressed, science exists only by virtue of its perception of the one in the many.

Now, before leaving this point, let us advert once more to the circumstance, already rendered obvious, that the universal, to which physical science leads us, is an abstract one. Not only does pure physical science make abstraction from all inquiry or profession of knowledge concerning the fundamental ontological conceptions of absolute or substantial *being* and *power*, but also, in ideal or tendency, from the infinitely varied forms of sensible existence itself, as contained in our actual experience. In the language (substantially) of a recent German writer, the world, as it exists for all the other senses, is reduced to the blank monotony of a world existing only for the one sense of sight,—and this, too, not for our actual, living, varied, color- and form-distinguishing sight, but for an "ideal eye," capable of seeing everywhere nought but moving lines and points in space.[4] To this monotonous description is *omne scibile* reduced in the ideal of physical science. The physical universe, thus viewed, is originally nothing but an indefinite aggregate of undifferentiated parts—a side-by-side of particles, indifferent to each other—not an organism of differentiated members, which imply and point to each other. *Being* is reduced to its own *shadow.* But, now, suppose that such a conception be, for whatever reason, adopted as the final and absolute, universal and all-comprehensive conception of existence. Here the abstract finite and particular are elevated into the rank of strict identity with the concrete infinite and universal, or, rather, the latter is degraded into identity with the former. This is the ideal of that kind of "pantheism," which the religious consciousness universally and violently repudiates, and which, on grounds of scientific, experimental demonstration, is rejected by philosophy

itself. This is the pantheism of purely phenomenalistic mechanism; and it is real atheism, because it
banishes spirit from the universe. Generically one
with this—in spite of apparent differences—is the
pantheism of the First Book of Spinoza's " Ethics."
The fault which philosophic science finds with such
a doctrine, is not that it asserts (in terms and in
form) the unity of being, but that in it being is
really not comprehended. The conception of "being" employed is formed by *abstraction from reality.*
The real and truly substantial is not included in it.
As a consequence, the "unity" in question is not
the true unity of real being, but an abstract and
formal one. It is derivative, and not primary—a
quasi-unity, or a so-called mechanical unity, not a
real, viz., an organic one. More than once has philosophy furnished the demonstration that the condition of all perception or conception of mechanical
unity—the unity of a mere sensible, or time-and-
space-conditioned aggregate—is the express or implicit perception and conception of organic unity.
Mechanical unity is abstracted from and hence
always presupposes organic unity, and the true
unity of being must hence be of this latter kind.

Our present inquiry concerns immediately and
especially the "absolute object of intelligence, or,
the philosophic theory of reality." In the phrase,
"object of intelligence," it is important that we put
stress on both of the substantives employed, "object" and "intelligence." That abstract quasi-philosophic science which, borrowing its method and

presuppositions and hence receiving its limitations
from mathematical and physical science, issues variously in Spinozistic dogmatism, in materialism, and
in English agnosticism, stops short with the demonstration of an apparent "*object* of (so-called) intelligence," but does not raise this into an "object of
(true) *intelligence.*" The expression "agnosticism,"
adopted by a large section of the votaries of such
"science," is a voluntary and truthful confession of
this fact. That intelligence has, and must have, an
object, it requires little or no science to demonstrate.
Any one capable of the slightest degree of analytic
reflection, recognizes at once the truth in question.
Apparently the simplest, and certainly the first and
most obvious illustration of it, is furnished in the
case of sensible knowledge. Every one knows that
there is no *sight* without *objects* of sight, and, in general, no sensible knowledge without *objects* of such
knowledge. Every one, too, is endowed by nature
with the power of looking at and directing all appropriate senses upon such objects, and of distin-
guishing them, comparing, recognizing them, and
describing the phenomena with which they present
themselves. This one may do without necessarily
inquiring or in the least knowing *what* that process
of intelligence is, whereby he knows—and what are
its implications—any more than, in order to walk,
one must first explicitly know all about the mechan-
ics of walking and the anatomy and physiology of
the human frame. Now this process of analytic
description may be carried on indefinitely, or up to

the very final limit of purely sensible knowledge (or, what amounts to the same thing, of "pure physical science,")[5] with the like essential ignorance of the science of knowledge as such. The question constantly is, and is only, respecting that which we either actually or constructively *see*, what we *find*, what is mechanically *presented* or *given* for external observation. And the knowledge, which we thus acquire, seems to us so satisfactory—so certain, so real, so final—that we heartily and credulously take it for the type and standard of all true knowledge—exclaiming, with the poet,

"Knowledge is of what we see,"

thus, as it were, making mechanical *sight* the genus of which knowledge is to be considered as a species, or, making knowledge a mechanical result of seeing, rather than sight a spiritual-organic function and dependently instrumental condition of knowledge or intelligence. And yet this very "knowledge," carried to its final issue, corrects and refutes itself. It corrects and refutes the assumption of the eye that it *sees* colors, of the ear that it *hears* sounds, of the mouth that it *tastes* sweet and bitter *objects*, and of sight and touch combined that they see and feel absolute, objective, *per se* existent matter. It denies that we sensibly perceive and hence (from *its* point of view) know the power of the mind or any other power or force whatsoever. Sensible knowledge, apparently so rich and full and concrete, thus again demonstrates itself to be in reality, when taken purely

by itself, in the highest degree abstract and empty.
Not only, namely, does it, as above noted, abstract
from the ontological conceptions—and *realities*—of
essential, substantive *being* and *power*—the *"belief"*
in which accompanies the sceptical physicist or agnostic to the very end of his inquiries, but his ultimate positive conceptions ("configuration and motion,") or the final *"object of* his intelligence," remain
empty of significance *for intelligence.* And "empty"
in a double and triple sense: (1) by reason of the abstraction just noted; (2) because " configuration and
motion" are not themselves principles of or for intelligence, whereby the so-called evolution of the actual
universe from them may be explained; they are abstract modalities, and not real and efficient essences;
(3) because the so-called sensible ultimates, motion
and configuration, when closely viewed, as objects
of purely or characteristically sensible knowledge,
turn out to be, not what they were first supposed,
viz., absolutely non-mental *objects* of intelligence—
separate from and independent of the latter—but
"modifications," and so identical parts of intelligence (= here, *sensible consciousness*) itself.

   Sensible knowledge thus finds itself finally confronted with a paradox, which, as our last lecture
showed us, it is, of itself, unable to explain, viz., that
its object is no *real independent object*—is not *independently objective*—but is, the rather, identical with,
or "a modification" of, the subject. Even its alleged
"object of intelligence," appears not to be a true *object.*
But the point which it is more important for us to

note here is that, admitting the alleged object to be, in its way, a true object, it is yet not an " object of *intelligence.*" For this is what we must say respecting all objects which appear in the guise of *mere* objects, inherently unrelated to or separate from the subject,—or respecting all objects concerning which the utmost which we can say is that they are *given.* And this is the case with " configuration and motion," *regarded from the point of view of pure physical science, or sensible knowledge, alone.* They are given, are facts, presented, apparently, in independence of intelligence. Intelligence simply accepts them. With reference to intelligence they are accidental. Something else might just as well have been given, for aught intelligence here perceives. They present (from the point of view which we are now considering) an inherent contradiction, inasmuch as they assume the *form* of *unintelligible* objects of *intelligence!* The state of the case with reference to the objects of sensible knowledge, *as such*, is sometimes aptly expressed by saying that they are *facts* and not *truths.* But the field and the true atmosphere of intelligence are truth. Intelligence is the active and living organ of truth—its true nature being embedded in truth—its only possible and real objective nourishment being the truth. Mere *facts* are only signs of truth, not truth itself, and the latter alone can be and is the true and final—not merely quasi and provisional—*object* of *intelligence.*

The predicate *being* is applied to the *object* of intelligence. The object (in the first instance) is

alone held to be *real.* In other words, that *is*
which is *known.* Knowledge and being are correlative terms. When we know therefore what is the
true *object* of *knowledge*, we know what is the final
and absolute significance of the terms *being* and
reality. We have just spoken of *truth* as the true
object of intelligence. If, in so doing, we spoke
truly, then it will follow that *truth, being,* and
reality, are synonyms. Only, it will be necessary
to determine in what sense the word truth is to be
understood. Obviously, we may anticipate that it
cannot have, as thus ontologically applied, the abstract and dead significance which belongs to the
term in purely formal logic. In what sense it is to
be understood, will presently appear.

That "configuration and motion," as the ultimate
facts of sensibly-conditioned—or pure physical—
science, are not *per se,* or independently considered, *intelligible*, or true and final objects of, or substantial truths for, *intelligence*, is shown by the circumstance that the physicist himself is compelled,
in his description and explanation of the physical
universe, to speak the metaphysical language of
materialism and dynamism. In other words, he
speaks, and is practically obliged to speak, in every
breath of "matter" ("atoms") and (blind) "forces."
He *knows*, and confesses that he knows, nothing of
absolute matter and force, and that in employing
these terms he merely employs artificial symbols,
like the x and y of algebra. But sometimes physical science forgets its own limitations—or rather,

its self-appointed interpreters forget them, and then speak as if matter—intrinsically inert and atomically constituted—and blind force were known as that in which true, objective being resides.⁶ Still more often is this error committed by the popular consciousness, which knows little or nothing of the limitations of physical science and is too generally accustomed to look to the latter for final and authoritative illumination respecting the ultimate problems of intelligence. But even if matter, as above described, and blind force were known to exist—and in a certain, relative way of speaking, it is true to say of them that they do exist—yet it could, and can, only be said of them, as of motion and configuration, that they exist only as immediate, relative, and dependent *objects*, but not as objects of *intelligence*—not as constituting *the* object of intelligence, not as *the truth*, but only as signs and symbols, or "the language" in which truth and reality are expressed.

It is time for us, after all this negative preparation, to revert to the results of our inquiry (in the preceding lecture) respecting the science of knowledge, and on this the only solid basis for our present inquiry, to develop succinctly the positive results, of which we are in quest.

The science of knowledge shows us subject and object, or intelligence and being, in organic unity. It follows hence (1) that the distinction made between intelligence and being is a purely formal or logical one, not real. Being, in other words, includes intelligence, or intelligence and being have

something in common. But, (2) if this be so, then
the nature of being is primarily revealed *in* intelligence. It is revealed, I say, in other words, to
intelligence from within, from the inner depths of
its own nature or precinct, and not from without.
A revelation absolutely and unqualifiedly from without were impossible and is a pure, or rather, an im-
pure, figment of the unreflecting imagination. Such
relative revelation of being from without as is made
to us in sensible perception is only initiatory, superficial, and symbolic, and *possible* only because that
which is symbolized is organically one in its being
with the being which is revealed within intelligence.
(3) The revelation of being in intelligence necessarily takes—as must at once be seen—the form of
self-intelligence, self-knowledge, or self-consciousness. These various terms are all designations of
one and the self-same activity, and this activity is
the fundamental activity of living spirit. They are
designations, I say, of *one* activity. But when I say
one, I do not mean *mechanically single* or *simple*, as
though the activity in question were like the motion of a point in a straight line; (such *motion*, for
the rest, is in no true or fundamental sense an *activity*, but at most only the sign and effect of one)
It is not simple, but complex. And not complex,
again, in the sense in which a so-called system of
motions, that tend to one end, is complex; for (not
to mention that a complex system of mere motions
no more constitutes a true activity than does a single
motion) the unity of such a system is not organic,

internal, and essential, but mechanical, external, and superficial; it is only the apparent and perishable unity of parts which are *per se* indifferent to each other and may conceivably be separated without losing their identity. No, the unity in question is a *living* one. It is a unity, not simply in spite of, but by very virtue of complexity, an *identity*, the very condition of whose existence is *diversity*. The *one* and indivisible ego, self, or spirit, whose function is intelligence, is *one in, through,* and *by virtue* of its self-intelligence, which latter is a complex process: the same permanent reality—variously styled "subject," "spirit," "self," etc.,—*distinguishes* itself as subject and object (*it*, as subject, knows itself as object), and this as the very condition upon which alone it can know itself to be *one*, and can in fact be one. Here we have an *ideal activity* which (paradoxical as this may sound) constitutes the *agent:* the agent *is* only through its *activity*.[1]

(4) Being, like knowledge, is thus primarily revealed as a spiritual *activity*. Almost the first lesson which the beginner in philosophy has to learn is this, that nought essentially exists by mere *inertia*. Existence, *as such*, or absolutely and truly considered, is in no sense whatever *passive*, but is absolutely and only *active*. When Leibnitz declared activity to belong to the very essence of substantial existence,[8] he seemed to utter a paradox, but expressed in fact a truth which has been, in substance, familiar to, and demonstrated by, real philosophic science, in every age in which such science has

existed, and which deserves to be set down as first
and foremost among the permanent achievements
of genuine, truly experimental *philosophy*. The difficulty of learning it arises only from the force of a
prejudice or habit, precisely like that which stood in
the way of the acceptance of the Copernican as-
tronomy. Just as, *per* demonstrations of physical
science, the whole sensible universe would at once
collapse into the blank nothingness of indistinguishable night, were all motion to cease, so philosophic
science demonstrates that were *activity*—*i. e.*, the
Life of Spirit—to cease, existence itself, including
time and space, would absolutely vanish. Where
there is no *doing*, there is no *being*. It is doing,
activity—the Aristotelian ἐνέργεια and ἐντελέχεια—
which constitutes *being* or *reality*;—and activity, I
have just said, is "Life of Spirit" (reversing Aristotle's phrase, "Life=Activity of Spirit"); [9] or, it is
the *reality* of Spirit. Or, in other words, absolute
being, and all "*being as such*," is spiritual.

It is the application of these truths to the interpretation of physical science and its conceptions,
that excites at once the greatest curiosity, the most
invincible incredulity, and the most passionate resistance. *Curiosity* and *incredulity*, because a spiritualistic interpretation of the physical universe,—
nay, the very pretense that it is susceptible of such
interpretation, (not to say, that this is the only
possible one,) runs so decidedly counter to that
which, to most men, seems at first most immediately
and irrevocably certain. But the incredulous forget

in this connection, that certainty and truth may be, and, in the present case, are, separated by a wide interval. All of our immediate sensible consciousness is *certain;* it certainly exists; we are directly and unqualifiedly certain of it. But, in possessing this *certainty*, we are not necessarily in possession of any substantial *truth*. This distinction, between certainty and truth (the same as the one above mentioned, between fact and truth,) is of the greatest practical importance, and is one which we easily forget, if indeed we ever reflect upon it or even become explicitly aware of it at all.[10] And yet the distinction does not necessarily amount to real opposition. On the contrary, in spite of the wide interval which *may* separate them, certainty, rightly viewed, is but implicit truth; and truth is developed —explicated—certitude. The opposition between them is in reality only apparent, not real, and exists rather between a premature and unscientific— hence inexperimental and unjustifiable—interpretation of that which forms the immediate subject-matter of our certitude and the true interpretation, than between this subject-matter and the truth which philosophy—or absolute scientific inquiry—establishes concerning it. In our immediate sensible consciousness we seem to be directly certified of the existence of a world of absolute matter, the scene of blind physical forces, and it is to this apparent certitude that we tenaciously cling, incredulous of a truth which not so much merely overthrows, as purifies and explains it. Our immediate sensible consciousness, then, is unquestionably "certain," but this by no means carries with it the certainty of the existence of an absolute form of being, called matter, whose fundamental attribute consists in an inert and impenetrable occupation of space. On the contrary, physical science itself, which presents nothing but the results of an exact analytic exploration of the immediate content of sensible consciousness, declares, as we have seen, that such consciousness contains—so to express it—nothing but itself, or its own modifications—which latter, in their subjective aspect, are called mental phenomena, and in their objective aspect, are all comprehended, not under the conceptions of absolute matter and force, but only under those of configuration and motion.[11] Sensible consciousness, now, can be certain or can give rise to true certainty, only concerning that which it really contains,—this, surely, no one will doubt,—and if it contains no real evidence of the existence of an absolutely non-spiritual, *material* world, it certainly must be a mistake for us to suppose that through it we are made certain of its existence. The fact that we assume and pertinaciously believe in the existence of absolute matter, in spite of the fact that it is not contained in our immediate sensible consciousness, simply shows that sensible consciousness does not fill up the whole circle of human intelligence and requires something outside of itself for its own complete explanation.[12] And in the case of any explanation to be offered, all that can be demanded in the name of sensible consciousness—or "pure physical science"—is that the principle of explanation shall not directly or indirectly conflict in its application, with the immediate facts—phenomena, laws—of sensible consciousness itself. The "passionate resistance" above mentioned as being made to the spiritualistic interpretation of physical conceptions which philosophy offers, is inspired mainly by the fear lest the foregoing demand should not be respected—a fear which is surely wholly needless.

The conception of absolute unspiritual matter is an unrealizable one and absurd, because in direct conflict with the fundamental law of intelligence as established in the science of knowledge. This law requires subject and object, while different and apparently opposed, to be nevertheless organically one. The difference, in other words, must be only relative, not absolute.[13] But the supposition of absolute matter, and of this as known, or as an object of *intelligence*, is an hypothesis in direct and absolute conflict with this law. No wonder that the putative object of this conception—matter—remains wholly unthinkable, "unknowable," and its existence without shadow of demonstration. But the unthinkableness and indemonstrableness of absolute matter by no means demonstrates the truth of subjective idealism, or that the physical universe exists only in the form of transient phenomena of individual consciousness. This supposition is no less unthinkable than the former and is opposed to another part of that same law of intelligence, with which the

supposition of absolute matter conflicts. For if one
part of that law required that subject and object
should be joined together in a bond of essential
unity, (and thus excluded the supposition of absolute matter,) another part of the same law requires
that subject and object shall be really distinct; and
with this requirement the doctrine of subjective or
phenomenalistic idealism stands in conflict. No, the
physical universe is not a mere dream or phantas-
magoria; it is not a picture in my and your brain,—
a picture, for the rest, which, if the theory of absolute subjective idealism were true, would have to be
regarded as a picture of nothing. The physical or,
as it is called, the material universe is a true and
ideal object of intelligence. As such it possesses
being, but not, as *per* results of the science of
knowledge, a being which is incommensurate with
or opposed to intelligence, but a being which is, in
spite of difference and distinction, of the same kith
and kin with intelligence itself. Its being, in other
words, is in its foundations—its source and its goal—
living and spiritual—it is a manifestation of the " life
of spirit." It is a manifestation of this life, not con-
centrated in the form of personality, but dispersed
in the form of externality, and realizing itself subject
to the law of a temporal process. Its being, therefore, is not independent and original, but dependent
and derived.[14]

The most fundamental physical conceptions are
those of externality, or Space and Time. The existence of space and time, it is said, is the condition

of the existence of matter. And those who believe (or, rather, think they believe) in the being of absolutely non-spiritual matter, find, or have often found, a difficulty in conceiving how any existence whatever—and especially the existence of God—was conceivable, unless it were supposed to be conditioned by space and time, and hence "material." Such persons show that their whole and only conception of absolute being is materialistic, sensible, mechanical, *i. e.*, in fact, abstract, inexperimental, "*a priori*," and "metaphysical;" of spirit they know nothing but the name. Matter exists only in space, as the contained exists in the container. This is the first and obvious state of the case, as it presents itself to immediate sensible consciousness. Matter—thus the case is substantially viewed—exists as one thing, and space exists as another thing. If matter exists, much more must—in the estimation of a naïve materialism —space be held to possess absolute and independent existence. But how it, the impalpable, can exist, and that as the condition of all palpable existence, this is one of the questions which materialism is never able to answer, and remains as one of its final "inexplicabilities." It can only continue with blind and pertinacious obstinacy to assert the *fact* of the existence of space (and time), while confessedly unable to utter one rational word with reference to its how or what, or with reference to its "truth."[15]

Materialism, with its naïve, inexperimental, and unscientific way of looking at ontological questions is compelled to regard space and time as two pecu-

liar and special kinds of being; whereas they are not
(independent) kinds, but only dependent modes, of
being. Such existence as matter possesses, it possesses indeed only in dependence on space and time,
and so the existence of matter is a doubly dependent
one. Space and time are the proximate condition
of matter; but the condition of the existence of space
and time themselves is the absolute being of living,
active spirit.

The being of space and time and matter is revealed
to experimental, philosophic inquiry as dependently
and organically one—not mechanically or numerically identical—with the absolute being of Absolute
Spirit.[16] Materialism, in its conceptions of matter
and space, errs with blind and absolutely unscientific, unintelligent dogmatism, against the first and
simplest principle of ontology and of intelligence,
viz., the principle of the unity of being. Space, in its
view, is one kind of being, and matter is another,
and the two are conceived as indifferent to each other.
Thus it is imagined that the nature of matter is out
of all relation to the nature of space, so that space
might contain it just as well, even if its nature were
quite different from what it actually is, and so that, as
matter of fact, it does "contain" indeed another kind
of being, viz., spiritual being (provided, of course,
that such a kind of being actually exists at all).[17]
But this view is wholly and naïvely dogmatic, being
flatly opposed to the results of scientific, experimental
inquiry and in absurd and violent contradiction with
the first principles of thought and of being. (Unity

of being and unity of knowledge.) Philosophy demonstrates the ideal-real—*i. e.*, the spiritual—nature (the spiritual derivation) of space and time. It shows them to be equally subjective and objective, hence, *in their sphere*, universal, or at once independent and inclusive of the particular (individual) subject and objects of our sensible consciousness. They are, therefore, living, constantly-maintained products of an absolute activity, which transcends and includes all subjects and objects,—the activity (in the last resort) of absolute spirit, or, rather, of *the* Absolute Spirit, of God. I cannot, of course, be expected or permitted to enter here into all the details of the explanation of matter, as furnished by philosophic science. It suffices to say that the proximate root of matter is found to consist in "force," and force is, for philosophy, nothing but a function of spirit. Materialism says, Where there is no matter there is no force—making matter the creative condition of force. Philosophy says, on the contrary, and proves that force is the creative condition of "matter." It shows the necessary and conditioning relation of force, as a spiritual function, to space and time, as themselves also spiritual functions. It finds in the sensibly observable manifestations of force, with their fixed mechanical laws, evidences of the omnipresent and ever-present and all-sustaining activity of immutable, effective, spiritual being. The "mechanical" means, etymologically, much the same as the "instrumental." And so philosophic science finds, indeed, that the mechanico-physical universe, as such, is instrumental. It is instrumental as serving to express symbolically,—and hence, like all symbolic expression, in a way which "half reveals, and half conceals"—the thought, *i. e.*, the power and nature, of the Absolute Spirit, which is the Being of all beings, the original and originative essence of all existence. But it is also instrumental in a more immediate and obvious way. The whole mechanism of material or phenomenal existence reveals immediately its teleological nature, or that it exists for a use or purpose, and that use not a remote and extrinsic one, but an immediate and intrinsic, or "immanent," onè. Aristotle of old saw clearly, and pointed out, how every thing that exists "by nature," exists only as it actively *realizes* its existence, and realizes its existence only as it fulfils a law, or process, which is the law or process of its existence.[18] It performs a "work"—or, a work is performed in it—and this work is none other than the realization of its peculiar type or idea, its good, or purpose. Indeed, Aristotle perceived how motion itself, (which we are accustomed to think of only in its most abstract form, as mere change of place, or, at most as a merely "mechanical" product of time and space,—viewing it, for the rest, simply as a brute, inexplicable "fact," and not seeing, or, perhaps, ever imagining that any one ever did or could see in it anything else, any "*truth*,") Aristotle, I say, perceived how motion, even thus conceived in its most abstract or ideally empty form, presupposed and was conditioned by that other kind of "motion," which consists in the

realization of a type or idea, and which is thus shown
to be an ideally conditioned and hence a spiritual
process; or, otherwise expressed, Aristotle saw, or
at all events saw and said enough to enable us, if
we will, clearly to perceive, that the genus of motion is not change of place, but fulfilment of purpose.[19]
However this may be, the activities of organic nature
present to us a scene, in which not only the "fittest"
—which is nothing other than that which is best
adapted to its purpose—"survives," but also (which
is much more to our present purpose) in which the
law, type, and nature of intelligence are visibly re-
produced, in a magnificent "object-lesson," before
our very eyes. Intelligence, self-consciousness, is,
as we saw, a process in which the one subject identifies with itself its many objects. It goes out among
its objects and never loses itself. It makes them at
once instrumental to, and also integrant portions
of, its own life and being. This process we have already termed "organic." For indeed it is just such
a process, in kind, that is set before us explicitly in
what we are pleased to term, especially, "organic"
nature, (as though all nature and all existence were
not in a radical sense organic—*i. e.*, rooted in and
illustrative of the law and nature of intelligence).
For, in every living physical organism all the "cir-
culation of matter," all the oscillatory tumbling and
jostling of atoms, is inexorably subject and subservient to the law of a process, whereby one idea, one
life, one law, maintains itself through the multitude
of parts. Here Nature shows explicitly that her

being is grounded in spirit, that her life is the life (Plotinus used to say, the "sleeping life") of spirit. She thus points everywhere backwards and upwards to the Absolute Spirit as the ever-present and omnipresent ground and creative source of her own existence. But also, and in particular, through the series of her forms, which advance through a rising scale in ideal content, worth, and significance, she points to the full and explicit development of finite self-consciousness, as in man, as the proximate end to which all her varied activity is (again) but "instrumental."

The application of our ontological principles as founded on the science of knowledge to the conception and interpretation of human existence, or the explanation of the nature of man, is obvious. For the science of knowledge discloses—demonstrates—knowledge as, in its fundamental and all-conditioning nature, a spiritual process. And the "subject" or agent in this process is, as we have seen, not something mechanically separate or apart from the process. The rather, it is organically one with and even constituted by the process itself. It is therefore itself spiritual. But the "subject" or "agent" is man. Man, therefore, is primarily, fundamentally, and essentially a spirit. And *if* a distinction is to be made between spirit (or "soul") and body in man, we must say that man *is* a spirit and *has* a body, rather than that he *is* a body and *has* a soul. In short, man is *man*, only as he is spirit. What the relation of the knowledge of man as a spirit must be to the solution of the problems of moral philosophy, which is the true science of man,—and how, indeed, no solution of these problems is possible except on the basis of such knowledge,—all this will be accepted, without further explanation at this point, as obvious enough.[20]

Not less obvious is the relation of the principles in question to theism. Indeed, the recognition of the principles is nothing other than the recognition of theism itself. The " unity of being" (meaning of the absolute *"object"* of intelligence), which philosophy in the name of the very possibility of thought itself inexorably demands, can be for us, and is indeed for philosophy, none other than the unity of Absolute Spirit.

We have seen the absolute condition of knowledge to be the organic union or " identity " of subject and object. The subjective must bear the character of the objective, and the objective of the subjective. In the realm of the relatively objective—the world of sensible phenomena—we find this condition only measurably or, as we may say, potentially fulfilled. In the realm of absolute objectivity the condition must be absolutely fulfilled, and the absolute object of intelligence can, accordingly, only be, and be conceived and known, as Absolute Spirit. The absolute object of intelligence must, like the human subject, be itself a subject; and man who knows, must himself also—as the supreme condition of all his own knowing—be an object of knowledge to the everlasting and absolute Subject.[21]

The " unity of being," then, is, I repeat, for phi-

losophy, the unity of Absolute Spirit. What such a
unity is and what it implies, has, I trust, already
been made sufficiently obvious. It is not an abstract
unity, like that of the mathematical point, or of
"homogeneous matter," nor a unity without inherent
difference, like that of space or time. It is a concrete unity—a unity through and by virtue of difference,[22] and hence active and living. It is, in virtue of
the principles of the concretely experimental *science
of knowledge*, a unity of intelligence and of power. It
is a unity which is centred in personality and self-
consciousness. It is the unity of God. From the
ascription to the absolute being of self-conscious
personality, many persons have in modern times
professed to find themselves deterred by what seem
to them insuperable scientific difficulties. Personality appears to them to be a special mark of finitude
and hence something which must not be attributed
to the Infinite Being. These objections are raised
mostly by those whose eyes have not been trained
to discern, and whose intelligence is equally un-
trained to comprehend, spiritual—*i. e.*, living, actual
—relations. Their thought being accustomed to move
only among sensible categories and consequently to
take in none but mechanical relations, is either wholly
at a loss or is completely blinded and misled, when
occasion arises for the apprehension or recognition
of anything whose essence is "supersensible," *i. e.*,
genuinely vital and hence spiritual. Such persons,
therefore, identify personality, which is essentially
a spiritual category, and so transcends and condi-

tions space and time and their relations, with sensible, numerical individuality, which is an affair merely of limitation in and by space and time. By such *individuality*, one is *pro tanto* cut off from connection with all the rest of existence, and is indeed preeminently finite. But by his *self-conscious* personality, on the contrary, man finds himself, not cut off from, but indissolubly bound up with, all the rest of existence, including the Absolute (God) itself.[23] It is thus precisely by his personality that man finds himself taking hold upon the infinite, joined to it, and capable of becoming organically one with it, So it is through his personality that he is the image of the infinite, or made as the Scriptures have it, "in the image of God." "In the image,"—this implies, not that the personality of man is a perfect reproduction of the self-conscious existence of God, but only that it is more or less like it, and that the more perfectly, the more perfectly the human personality, with its necessary moral and intellectual attributes, is developed. What man, therefore, through his personality is finitely, imperfectly, dependently, that God—the Absolute—is infinitely, perfectly, independently. With this view of the divine nature, which philosophic science—the science of man's absolute experience—forces upon us, and with this view alone, can we, while holding fast to the necessary and fundamental doctrine of the unity of being, still maintain and comprehend the true and morally responsible independence of man. This view is the only one, which does not necessarily lead to the errors of atheism and pantheism. It is also the only one, with which the doctrine of the unity of being is experimentally consistent. If God is a spirit, and if man is a spirit, and if the root of all existence whatsoever is spiritual, then, and only then, can unity—organic, living unity, namely—consist with real difference and plurality, and the independent absolute with the dependent relative. Upon any other than the spiritualistic (and experimental) view of the nature of absolute being, the plurality of particular, finite existence is reduced to the rank of a mere insubstantial phenomenon, or of a mere irresponsible "bubble on the ocean of existence," as pantheists like to express it.

But to this and other points, which have been suggested or which will readily suggest themselves, we may have occasion to return in subsequent lectures. Let us hope, only, that the basis of doctrine, which we have now won, may serve to facilitate our subsequent progress.

LECTURE IV.

THE BIBLICAL THEORY OF KNOWLEDGE.

THAT, in planning and preparing the present course of lectures, I should feel an irresistible tendency to go back in thought to the time, years ago, when, for a limited period, I too was registered as a student of theology within these walls, to reflect on the intellectual experiences through which I then passed, and, judging of your needs by what my own then were, to seek in some measure to minister to you even as I would gladly have been ministered to,—all this you can readily understand. The position of one disposed to thoughtful and thorough study of "the faith delivered to the saints," or of what currently and worthily passes for theological truth, was then, and is still, beset with many difficulties and perplexities. Here—so one must argue to himself on contemplating the body of doctrine which he is beginning to study, and which he has already nominally accepted before beginning to "study" it—here is a body of doctrine which claims to be the truth, the truth *par excellence*, or, at all events, to rest on and so, directly or indirectly, to contain the revelation of such truth. But what is

(89)

truth? Truth exists for intelligence; it is the proper object of intelligence, of knowledge. Truth is truth of fact,—that is to say, it has in immediate fact its warrant and evidence. But—so one must go on to say to himself—is the truth which I accept as "re-vealed" indeed truth for my intelligence? Is it really an object of knowledge to me? Has my intelligence passed, with reference to the alleged facts of "reve-lation", from the state of mere information respect-ing the facts as reported or alleged, to the state of knowledge that the facts are indeed facts, or that they contain indeed the truth which they are reputed to contain? And here, of course, the question is not simply concerning the outward historical credi-bility of sacred narratives, or details of dogmatic definition, but, rather, concerning that which lies both deeper than and above all these things and about which, if any doubt remains, all time devoted to narratives and definitions is wholly wasted. The "truth" in question is often—and rightly—termed "spiritual truth." It is ostensibly truth about man as a spirit, about "God," the absolute and everlast-ing Being, as also a spirit, and about the relations which, as matter of immediate fact, actually subsist between the two, or which, as matter of right, duty, or privilege, should and may exist between them. Thus it is also termed peculiarly religious truth, and with absolute right:—for, as we shall subsequently more fully see, religion and, hence, religious truth are an absolute illusion, unless man be really a spirit and unless God, the universal and eternal source of

all existence, be also, and be known to be, a spirit.
But, now, if man is a spirit, and if he is the subject
of spiritual—which are vital, organic, and substantial
or essential—relations (not dead, mechanical, and
purely phenomenal or insubstantial ones,) he may be
expected in some way to be aware or assured of the
fact. For of what should man have knowledge, if
not of himself and of that which stands in vital and
essential relation to himself? And so, indeed, the
sense, either clear, conscious, and explicit, or, more
usually, obscure, more or less unconscious, and inexplicit, of man's spiritual nature furnishes the inexpugnable and indestructible root, from and upon
which, in the universal consciousness of mankind,
religion imperishably thrives. So long as his spiritual nature is to man not an object of clear, explicit,
reflective and scientific knowledge, it takes for him
the less hardy, but scarcely less persistent form of a
"faith," on which he dares to found all his hopes
and by which he is more than content to be guided
in all his conduct. But faith is only inexplicit knowledge. If it be any thing other than this, it is worse
than worthless. It is, or it marks, simply the state
of innocent childhood, but not, for that reason, necessarily of error in understanding. But the professed
student of Christian knowledge, he who is studying
with the openly confessed intention of becoming a
teacher of others,—he, I say, whatever may be true
of others, cannot remain unmindful of the Apostolic
injunction, " Be not children in understanding: . . .
. . . but in understanding be men" (1 Cor. xiv. 20).

He must—on penalty, if he do otherwise, of contradicting the very nature of his intelligence and so stultifying himself—seek to have his faith thoroughly "rooted in knowledge." And so, if he understands himself and his own needs, and means to be thorough and complete in the work which lies immediately before him, he not unnaturally turns to those who have sought to determine, on grounds of universal fact and experience, what knowledge, as such, is, what are the limits or what is the range of knowledge, what is and can be known. He asks, What does philosophic, or absolute, unqualified science demonstrate respecting the universal nature of knowable being? What is the utmost that it finds in the facts of existence? What is its final interpretation of the facts of man's conscious experience?

And now it is, I say, when the theological student, following a requirement which flows immediately and necessarily from the peculiar nature of his work, comes to put to himself these questions, that he is likely to find his way beset with perplexity and difficulty. He turns to "science," he turns to "philosophy," and naturally his first supposition is that he will hear the last word of philosophy or of absolute science, if he only listens intently to those whose names happen to be sounded most frequently and with most praise at the present moment. He listens, and what does he hear? He hears that all knowledge is sensation, or is the mysterious, but purely mechanical, result or accompaniment of molecular motions; that it is confined, in its ontological range, to sensible phenomena, and extends to naught that truly and absolutely is; that, while nothing can be known or determined respecting the nature of matter *per se*, or whether there be indeed any matter *per se*, all phenomena, so far as knowable, are in the last analysis *material in form* and can rightly be described only as phenomena of the "redistribution of matter and motion;" and that, finally, all knowable relations are mechanical, are relations of and in time and space as such, and are, accordingly, external and extrinsic, not internal and intrinsic,—accidental, (or, what is the same thing, fated,) not essential and self-determined,—dead, and not living. All this, I say, is what the young student, in quest of philosophic wisdom, is most likely to hear at the first, and is sure to hear, if he consults those supposed—and at all events, widely accepted—oracles of philosophic science, who have been enjoying in our day the most brilliant and influential notoriety among English-speaking peoples. And if, with the historic spirit, he follows back the main currents of scientific and ostensibly philosophic thought in Great Britain to their beginnings, and then follows them again from their beginnings down to the present day, he finds an unbroken line of ideal continuity connecting the men of the present with those of the past: the Mills and Spencers, the Bains and Leweses of to-day are the true intellectual descendants and heirs of the Bacons and Hobbeses, the Lockes and Humes of the past. The voice of the former, as regards philosophical questions, is in reality but an amplified and prolonged echo of the voice of the latter.

Recalling, now, the most general and universal presuppositions of his religious faith, viz., that man in his true and indestructible nature is a spirit, that the Absolute is a Spirit, and is God, and that real, spiritual relations unite man to this Absolute Being, our inquirer, by a natural necessity, goes on to ask those to whom we have imagined him as applying for information, "What, then, have you to say about spiritual existence? Is no such existence known or knowable? Does nothing spiritual exist for strict science, or as a literal, demonstrable object of knowledge? Is there at least no indirect evidence of the reality of such existence?" And to the complete intellectual discomfiture of faith—just so far, namely, as trust is reposed in the knowledge and authority of those to whom the foregoing inquiries are supposed to be directed—there comes to each of these questions a negative answer. Faith approaches the door of what she has taken to be the audience-room of pure intelligence, only to find herself absolutely refused admission. There—such is the apparent decree—she is not, and can not and must not be, at home. If her objects exist not—or, what amounts to precisely the same thing, if there be no evidence to intelligence of their existence—how shall she justify her own further existence? What is to stand between her and suicide? Whatever the issue in any particular case may be, it is obvious that it can never be a healthful one for faith, so long as the apparent conflict between it and intelligence remains unremoved. No, the foundations of faith must be scientifically justifiable, or else in the long run faith must vanish from the earth, perishing by inanition. For man is a thinking being. By his thought he is what he is.[1] By his intelligence he is led to do whatever essentially good thing he does. Nay, he " believes " only in accordance with the real or fancied dictates of his intelligence: he believes only because he knows, or thinks he "knows what he believes." And now, I have entered upon the course of inquiries, which have led us to the present point in our discussion, because the schism, which British sensationalism and agnosticism tends to establish between intelligence and a spiritual faith, is falsely and misleadingly regarded and proclaimed as the work of pure or "advanced" science and of philosophy, and the theological student, above all others, needs and has a right to know and to have it pointed out to him that this is so. Great Britain is an island, and not the whole world. And the seventeenth and eighteenth centuries of the present era—beyond which, in philosophy, such British "leaders" of to-day as Mr. Spencer have scarcely advanced one whit—constitute but an island, and that a very barren one, in the history of philosophy. Philosophy, as absolute experimental science, as the science of the whole and fundamental nature and content of man's actual experience, has demonstrated and still demonstrates—*i. e.*, points out, as truth of immediate and ever-present, experimental fact—that the spiritual exists and how and as what it exists; that the condition of all knowledge whatsoever is a spiritual process, and that the condition of all existence whatsoever is spiritual existence. The apparently contrary opinion of so many British leaders arises from the circumstance that they do not really know what the science of knowledge is, or how to study it. For this science they substitute, as I have previously pointed out, empirical, descriptive psychology, for the method of absolute science the mathematico-physical method, and for its results the highest generalizations of mathematico-physical (*i. e.*, sensible, phenomenal) science itself. Such errors and misconceptions philosophy, with its broader vision and more concrete method, wholly repudiates; and it is time that philosophy should assert its true nature among us and make known and defend its real achievements, and that true, spiritual religion—the religion which declares that God is a Spirit and that there is also a spirit in man, and that man, according to his true intention, is a son of God—should reap the benefit of such support as philosophy is thus prepared to give it. In philosophy, properly understood, religion is to seek and find its scientific justification.

The student of theology, then, has a right and it is his duty, to ask whether religion is scientific, is philosophical, is in agreement with the results of science and philosophy, and, consequently, to inquire what science and philosophy, as such, are, what results, relevant to the subject-matter of faith, they have reached, and how and on what grounds they have reached them. And he is entitled to have the path of his inquiry made easy for him, so far as this can be done by the explosion of false, though popular, notions as to what science and philosophy really are, who the true or properly accredited votaries and representatives of philosophic science really are, and what results have actually been reached by them. He is entitled, so far as this is possible, to be saved from the danger of wasting precious time in searching for the living among the dead, and it has been partly with a view to performing such a service, that I have followed the line of discussion, which has led us to the point where we now are. But more, if religion is a domain, not of pure fancy, error, or illusion, but of solid and everlasting truth and reality,—if the fact which it presupposes and proclaims is, not in discontinuity, but in continuity with the fact which philosophic science, with its strictly experimental and unbiased method, discovers and declares,—then religion is surely entitled, and theological students are entitled, to be assured of the fact, and that, too, in the name of science and philosophy themselves. And this assurance, also, I have been seeking to give,—or, rather, I have been seeking to provide the basis upon which, in the rest of our course, such assurance may be made, in all its leading details, doubly sure.

I desire, now, in the remaining portion of this course of lectures, to point out how Christianity, as the most spiritual of all religions, is also, and for that reason, the most philosophical, and to show, in

particular, that Christianity, in its Scriptures, either
directly contains, or else immediately and obviously
presupposes, a theory of knowledge and of the objects of knowledge—of the Absolute (or God), of
the finite world, and of man—which is not only confirmed by the results of philosophic inquiry, but also
has positively contributed, in the most marked way,
to the enrichment of philosophic science itself.

That Christianity is the most spiritual of all religions,—and this by universal confession,—we may
safely take for granted. Wherein the concrete and
intrinsic evidence of this consists, we shall have
abundant occasion to see, as we proceed with our
examination of its fundamental doctrines. It may,
even at the risk of repetition and anticipation, be more
to our purpose to say a word here as to the difference
between religion and philosophy, and more especially
as to how philosophy conceives and defines religion
and, so, by what standard she judges of the worth
or perfection of different religions, or, rather, forms
of religion.

It has no significance, or, at all events, no interest, to speak of the difference of things, which are
not at the same time in some way specially related.
Since, by way of very familiar example, there is no
special relation between a hat and an umbrella, it is of
no scientific interest to attempt to define the "difference" between them. But religion and philosophy
disclose a peculiar relation subsisting between themselves. They belong, we may say, to the same genus
and hence each is distinguished from the other by

an important and scientifically relevant specific difference. Both of them are works or functions of spirit, and of intelligence, *as such.* The fundamental condition and the final and highest end, result, or work of intelligence is, in different senses, self-consciousness. We have seen, namely, how the scientific examination of the nature and process of knowledge discloses, as the condition of knowledge in its lowest and simplest form (the form of mechanically-conditioned sensation), the formal presence and activity of self-consciousness. Here self-consciousness seems to be purely and only formal. It does not yet recognize and possess the content, with which it is filled, as peculiarly and explicitly its own. The content or matter of consciousness appears as something foreign to the self. But the final and highest end, result, or work of intelligence, on the other hand, consists, as we have also seen, in the discovery, and detailed demonstration of the fact that the whole realm of intelligence and, consequently, of reality is but the manifestation or realization of universal Self, or Absolute Spirit, so that all reality is, directly or indirectly, the reality of a Self, or is spiritual reality, and all intelligence is in like manner self-intelligence. Human intelligence realizes its full nature, when it recognizes itself as organically one, on its universal and fundamental side, with the Absolute Intelligence, so that its truest knowledge of itself is the knowledge which it has of itself as thus dependently one with God, and of all things as, through God, organically one with and in this sense

a part of itself. Philosophy, now, is the explicit, reflective, scientific demonstration of this relation of
finite to the Absolute Intelligence and of finite forms
of being to the Absolute Being. Or, philosophy is
in kind and in ideal, the realization of absolute self-
consciousness and so the apprehension of absolute
reality, in the form of pure thought. Religion, on
the other hand, substantially considered, is the realization of the same thing—*i. e.*, the realization of
man's true nature as organically, but dependently,
one with the Absolute, or God—not simply, or even
predominantly, in the form of pure cognition, but in
every form of actuality, or in one's whole, and actual,
and living being. Religion, thus concretely viewed,
pre-eminently *is*—or, since "being is doing," it actively *realizes and exhibits*—the truth which philosophy reflectively recognizes and demonstrates.
Religion is organic unity with God—in heart, in
will, in conscious thought, and in life.

Considered more abstractly and superficially, or
with reference to the images and stories, the rites
and usages, in which for thought and imagination its
substance is usually bodied forth, religion is in form
a non-scientific representation (through the aforesaid means) of the substantial truth of things—of
man, the world, and their relation to the Absolute,
—in accordance with that stage of intelligence and,
more especially, of religious life or of normally developed and perfected humanity, which its highest
representatives have reached or been able to recognize. It is especially noteworthy that the Christian

religion finds its first and fundamental expression, for all those who have lived and shall yet live after the death of its founder, in the simple story of a perfect life—a life of perfect union with God, the Absolute Spirit. Religion, then, in its various "scriptures," deals primarily, not in definitions, but in images and narratives. It is the work of an abstract or, as it is called, "dogmatic" theology, to define the truth which the images and narratives contain. Hence the fact that theology always tends to assume the form of a philosophy,—for philosophy is definition; it is the *definite recognition*, namely, and *demonstration of truth*.

Philosophy, then, recognizes that religion, substantially considered, as most perfect, in which the spiritual, substantial, vital, all-pervading union of man with the personal, spiritual Absolute is most perfectly realized—and realized through the unconditioned love, the unfaltering and energetic will, the clear intelligence, and the beautiful life of the individual. And that religion, formally considered, or viewed with regard to its symbolic expression, is, for philosophy, most perfect, in which the corresponding truth is most perfectly and distinctly symbolized. That, judged by these standards, Christianity stands at the head of all religions, as the one absolute and perfect religion, to which all others are related as relative and imperfect ones—this is a truth to which philosophy has borne willing witness.

With a view, now, to examining whether this witness is indeed true, let us first briefly consider, in the remaining portion of this lecture, that theory of knowledge, which is directly implied in the theory of the Christian life, as portrayed in the Christian Scriptures;—reserving for subsequent lectures the consideration of Christianity on its other philosophico-scientific sides, as a theory of the grand objects of knowledge—of man, the world, the Absolute, or God, and their mutual relations.

That the Scriptures represent the Christian life as most intimately—nay, indissolubly—bound up with a knowledge of some sort, no one of course, who looks at the subject even in the most superficial way, can for a moment doubt or deny. He who is the Alpha and the Omega of this life to all those who share in it, declares concerning himself, "I am the Way,"— the "Way," that is to say, obviously, for living, intelligent men, not for unconscious automata or machines; the "Way" for those who can perceive and know it and who, by an intelligent and sustained exertion of will, have the power to adopt it and to persevere in it. "I am," he says further, "the Truth." But truth is nothing out of relation to intelligence. Only through intelligence can it be possessed, and possess it we must—we must share in, or "be partakers of" Christ, "the Truth"—if we would enjoy that "Life," which, in the very next words, Christ goes on to say that he is. The truth which Christ professes to "be," is the absolute truth, the truth without qualification, the truth concerning the Absolute, the truth of God and of all things as existing and explicable only through him. It is the truth, the knowledge of which is the condition of our "liberty," our freedom—and true freedom is by no means a purely mechanical condition, as when we say of water, for example, that it is "free," if unobstructed, to run down hill, but is something far higher; it is a spiritual condition, or, better, activity, which can be realized only through intelligence. And so, too, finally, the knowledge of the same truth, the knowledge of God, is said to be eternal life,—not simply the condition of such life, but identical with it. The life in question—please observe—in being termed "eternal," is not designated as simply a life to come, a future life, a life which may yet be, but has nothing to do with the present. No, the eternal is an everlasting Now; in it there is no distinction of past, present, and future; in this sense it is superior to time. Time is the emblem and the condition of mutability, of change, of impermanence, so that every thing which is, as such, subject to the condition of time, has for its law that it shall "pass away." Thus whatever is characteristically subject to the condition of time, is *pro tanto* unreal, insubstantial, purely phenomenal, and man, so far as he is subject to this condition, is without true and abiding reality. It is only through his participation in an eternal life, that he has in him true substance or reality; and so it is—if the Scriptures are to be believed, only through the knowledge of God, more especially as presently and eternally revealed to the human spirit in the spiritual person of Jesus Christ, that man ever truly *is* himself. Mani-

festly, Christian knowledge, whatever this may prove
to be, is a most important thing in the theory of the
Christian life. The latter is represented as being a
life through growth in the knowledge of Jesus Christ
and of the Eternal Spirit whom he, not merely verbally, but actually, livingly, spiritually, reveals. It
is a life of sanctification—not through error, nor
through ignorance, nor through indifference to the
truth, nor, again, through a mock humility which ag-
nostically renounces the knowledge of the truth, on
the plea that such knowledge is too wonderful and
exalted for the finite vessels of our intelligence and
would, if once attained, be sure to work rather our
ruin, than our everlasting salvation; no, it is no such
sanctification as that; it is sanctification through the
truth, through a partaking of the Holy Ghost, the
Spirit of truth, who leads, not away from, but into
"all truth";—the Spirit who inspires, not a dread or
a despair of the truth, but the love of it, and the confident hope—nay, more, the assured knowledge—of
possessing it. And of its promised pastors—the pastors according to Jehovah's heart—it is declared, that
they shall feed their flock " with knowledge and understanding" (Jer. iii. 15).

Finally, St. Paul, "rude in speech, yet not in knowledge," confessed to a "great conflict" or agony of
prayerful desire, that the Colossian disciples might
attain to "the full assurance of understanding," *i. e.*,
to that completeness of assurance which understanding alone can give, so as to know the very
" mystery of God, and of the Father, and of Christ;

in whom are hid all the treasures of wisdom and knowledge" (Col. ii. 2, 3).

We remark, now, first, that, notwithstanding all this insistence on the dignity, value, and indispensableness of knowledge, there is yet recognized by Scripture a kind of knowledge, which is essentially vain, and which, accordingly, instead of building up, only "puffeth up." It brings, not the fulness of true, solid, spiritual substance, but only essential emptiness. This knowledge is that which has the appearance of being purely, as indeed it is primarily, individual. It is the knowledge of the "natural man," of man the sensible individual, in the intellectually and morally untutored condition, in which he is by physical nature launched into the existence of space and time. Its vanity and imperfection are declared by one of Job's questionable "comforters," who says roundly, "We are but of yesterday and know nothing, because our days upon earth are a shadow" (Job viii. 9). It is not knowledge *per se*, not knowledge without qualification, not absolute, substantial knowledge, but knowledge viewed in that aspect of it, whereby it is, as such, limited and determined by the conditions of space and time. It is the "form of knowledge" only, severed from the absolute content or substance. It is relative, phenomenal. It has for its immediate and only object that, whose very nature is, not to be, but to change and to pass away. It is a knowledge, therefore, which "cometh to nought";—it "cometh to nought," namely, when it is either in practice or in theory treated as the all in all of knowledge. Its theoretical end is (as we noted in our first lecture) the familiar spectre—and idol—of "agnosticism." And its practical end is, not the much-vaunted "lesson" of intellectual modesty on man's part, but the blasphemous imputation to God, the Absolute One, of its own limitations, saying, (Job xxii. 13), "How doth God know? can he judge through the dark cloud?" As though all knowledge were, as such, wholly an affair of sensible perception and consequently subject to the limiting conditions of such perception, rather than—as is indeed the case—mistress of them. As though "sensible affection" were the imperiously determining and conditioning principle, and not rather, merely an instrument of intelligence, and that for the absolute and perfect intelligence of the Almighty and Universal One—the "all in all"—as well as for the inchoate and undeveloped quasi-intelligence of the "natural man," or, the purely *sensitive individual!* And as though "the dark cloud," or any other purely sensible phenomenon, were an outermost or absolute boundary for intelligence—be that intelligence termed either "human" or "divine"—and not, rather, as it were, a mere stake, set, whether casually or necessarily, within the field of intelligence by intelligence itself.

And yet the Christian Scriptures do not pass, with reference to sensible knowledge and its objects, to that exaggerated extreme of abstraction and denial, which is illustrated in the Phenomenalism of Hindu religious philosophy. It is not that sensible knowledge and sensible existence are an unqualified illusion, or that, rightly understood, they are any illusion at all. The realm of such knowledge and of such existence is indeed a realm of "appearance," as distinguished from absolute and independent reality, but it is not therefore one of inherently false appearance. "The things which are seen were not made of things which do appear" (Heb. xi. 3). But it does not thence follow that they were not "made" at all, and hence that they have no sort of *real* existence whatever. It follows simply that they were "made" by, or have the necessary ground of their existence in, that which does not appear. The apparent has the root of its existence in the sub-apparent, the sensible in the non-sensible and intelligible, the mechanical in the organic and spiritual, the dead in the living. "The worlds were framed by the Word of God" (Heb. xi. 3), which "Word," as Reason, Life, Power, and personal Spirit, is to "the worlds," not merely as a "First Cause" in point of time, but as the everlasting, ever-present, ever-active, living principle of their existence and of their reality. If the worlds are to be designated as "appearance," it is the divine Word that appears in them. Their very nature is this, namely, to *be* the appearance of the divine, the absolute, word, reason, power, spirit, purpose. As their existence is dependent, it is thus also instrumental. It is the mechanism for the accomplishment of a divine purpose, the manifestation of the divine word or nature—*i. e.,* the manifestation of absolute being—which latter, accordingly, the Scriptures declare that they in fact

declare.   The sensible heavens declare the glory of
God (Ps. xix. 1).   Their very existence is a "language" or "voice," so that "there is no speech or
language, where their voice is not heard" (Ps. xix. 3).
"For the invisible things of him [God] from [and
including] the creation of the world are clearly
seen, being understood by the things that are made,
even his eternal power and Godhead" (Rom. i. 20).
Evidently, any criticism which the Scriptures pass
upon sensible knowledge, is directed to it only as
understood in that superficial sense in which it is
understood by a purely sensational theory of knowledge, where, in the phrase, "sensible knowledge,"
all stress is laid upon the epithet "sensible," and
the word "knowledge" is kept as much as possible
out of sight and thought and, for the rest, is left
almost wholly uncomprehended.   If sensible knowledge means simply immediate sensible perception—
the immediate consciousness, the mere "being
aware," of a sensible affection as a present fact of
individual experience, and nothing more—then, as
Bildad the Shuhite said, in agreement with the
sensational Agnostics of to-day, "we know [in the
absolute sense] nothing;" our "wisdom" comes finally to nought; and this the Scriptures, confirming
the voice of philosophy, declare.   But the Scriptures
also perceive, and, in the passage from Romans
above cited, plainly indicate, that sensible KNOWL-
EDGE is something more than mere sensible perception; that the world of sensible consciousness is
not *known* through the mere fact of our being sensi-

bly conscious of it, but through an active process of intelligence, to which the data of sense serve simply as that which they are, namely, *data* in a problem which can be solved only by going beyond the data, but to the true solution of which the data themselves, when truly apprehended, directly point.

But perhaps we are approaching too near to an anticipation of our conclusion, or of discussions which are announced to follow in a subsequent lecture. One of the defects of purely sensible knowledge is that it is, at least in form and appearance, exclusively individual. But purely individual knowledge, as the science of the subject shows, is, as such, an absurdity and an impossibility. Of this truth, too, the Scriptures would seem to manifest the most positive and explicit consciousness. Saint Paul's declarations to this effect are especially pointed. "I know nothing by myself," he says (1 Cor. iv. 4). And again, "If any [*individual*] man thinks that *he* [as *individual*, purely] knoweth any thing, he knoweth nothing yet as he ought to know" (Ib. viii. 2). And still again, with even greater explicitness, he declares that we are not "sufficient of ourselves to think any thing as of ourselves" (2 Cor. iii. 5). How truly these words are spoken—judged from the point of view of the science of knowledge—our previous discussions will, I trust, amply have prepared us to perceive. But does it then follow that we have no "sufficiency" or ability to "think" and to know at all? By no means; for the obvious fact is that we do think and know, in one fashion or another, and that it is only in consequence of this fact that *we* as self-conscious intelligences, exist at all. No, it is not that we have no sufficiency to think at all, but simply that it is important for us to recognize wherein that sufficiency really consists, and whereon it is truly founded. " Our sufficiency is of God " (2 Cor. iii. 5; see also 1 Cor. ii. 10–12). True knowledge, knowledge in the absolute sense, knowledge proper, is a spiritual process. It is possible for man only because and in so far as he is a spirit. " There is a spirit in man, and the inspiration of the Almighty giveth them understanding " (Job xxxii. 8). Were there no spirit in man, there were no understanding; and were there no inspiration of the Almighty, there were also no understanding. " The spirit of man is the candle of the Lord " (Prov. xx. 27). The individual man, through his spiritual nature, is *essentially* connected with and dependent on the Universal and Absolute, and in his intelligence, which is a spiritual process, this connection and dependence is consciously reflected, and is spoken of, in language which philosophic science also employs, as " a light." The light of our so-called individual —the rather, of our *personal*—intelligence is not self-lighted. It is not the light of the individual as such; it is, as the philosophy of knowledge has always perceived and declared, the light of the universal: science, knowledge as such, is only of and through or by the universal;—this we have found philosophy asserting ever since the day when, with Plato and Aristotle, scientific reflection concerning the subject began. But the universal, in the category of living reality, is, when carried to its final issues, or probed to its deepest foundations, nothing other than Absolute Spirit, or God. Here, then, in the realm of intelligence, is proved true, that which is declared by the Christian master: "He that findeth *his* [individual] life shall lose it; and he that loseth his life shall find it" (Matt. x. 39). "*Our*" life, as pure individuals, in the matter of intelligence, as in other weighty respects, is nought. To "find" it, is to find nothing, and less than nothing. Our intelligence is in proportion to its genuineness, not *ours* alone, but that of the universal, of God.[2]

The individual spirit of man, therefore, is, in respect of its intelligence—and without the function of intelligence it is no real spirit—a lighted "candle of the Lord." "The Lord giveth wisdom," even to them who consciously know it not.[3] Who, that is acquainted with the course of philosophic inquiry, is not reminded of Aristotle's declaration, that the "active reason" of man—the very root and basis and presupposition of all his intelligence, the functional condition of all knowledge of the universal, *i. e.*, of all true science—is "something divine," or is of divine origin, and may be symbolically described as entering into us, *as individuals, or quasi-individuals*, from without, "as through a door?" And who does not involuntarily recall how the post-Kantian inquiry, in the history of German philosophy, taking its immediate, historic cue from Kant, (who had demonstrated anew that all knowledge is the depend-

ent result of what we must term a distinctively spiritual process,) but, above all, and more especially, being
guided to its conclusions by the nature of the case itself, as revealed to experimental inquiry, was brought
directly to recognize the fact that knowledge, as an
affair (to first appearance) of purely individual origin
and nature, (or of the "individual ego") was wholly inexplicable without reference to an "Absolute Ego,"
which indeed transcends the individual ego, but in
and through which alone the intelligence of the
latter "lives, and moves, and has its being?" Nay,
more, to what but to the necessity of recognizing
some such truth as the one we are now contemplating does the mechanistic evolution-philosophy of our
day point. In this "philosophy" it is Evolution that
stands, practically, for the Absolute. For Evolution
is conceived as the law and process which determines
all (knowable) existence. It is not regarded as the
law or fancy of the individual subject of knowledge,
merely; it is viewed as the law of the universal and
final Object of Knowledge. And what is the "philosophy of evolution" but the Absolute, as thus poorly
conceived, thinking itself, as it were, in and through
the individual, and becoming thus not only the principle of the individual's knowledge of it (the "Absolute"), but also of the true knowledge and explanation of himself and of all things as determined by
and according to it? And if evolution-philosophy
stops short with the recognition of such an "Absolute" (and thus suggests a conception of knowledge
which is so essentially pantheistic), we have already

learned that the reason for this is to be found, not
in the intrinsic limitations of human intelligence, as
such, but in the limitations with which the evolu-
tion-philosopher voluntarily and arbitrarily surrounds
his own particular intelligence.

The knowledge, then, which the theory of the Christian life, as expressed in Scripture, implies and requires, is " spiritual knowledge." It is a knowledge
which the individual possesses, not as mere individual, but only by virtue of his organic, living connection with the universal and absolute. It is a knowledge, which, in form and kind, corresponds perfectly to
the definition—universally accepted, either expressly
or implicitly—of scientific knowledge. It is not, as is
too often supposed, something absolutely *sui generis*,
inexplicable, miraculous, and without scientific rhyme
or reason. No, it is not discredited by the science
of knowledge. The rather, it is the living, practical fulfilment of knowledge, according to the ideal
requirements and presuppositions of such science.
"The practical fulfilment," I say, just as we might
say that breathing, digesting, and all other physiological processes, as actually carried on in the human
body, are carried on in "practical fulfilment" of the
"presuppositions and requirements" of physiological science, just as well in the case of those who are
wholly ignorant of physiological theory, as in the
case of the accomplished physiologist himself. The
functions of the human spirit may proceed normally
and accomplish their due result in the practical knowledge and possession of the truth, and of eternal life

through such knowledge, even in the absence of explicit knowledge (scientific information) respecting the process of its own intelligence. But this does not prove that religious disciples, and, above all, religious teachers, can afford to slight or to undervalue the benefits of such scientific information. For although, without it the truth *may* be lived, felt, and even correctly spoken, yet, being unable to give a rational account of itself, it is, as history is ever showing, thus rendered liable to wander in all sorts of devious and unwholesome ways, and, above all, is unable to defend itself before that very forum of intelligence, before which, by virtue of its very nature, as an ostensible function of intelligence, science is with justice ever citing it to appear. Religion is robust and really mistress of itself, only when it is "always ready to give an answer to every man that asketh a reason of the hope" that it inspires.

The Christian life is, according to the Scriptural theory, a "partaking of the divine nature." Our examination of the Scriptural theory of knowledge shows, in particular, that Christian knowledge—the true knowledge—is held to be realized only through a participation in the divine, the absolute, intelligence, and that this claim of Christianity is in no sense unscientific. We only remark, in this connection, that the theory and the facts in question bring vividly before us the truth, at once religious and philosophical, that God is a being "near at hand, and not afar off" (Jer. xxiii. 23), and that the more human thought realizes its true nature, becomes true to itself, or is indeed true thought, the more distinctly does it recognize the literal fact that all its works are "begun, continued, and ended" —not in a mechanical and pantheistic process of evolution, merely, but—in God. Just as, universally, the intelligent "service" of God is "perfect freedom," so, in particular, the thought which is begun, continued, and ended in God is the only perfectly "free thought." It rests on and is filled with the absolute substance of thought. What is often termed "free thought," is free only in this secondary and insubstantial sense, that it is contingent. But contingency is not the element in which true freedom lives or can live. *Its* service is essential bondage. The contingent is the incalculable, and that thought which is at its mercy, is free only in name. No wonder that its final issue is, and has always been, not the free and masterly assurance of knowledge, but scepticism, or agnosticism. "Free thought," thus miscalled, is thought remaining at that point of view which—according to the distinction rightly made by Hegel—distinguishes the "religions of nature" from spiritual or absolute (and, in particular, from the Christian) religion. It is that point of view which separates mere agnostic sensationalism from philosophy. It is the point of view of "consciousness," as distinguished from "self-consciousness." It is that point of view, from which the knowing subject appears as a purely individual agent, (or *recipient*, rather), set over against an indefinite aggregate of objects, called a "world," and between which and the knowing subject none other than superficial mechanical relations either do or can exist,—so that knowledge is and can only be conceived as the purely mechanical result of contingent impressions. Here one man's impressions are as good as another's, *i. e.*, they are good for nothing, as keys to absolute *knowledge.* From this point of view, the farthest that one can or ever does get, in the way of an absolute, objective, conviction, is to the belief—subject to the caprices of "argument"—that there is somewhere "a God," not to the present knowledge of him. A "First Cause" existing before the world, and now remaining afar off from it, is postulated or conceded," but all knowledge of him is regarded as a matter of indirect and more or less credible information, or of "argument," and not of immediate and necessary intelligence. Or if, as in the conceptions current in the religions of nature, God is thought of as standing in any sort of present relation to men, he is regarded merely as one brutely possessing all power, so that he may, if he will, mechanically adjust circumstances in the world in a manner to conform to our desires, *i. e.*, so as to secure for us the reception of a pleasant series of impressions from the objects that surround us and from the situations in which we may be placed. At this stage of thought, which survives so widely to-day, the spiritual foundation of all existence and of all knowledge is not known, and consequently God, as the Absolute Spirit, by whom and through whom are all things, who keeps no holiday, but "worketh

hitherto" and still works,—God, who is not far removed from any one of us, but is absolutely near,—
God, in the true and literal, present and everlasting
knowledge of whom "standeth our eternal life,"—
is not known: He is worshipped, if at all, only in
name, not in Spirit and in intelligent and everlasting possession of the truth. And above all, the
truly ethical element is banished from the conception of him and of his relation to the world. For
all really ethical relations are spiritual and only
spiritual. Man is a moral being only because he '
is a spirit; and hence those ostensible "moral systems," which take no account of man in his spiritual nature, but regard him purely as a so-called
"natural being" or mere physical and psychical
automaton, are easily, and have often been in fact,
convicted of being "moral systems" only in name.
And so, too, it is only when God is truly known as
an Omnipresent Spirit, that he becomes, for human
conception and praxis, a moral being, so that man
can be conscious of moral and truly religious relations as binding him to God and can see in God a
true, *i. e.*, a moral, Governor of the universe, and not
simply, as pure mechanism would require, a mere,
irresponsible tyrant (in the Greek sense of this
term). So fundamental and far-reaching are the
interests which are bound up in the Christian theory of knowledge, or indeed, as we may well and
truthfully say, in the theory of knowledge, taken
without any qualifying epithet.

It remains only for us to say a word respecting the

connection of the results which we have reached
with the conception of "revelation."

And first we remark, that from the point of view
of the mere individual, all true knowledge, all genuine
science, is of the nature of revelation. And first
this revelation has the appearance of being purely
mechanical. The object of knowledge first has the
air of being mechanically brought or *shown to* the
knowing agent. It does not appear to belong to
him as his own, or as a part of himself. It does not
seem to lie within the territory which is covered by
his proper self. It does not appear to him as something which it is a part of his very nature to know,
and not knowing which he were something less than
˙s own complete and proper self. It seems to be
mechanically revealed to him, as by special but inscrutable grace, and as from without. But we now
know, on the authority of philosophic science, as
well as of religion, that all this is so only in appearance. We know that a revelation, purely on the
terms and in the form just mentioned, is an impossibility; for no knowledge whatsoever is possible
on purely mechanical conditions. The Scriptures,
therefore, when received in a purely mechanical way,
are no revelation. They are then simply a dead
letter, which kills, instead of enlivening and quickening, intelligence. The only authority which such
a "revelation" possesses is that of accidental might,
but not of real and effective, because recognized or
recognizable right.[4] It may be accepted through
fear, but it may also, as daily observation informs

us only too well, be rejected and shaken off through arbitrary and capricious wilfulness. No, the mechanical reception and possession of the Scriptures is only the first and necessary precondition to the further reception of them with the eyes of an opened "understanding" (Luke xxiv. 45), so that they may become to us truly a word of life.

But again, our studies have further informed us that, in the view both of philosophic science and of Scripture, all " understanding " or knowledge proper is of the nature of revelation in another and truer sense. It is of the nature of self-revelation. And here we may lay it down as an axiomatic truth for all intelligence,—whether the latter be termed " religious " or " philosophical,"—that all genuine, or complete and effective, revelation is, *in form and kind,* self-revelation. For it must have the form and be submitted to the nature of self-consciousness.[5] Revelation is of the same nature or genus as intelligence itself. If philosophy means simply being everywhere —in all fields of intelligence or of the " objects " of intelligence—" at home," so that in all one's true knowledge one knows only one's own (larger) self, and in all one's findings finds only that same Self, religious " revelation " means the same thing. The " larger self," it will be remembered, is divine, and is graciously bestowed on man as the precondition of his true existence, as well as of his intelligence. We truly are, and we truly know, only as we become " partakers of the divine nature." If, therefore, it is the voice of God which is heard in the

word divine, it is also, and for that very reason, also
the voice of man,—the voice of man, namely, according to his true nature and intent; of man as he is at
once revealed to himself and as God also is revealed
to or set before him, not in an abstraction, but in
the living, spiritual person of the Incarnate Word,
the Son of God and Son of Man in one,—or, finally,
of man in his—not individual, but—personal or organic union with God, the Absolute.[6] And as the
bond of organic union for spiritual personalities is
and can be nothing other than Love, the voice is
the voice of love and the effective hearing of it is
conditioned by love.[7]

From all this it follows that the true revelation
does not fundamentally consist in the communication of dates and figures or of any other sort of purely
historic information. It may be given through these,
but is in no sense merely identical with them. It is a
revelation by, of, and to the spirit, and can be only
spiritually discerned. Its proper content is the absolute and not the relative.

It follows, further, that the content of revelation
can be nothing which is essentially out of relation
to intelligence. It must be of, from, and for the
world of intelligence as such. In this sense it cannot be essentially "mysterious." To the "natural
man" it may indeed be mysterious. To the sensational agnostic it not only may be, but is confessedly, mysterious, and for that reason incredible.
But so also, to him, all philosophy proper, all absolute truth, as well as all absolute religion, is a

mystery and theoretically incredible. But it is not of such that we now speak. We say only that for the true and proper man, for him who has reached the stature of real, and not merely nominal, spectral, manhood—in other words, for him who has become and is a true spiritual being in fact as well as in name—for him, and for his intelligence, be the latter called philosophic or religious, no truth is or can be essentially mysterious, and none can be revealed as such. It may not, in all its details, be completely apprehended, but it must in its substance be comprehended.[8] Intelligence must find its own larger lineaments reflected in its every dogma. Truths which, as ostensibly absolute and of the absolute, are therefore truths which are of the very essence of reason and of reality, cannot be revealed, as they cannot be known, except as in harmony with both reason and reality and as throwing an illuminating light on both. Absolute truths must be all-explaining and all-illuminating. They must really enlighten, and not simply mystify, intelligence.

That, now, with these explanations, it should be possible and conceivable that through the mouths of holy men truths have been spoken, which they, of their individual selves were incompetent to know and to speak, and that the knowledge or inspiration by virtue of which they did this was a knowledge and inspiration from the Most High, all this we may readily and gratefully admit and can now, as I trust, without too great difficulty understand.

LECTURE V.

BIBLICAL ONTOLOGY;—THE ABSOLUTE.

"Denn das Leben ist die Liebe,
Und des Lebens Leben Geist."—*Goethe.*

THE Absolute is everywhere. It is strictly con
tinuous or co-extensive with all existence. To
treat of it exhaustively were, therefore, in one sense,
the same as to treat of *omne scibile.*

The Absolute, I say, is omnipresent. This is the
doctrine of religion as well as of philosophy. "Whither
shall I go from thy Spirit? or whither shall I flee from
thy presence?" (Psalm cxxxix. 7.) And the Psalmist who puts these questions immediately answers
them in language which indicates that the omnipres-
ence of God is not simply a mechanical, external
presence, without influence upon that to which he is
present, but that it is a presence in effective power
and reality. It is a presence to "lead" and to uphold.

No superstition—I use the word advisedly—no superstition is, from the point of view of absolute science, more groundless, and yet none is, in our day,
and among those who lay claim to a certain degree
of scientific illumination, more common, than that
which finds expression in the theoretical or practical

treatment of sensible "nature" and of her supposed "blind forces" as if they were complete and independent in themselves; so that, if there be aught which is more absolute than they, it must nevertheless find in them a foreign and limiting and resistant obstacle, and not, rather, a connatural and pliant servant. The true Absolute, or God, is thus viewed as not at home in the universe. Here he has no longer power or right. Or, if the contrary is still admitted, the power is a foreign one and the right is, accordingly, one of purely arbitrary and extrinsic might. It is a *right* only in name, for in pure might there is no intrinsic right. This view has for centuries had, and still has, a considerable—and pernicious—currency in certain strata of the nominally Christian world. The basis for its scientific refutation has, if I mistake not, been furnished, in general terms, in a preceding lecture. We shall have more to say concerning it in the following one, for which place we also reserve the not difficult task of showing that the Christian religion repudiates it.

Nature is not foreign to the Absolute. It has its very life and being in and by it. The Absolute is present in nature, and if you would know what the Absolute is, you may, if you choose, look for it, and study it, and find it in nature. But not in its completeness and purity. For the Absolute is not absorbed in nature. Nature, on its most characteristic side, is an "other" than the Absolute, although it is *its* "other." If it points to, and even, to the eye of a true and patient intelligence, presently reveals the

Absolute, yet it, as such, is not the Absolute. If the omnipresent root of its being and of its reality is the Absolute, yet it is not itself that root. Or if, again, in the language of Scripture, God "filleth all things," yet it does not thence follow that all things are God. To-night then, in dealing with "The Absolute," we wish to fix attention on the Absolute not so much in the aspect of its oneness with nature, as in its separation and distinction therefrom. We desire to fix attention, in other words, on that which 'fills," rather than on that which is filled.

Philosophic science, as we have seen, finds the Absolute disclosed, not to mechanical sense, but to spiritual intelligence. Its nature and reality are known through the ever-present witness which it bears of itself to and in the living, intelligent spirit of man. Such witness nought but spirit can give, and, on the other hand, nought but the witness of a spirit can the human spirit truly receive. Philosophy, therefore, as the expression of absolute or pure intelligence, finds, knows, and declares that the Absolute is Spirit, and is God. This we have already seen, and we have also seen in somewhat general terms what it is to be a spirit, at least on the side of intelligence or pure cognition. We have now to see what God, as the Absolute, and a Spirit, is for the Christian religion, and may hope, as we proceed, to find occasion to render our ideas concerning the spiritual nature still more explicit.

No multiplication of texts is necessary to prove that for the Bible the Absolute is God, and a Spirit.

"I am the first and I am the last," says the "King of Israel," speaking by the mouth of the prophet Isaiah (xliv. 6). The "heaven of heavens" cannot contain him. He is not bounded by time and space. The rather, he is himself their boundary and their condition. And so, as we have seen, one of the most solid, as well as one of the most important of the achievements of philosophy—and especially of modern philosophy—has been the demonstration of what is termed the "ideality of space and time," or the truth that space and time are, not limiting preconditions of spirit and of absolute being, but dependent functions thereof. And this demonstration—accompanied by the recognition of space and time as the peculiar and determining conditions of sensible phenomena, as such,—discloses itself at once as but an organic part of the demonstration, which was carried so far in ancient philosophy, to the effect that the sensible universally is but as the voice or language, or is the partial manifestation or actualization, of the intelligible; so that the sensible consists by the intelligible and spiritual, and not *vice versa*, while, on the other hand, the intelligible and spiritual exists in or fills the sensible, but is not wholly absorbed in it.

He who is the creative condition of space and time, must bear a like relation to all conceivable manifestations of power or force in the sensible universe. These manifestations take the form of motions, and motion is an ideal resultant of space and time. Indeed, it is only in and through motion that space and time realize themselves. A space and time which should not give evidence of their reality through motions, would not be known and would not concretely exist. Conceived independently of motion, they are pure abstractions. The condition of space and time must therefore be the condition of all motion, and this condition—or, in other words, the Absolute conceived with immediate reference to motion—is what men ordinarily term power or force. (This they do, as is well known, in agnostic systems of "philosophy," where, as the ground or source of all phenomena,—*i. e.*, cases of the redistribution of matter and motion,—a "persistent," but "inscrutable" and "unknowable," because non-sensible and absolute, "force" is postulated.) God, then, is for the Bible the Absolute also in point of power. "I am the Almighty God" (Gen. xvii. 1). Such is the character in which the Absolute is revealed and displayed in the magnificently simple and impressive first chapters of the Book of Genesis. The Absolute, God, is indeed power, is "force"; "power belongeth unto God" (Ps. lxii. 11); "without" Him "nothing is strong" (Collect for the Fourth Sunday after Trinity). But he is not for that reason mere brute or blind force, nor inscrutable. The Scriptures' no more countenance that impossible abstraction, which is termed blind or brute or mechanical force, than does philosophy. It is only from the point of view of purely physical science, as the science which has to do with the sensible as such, and with it alone, and which therefore rightly and necessarily

abstracts from all that is non-sensible,—including,
therefore, force itself,—it is only from this point of
view, I say, that force can come to be *spoken of*—I
will not say, *conceived*—as something "blind," "brute,"
or "purely mechanical." These epithets belong, at
most, only to the sensible manifestations of force,
but never to force itself. No, the conception of force
is not a mechanical, but a spiritual conception, and
so physics, which must needs speak of force and forces,
points, for its own ideal completion, to metaphysics,
just as the sensible, universally, points for its complete explanation to the spiritual. The Scriptures,
I say, countenance only a spiritualistic conception
of force or power. No doubt "In the beginning God
created the heaven and the earth" by his *power*. But
it is also just as indubitable,—as for philosophy, so
also for religion,—that "The Lord by *wisdom* hath
founded the earth; by *understanding* hath he established the heavens" (Prov. iii. 19). Just because the
power to create was there, the wisdom was also present; for power and wisdom are but names for two
ideally distinguishable, but really inseparable, aspects or functions of the one only reality which is
truly substantial and absolute and eternal, namely,
Spirit. As of wisdom, so of power, the ontological
explanation is living spirit. Power and wisdom,
taken by themselves, are dead abstractions. They
are real only through their organic identity with, or
functional relation to, Spirit. And if to either of
these two a primacy or logical priority is to be as-
signed, this must be given the rather to wisdom than

to power; for wisdom is a category or function which leads the mind by a less circuitous and indirect route to Spirit, as its ontological condition, than power. In the beginning was, unquestionably, the Power. This were a true saying; but to say it were undoubtedly—such is the havoc that a sense-begotten habit and necessity of abstraction plays with human conceptions—to express less unequivocally to the popular mind the truth about the Absolute than to employ another expression, which strictly includes the foregoing, and to say, with Scripture, "In the beginning was the Word." God, the Absolute, upholds all things "by the *word* of his *power.*" The Word, the Logos, the Reason or Wisdom, is the Power; and *vice versa:* who says the one, says also, by necessary implication, the other; since both—viz., power and "word," or "wisdom"—exist and are known only as organically one in and inseparable from the life or reality of Spirit. And so God declares, through the mouth of his prophet, that he is God, the Absolute and Eternal One, "not [primarily] by might, nor by power, but by my spirit" (Zech. iv. 6). As such, he is personal. He is not the everlasting "It is," but the "I am." "Before the mountains were brought forth, or ever thou hadst formed the earth and the world, even from everlasting to everlasting, thou art God" (Ps. xc. 2). The human spirit thus looks into the face of "the high and lofty One that inhabiteth eternity," and addresses him, not as a mysterious It, but, familiarly, as "Thou." It recognizes in him, the Absolute, the personal Spirit, the "dwelling-place for all generations," the ever-lasting Home, nay, the never-absent Father, of its own and of all spirits. Here it, the relative, and dependent, finds the secret and the source of all its own true life and reality, as of all its true blessedness. But now we may seem to be treading on ground foreign to our subject, which is God, the Absolute, as such, and not the special relations of man to him. And yet, if God is to be known by man, it is obvious that this very act of knowledge must bring him into relation to man. Not only is this so, but for the Christian consciousness God becomes truly known, or fully revealed and at last "seen," in the spiritual personality of a man,—the "man Christ Jesus."

We saw in our third lecture that, for philosophy, the knowledge of the infinite or absolute, as spiritual personality, is founded in and rendered possible through the spiritual personality of man. The conscious thought and knowledge of man, as such personality, involved, as we saw, the present power and light, and thought of the universal, living, and absolute Spirit. The relative and finite in human life and thought appeared, not as bounding, limiting, warding off, and repelling the true infinite—which were absurd—but as enclosed in it. And it was seen to be thus "enclosed," not in a purely mechanical way,—which again were impossible; the infinite is not a mechanical instrument; it is not a vessel made of space or time, or both,—but in an organic union, as it were members of a living ideal whole, to the very comprehension and existence of

which the whole is necessary, even if *they* are not
equally required as well for the existence as for the
comprehension of the whole.   It is only for an
essentially sensational theory of knowledge, and for
a philosophy or theology founded thereon, that
self-knowledge becomes a principle or occasion, not
of knowledge, but of necessary ignorance, concerning the Absolute or God.   Here, where the highest
conceptions and relations that are known or recognized are sensible and mechanical ones, the dictum is not unnaturally accepted and put forth, that
"All limitation is negation."   In the realm of purely
sensible relations this is obviously true.   Here the
limiting is *only other* than, or different from the
limited.   But to affirm that the same is true universally and without qualification, is, obviously,
simply to affirm, without demonstration and even
contrary to demonstration, that the absolute object
of knowledge is sensible, or that that, which is true
within the realm of sensible phenomena as such, is
true within the whole realm of all possible knowledge.   But philosophy, as we have seen, has a
demonstration to the contrary founded on experimental fact.   Philosophic science, as in ideal, the
pure and complete science of experience, finds the
absolute object of knowledge to be, not dead, but
living, not mechanical and sensible, but organic and
spiritual; and its highest conceptions are framed accordingly.   And so philosophy perceives and demonstrates that in the spiritual realm of absolute
reality limitation is not negation alone, but is

also, and primarily, affirmation. Here the dictum is, "All limitation is self-limitation, and so is self-affirmation." The limitation proceeds from a self, which, by the very fact and act of limiting *itself*, affirms itself. It is thus that philosophy finds in the very life and thought of the finite and relative individual,—nay, more, finds even in the lowest forms of sensible existence,—the true infinite and absolute, not negated and obscured, simply, but affirmed. The true finite, or the finite truly *known*, (not simply, *sensibly perceived*,) reveals the true infinite. It points toward the infinite, not away from it. And so finite man, in *truly* knowing and affirming himself, as a spiritual personality, knows also and affirms God, as the present Father of his spirit.

The Scriptures, now, not only recognize and confirm the general truth of this statement of the case, but also, and especially, in their account of the nature and work of the Christ, they furnish a concrete and special application of it, in which we may say that the whole and characteristic essence of Christianity is contained.

The Scriptures recognize, I say, the general truth in question. This they do, for example, through their conception of "a law written in the heart," and through and in which the nature of God, the lawgiver, is immediately made known. A writing in the heart is no mere mechanical writing. The heart is no mere dead tablet of stone. Nor is it merely the seat of blind and involuntary feeling. "The heart" is the living human spirit. It is organically one

with mind. Its functions are intelligent, for "with
the heart man *believeth* unto righteousness," and so
is "*wise* unto salvation." And so, then, this is the
promise of God, which is echoed from the Old Testament into the New:—"I will put my laws into
their mind, and write them in their hearts: and [so]
I will be [not simply appear, or be reported] to them
a God, and they shall be to me [in immediate, living
relation] a people: and they shall not teach every
man his neighbor, [as though the true knowledge
of God were a matter of casual information, to be
acquired by mechanical communication of 'ideas'],
and every man his brother, saying, Know the Lord
[as who should say, for example, I tell you that
there is 'a God,' and who and what he is, and
there are no data at hand in your own mind and
heart, whereby you might know him yourself, by
proper self-knowledge, unless I or some one else
told you]: for all shall [not falteringly and doubt-
fully believe in, but] know me, from the least [from
those whose stock of erudition, or of miscellaneous,
mechanical, and essentially contingent information,
is the least] to the greatest" (Heb. viii. 10, 11).

But, secondly, it is in the personality of a trans-
cendent Man that Christianity finds the true revelation, the present knowledge, and the perfect
exemplification of the nature of the absolute and
everlasting God. To the Christian consciousness
this man is "the image of the invisible God" (Col.
i. 15). Speaking in his own name, he says, "Neither
knoweth any man the Father, save the Son, and he

to whomsoever the Son will reveal him" (Matt.
xi. 27). And again, "He that hath seen me hath
seen the Father" (John xiv. 9). "He that believeth
on me, believeth not on me, but on him that sent
me" (John xii. 44). And yet the true sight of him
is not the sight of him, the human individual, as he
traverses the coasts of Judea, on his never-tiring
mission of good works and of love. And the true
belief is not identical with the intellectual admission
that he, as Son of God and Son of man, once actually
walked this earth. In language which, to the disciples, the eyes of whose understanding had not yet
been fully opened, doubtless seemed very paradoxical, he declared that they would first truly see him,
when he should have gone to the Father (John xvi.
16; and xiv. 19: "Yet a little while, and the world
seeth me no more, but ye see me ."). The true sight
of Jesus, that sight which involves the vision also
of the Father, or of the "invisible God," is, not
physically, but spiritually, conditioned. It is a sight
which is of, by, and for the spirit, and so conforms
strictly to the requirements and conditions of absolute knowledge. It is a sight, or knowledge, which
is rendered possible only through the present illumination of the absolute, living, and Holy Spirit
of truth. It is a knowledge, therefore, in organic
dependence on the Absolute Spirit. If all our "sufficiency to think" is "of God," more especially is
our ability to think and know the Christ divinely
derived; whence no man can say [knowingly] that
Jesus is the Lord, but by the Holy Ghost" (1 Cor.

xii. 3). "Through him we have access by one Spirit
unto the Father" (Eph. ii. 18). The true understanding of Christ is a "spiritual understanding" (Col. i. 9).
And the true witness concerning Christ is a witness
of the Spirit, and for the spirit. The "Spirit of truth
. . . . proceedeth from the Father" and testifies
of Christ (John xv. 26). He takes of the things of
Christ and shews them unto us (xvi. 15). And that
which He, the absolute principle of all intelligence,
the very "Spirit of truth," shall enable the true
disciples to see and to know, is—in the Master's
own words—"that I am in my Father, and ye in
me, and I in you" (John xiv. 20); and again, "as
thou, Father, art in me, and I in thee, that they also
may be one in us: . . . . I in them, and thou in me, that
they may be made perfect in one" (John xvii. 21,
23). Not miracles alone, or as such, nor what is
termed "credible historic testimony," but the reception of this witness of the spirit and of fact—the
fact of men "made perfect," perfected, completed,
rendered at last true, and not merely nominal, men
through actual, living, spiritual union through the
Son with the Father—this it is which according to
Christ shall make "the world" know and "believe
that thou hast sent me" (John xvii. 21). The kind
of being which is here known, corresponds to the
kind of knowing: both are spiritual; and we shall
have presently to inquire what light is thrown for
us upon the nature of spiritual being by the fore-
mentioned witness of the spirit concerning the Christ.

But first we mention that spiritual being, or the

Absolute, is often referred to in the Scriptures, not only in terms which express wisdom or intelligence, but also as "life." The gospel is spoken of as a revelation of life. In bringing to light the nature of God, it brings to light the nature of life. The peculiarity of the Father is that he "hath life in himself" (John v. 26). His being is life, the source and centre of which is in itself. Absolute being is absolute life. Life is not a mere physiological process, however much it may manifest itself in and by means of such process. Physiological processes are mechanical and sensible; life is organic and spiritual. "To be spiritually minded is life and peace" (Rom. viii. 6). Peace, to be at peace,—this is not to be asleep or dead, but to have reached and to be constantly and energetically maintaining the perfection of living self-conscious being. It is to have banished contradiction from within oneself, to have no longer one member warring against another, and that not through the cessation of activity, but through the harmonious and successful direction of all activities according to the true law of one's nature. Absolute peace—"the peace of God"—is absolute life; and absolute life is absolute doing. The life and being of the Absolute is not, whether in the view of philosophy or of Christianity, a life or state of "blessed indolence," after the manner of the gods of Epicureanism or of the "First Cause" of modern Deism. "My Father worketh hitherto, and I work" (John v. 17). "God is not the God of the dead, but of the living" (Matt. xxii. 32). What the Son of God brings to man is

more abundant life (John x. 10). Just as the Hebrew
Psalmist recognizes in God the Father the "fountain
of life" (Ps. xxxvi. 9), so he, who is conscious of and
declares his oneness with the everlasting Father,
calls himself the "bread of life" (John vi. 35), and
the bringer of "living water" (John iv. 14), of which
he who partakes shall "not die" (John vi. 50), but
have in him eternal, *i. e.*, absolute, unqualified life,
being, substance. But this life, I must once again
repeat, is not identical with mere inert existence
or mere persistence in time. Of such existence,
absolutely considered, neither philosophy, as the
scientific, analytic interpretation of experience, nor
religion knows aught. Life in all its absolute purity
is pure and unqualified activity. As such, it is not
identical with any purely blind, unconscious phenomena of motion in a sensible organism. Nor is it
aimless. That is no true activity which does nothing,
and there is no true doing in which no aim or end
is realized. No, the true and perfect doing, in which
consists the true and perfect living, is a conscious,
purposeful, and willing activity, which (on man's
part) accomplishes the will of God, the absolute law
of being, and so only effectually realizes its own
nature. It is, in the case of us men, a rising to the
stature of "a perfect man," or "unto the measure
of the stature of" that fulness of life and of being
which is in the Son of Man and of God (Eph. iv. 13).
True life, then, is an affair of the self-conscious spirit.
"The spirit giveth life" (2 Cor. iii. 6). "It is the
Spirit that quickeneth [en-liv-ens]; the flesh profiteth

nothing [or has, absolutely considered, nothing to do with life as such; its relation to life is, at most, only instrumental]; the words that I speak unto you, they are spirit, and they are life " (John vi. 63). " The words,"—not as a mere letter, or combination of letters. Thus considered, they profit as little as the flesh. " The letter killeth." It is only the words as apprehended by spiritual intelligence, that are at once a vehicle of " spirit " and of " life,"and organically identical therewith. " Whoso findeth "—not ignorance, not the stupidity of " the Unconscious," but—wisdom, " findeth life," while all they that hate her " love death " (Prov. viii. 35, 36). Who is not reminded again of Aristotle's beautiful and truthful definition: " Life is energy of mind," or, as we should say, "of spirit" (Greek *νοῦς*)? We conclude, therefore, under this head, that for the Christian Scriptures, God, or the Absolute, is life; that, as such, he is intelligent activity; and that this activity consists in an eternal and ever-complete process of self-actualization.

Finally, we have to notice that for the Christian consciousness God, the Absolute, is Love. God loves with " an everlasting love " (Jer. xxxi. 3). He draws with "bands of love " (Hos. xi. 4). "Love is of God; and every one that loveth is born of God, and knoweth God " (1 John iv. 7). It is love that fulfils the law (Rom. xiii. 10), and is the quickening and operative principle in "faith" (Gal. v. 6). Abiding in Christ and sharing his divine and eternal life is otherwise described as continuing in his constrain-

ing love (John xv. 9; 2 Cor. v. 14). Love is thus a
principle of knowledge; nay, rather, since love is
represented as the active condition on which our
apprehension of God, the absolute object of knowledge, is dependent, shall we not say that it is the
principle of knowledge as such, or *par excellence ?*
Love, I say, is represented as a principle of knowledge, of practical activity, of life and of genuine or
eternal being. "Life," in the words of a great
Christian poet, "is energy of love." God, who is
absolute life, is, for the Christian consciousness,
—which philosophy does not in this respect belie,—
absolute Love.[1]

Absolute being, then, is, according to the Scriptures
of the Christian religion, absolute Spirit, in the forms
of absolute intelligence, absolute life, and absolute
love. And these three are not mere accidental
modes, but essential and constitutive attributes of
the divine nature, or of absolute being. The interpretation and exemplification of them are offered to
us in the personality of Christ, the God-man, and in
those words which the Christian world accepts as the
true and perfect expression of his self-consciousness.
In the light of these words,—the most important of
which, for our present purpose, we have already
cited,—and in the light of philosophic science, let
us now see what sort of a conception they authorize
and necessitate respecting the nature of God, as
Absolute Spirit. Is this conception flighty, mysterious, and, if not positively irrational, yet at least
non-rational, in the curious sense of being utterly

"superior to" and so out of the reach of "reason"? Does it illuminate, and is it thus confirmed by, our experience, in the most comprehensive and exact sense of this term, or does it only confound and add to the mystery of experience? In and through it do we really know a God who is near at hand, or only "admit" one who is far off? Is God, for the Christian consciousness,—nay, more, is he for universal philosophic consciousness, considered as a transcript of the absolute content of human experience,—a present and intelligible reality, or a remote and unknowable "thing-in-itself"?

More especially, God, as absolute Spirit, is, for the historic consciousness of the Church, Triune. The Church has never wearied of proclaiming, and with all her energy insisting on, the fact of the divine Trinity. Is she right in this? Is the alleged fact indeed a fact, and if so, what sort of a fact is it? Is it one which, lying wholly beyond the realm of our conscious experience, falling, therefore, under none of its categories, and being altogether insusceptible of experimental verification, we must and do accept purely on the ground of credible testimony, just as we should accept and believe the testimony of a competent witness, who had been privileged to visit the moon and brought back the report that upon that satellite water exists in a fourth state, neither gaseous, nor aqueous, nor icy,—a state wholly unknown to terrestrial experience and which, by reason of the fixed limits of such experience, we are quite unable to conceive or imagine? Is the Trinity an attribute

of the known or of the unknown God? According
to the Church, it is essential to God, that he be
triune. Trinity is the eternal and constitutive law
of his absolute being. At the same time it is held
that God has revealed himself in his works. He is
believed to have made man in his own image, and
to have made "clearly seen" and "understood by
the things that are made," "the invisible things of
him." Is, then, man only a quasi-image of God, and
does the world furnish only a quasi-revelation of
him? Is that an "image," and is that a "revelation,"
which neither images nor reveals the essential character—*i. e.*, in this case, the divine Trinity—of the
original? These are serious and weighty questions,
on the right answer to which the whole edifice of
Christian doctrine would seem to depend for its
security.

A doctrine which expresses the essential truth
respecting the absolute principle of all being and of
all intelligence, cannot but be full of illumination
for all derived or dependent intelligence and for the
comprehension of all derived existence. In the absolute the derivative must find itself, not confounded,
but explained. In the knowledge of it, it should
find and feel itself at home, and not as if in an utterly strange and unknown land. The intelligence,
as well as the moral nature, of man should find in
God its "strength." The Church was, in my judgment,—and I believe that I express the true historic
verdict of philosophic science in this matter,—guided
by a true instinct, or a true inspiration, in making

the doctrine of the Trinity the corner-stone in the confession of her faith, and is right in praying that she and her children may evermore be kept "steadfast in this faith." It is, or involves, to my mind, the very key to all true illumination for the intellect as well as to all solid and saving comfort for the soul. But it certainly is not this,—on the contrary, it is purely and justly "a stumbling-stone and rock of offence,"—when it is preached only as a sort of mystic or magic formula, which all the faithful are to repeat, but into the meaning of which they are warned, as they value the stability of their "faith," not to inquire too closely.

And now, before proceeding with the positive portion of our inquiry, we may mention, first, that trinity does not simply mean threeness. Trinity means three in one,—a unity, the very condition of which is multiplicity, or, in particular, triplicity. Such unity is not unknown to experience. On the contrary, we have already, in a previous lecture, observed such a unity lying at the basis, and constituting the ever-present condition, of all our conscious experience; and we shall subsequently have occasion more amply to explain and illustrate it. But trinity, it must be noticed, is a spiritual category, and not a sensible one. It is a category of the noumenal and absolute, not of the sensibly phenomenal, as such, and "relative." The attempt to translate trinity into terms of the sensible, to find for it a purely sensible image, and to think or conceive it by means of such image, must and does therefore necessarily fail. What is thus imaged is not and cannot be trinity, or three in essential unity, but—if I may again be allowed this expression—mere three-ness, or three which are joined in a unity that is at most only accidental and superficial, not essential Sensible unity is unity in or of time and space. It is, as such, or abstractly considered, without inherent difference or even extension, and its type is the mathematical point. When several unities are joined together, their union, if we consider them purely on their sensible side, as conditioned only by time and space, is a union of mere aggregation. It is purely accidental and relative, not essential and absolute. Each unit is no less that which it is, or its inherent nature is not a whit changed, even though it be separated by an interval of indefinite extent in time and space from all the rest. Take, for example, three members of the human species, considered simply as so many different, sensibly visible individuals. You find them together and say that these constitute one group. But you would say the same thing if their number were four, or ten, or ten thousand, etc. Let them scatter to the four quarters of the globe, and the one group, as such, is no more, yet the individuals remain without change the same. Their common unity, considered as members of one group or collection, was accidental and superficial, and dependent on no particular number. There is, indeed, a unity which, after their dispersion, still holds them together. But this is not a sensible unity, but an intelligible one. It is the unity of kind, or of a common humanity. And yet this unity, too, is independent of any particular number in the sensible individuals comprehended under it. Humanity, considered as an ideal kind, is just the same, whether the race be restricted, in the number of its sensible individuals, to an original pair, or contain, as at present, its hundreds of millions of such individuals. In short, sensible analogies, or analogies subject to mechanical and sensible conditions, are absolutely incompetent to illustrate for us the notion of trinity. They have nothing to do with it. And yet most, if not all, of the difficulties which have been met in the attempt to comprehend it, have arisen from the obstinate determination to comprehend it only through the use of such analogies. The real difficulties thus lay, not in the notion itself, but in the subjection of the inquirer's mind to sensible prejudices. Trinity, I repeat, is not a sensible, but a spiritual category. It denotes, not a mechanico-sensible relation, but an organic and vital one. It is absolute and essential, and not merely relative and accidental, unity in and through triplicity. It is dynamic, and not static. Trinity is not mere three-ness, and "trinitarianism" is not mere "tritheism."

Trinity is, in a word, concrete unity. It is unity in, through, and by very means of difference. Its attribute is, like that which the Scriptures ascribe to God, "fulness," in distinction from emptiness. It has (unlike the "mathematical point") a content. It has a meaning. It *is* something, or has definite character. It is real; it is experimental; it is knowable; and it is, consequently, the type of the only sort of unity which is recognized in real objective science and philosophy. And it is all this in distinction from that abstract, inexperimental, contentless unity, which constitutes the empty ideal of theological agnosticism. A perfect specimen, I repeat, of this abstract unity is furnished in the conception of the mathematical point, which is, by hypothesis, something in and of space and time and yet has absolutely no content of space or time. The conception is framed, namely, by abstracting from all extension of space or time, *i. e.*, from all concrete or real space and time. It is a quasi-sensible conception, and yet it is wholly unreal, because wholly abstract: it is formed by abstracting from the fundamental and constitutive conditions of sensible reality and of sensible consciousness. Here, now, we have that which many are pleased to term absolute unity, or unity which is absolutely separated from intrinsic or extrinsic difference. But in having it, we have obviously nothing, except a shadowy figment of the imagination. Of this kind is the unity which theological agnosticism requires us to realize in thought, as a condition of the possibility of knowing God. We are called upon to abstract from all that is concrete, from all definite relation, or, in other words, from all the demonstrable conditions of objective and subjective experience, and the result is to be the One (so-called) God, whose nature is, obviously, to have no nature, whose existence is the illusion of existence, the everlasting Nay, Nirvana.

act. Here beginning and end cannot be separated
by space or time; otherwise there were no *self-*
consciousness. In the technical language of philosophy, the subject which starts out on this career
of self-conscious activity, must, throughout its whole
progress, nevertheless remain "by" or "with" itself,
or "at home." It goes out from the station termed
"subject" to the station termed "object," and at the
same time never leaves its starting-point. It "loses
its life" and in the same indivisible instant "finds"
it. In describing such a process, which is a process
of spirit, the language of sense and of sensible relations can be applied only metaphorically and at best
cannot but seem paradoxical. And yet nothing is
more demonstrably the language of absolute and
immediate truth, than this language as we have thus
applied it.[3] Moreover, the description which we have
given does not, as may perhaps at first be thought,
apply only to the case of an abstraction called "pure
self-consciousness," conceived in complete but imaginary, separation from all definite and particular,
empirical consciousness. On the contrary, it is of
universal application, since there is no consciousness
whatsoever that is not conditioned by and contained
in the organism of self-consciousness; and there is
no self-consciousness that does not realize itself in
"objective consciousness." The distinction of subject and object is not merely formal and artificial;
it is also, if I may use this expression, material; it
is real and essential. And yet their "identity" is
none the less real and essential. Only, this identity

is not abstract, but concrete. It is not a sensible identity. It is not the identity of a mathematical point with itself, nor of a line or surface or solid or any other sensibly individual object, as such. It is not sensible, but spiritual; not dead, but living identity. It is not identity excluding difference, but identity which is conditioned by, and so exists in and by very means of, difference. It is unity, but it is also trinity. It is true and living unity—real, objective, experimental, concrete, and not merely (like the unity of the mathematical point) abstract, hypothetical, and imaginary—for the very reason that it is trinity.[4]

(We may mention parenthetically, in passing, that the fate of the pure sensationalist, in dealing with the facts now under consideration, is full of negative and warning instruction for us. The sensationalist not only admits, to begin with, the distinction of subject and object, but insists on it also with exaggerated energy. Recognizing, and being able to deal with, none but purely sensible categories of thought and experience, distinction means for him absolute difference, and nothing else. Subject and object are different: this means, for the sensationalist, that they are completely and mechanically separate from each other: where the one is, the other is not. But then— such is the implicit argument—nothing can act where it is not: all action depends on contact. In view of the mechanical separation of subject and object, an action of the subject, whereby it should cognize the object, is impossible; and this is the first alleged ground of philosophical scepticism ! But then, having gone thus far, sensationalism is immediately compelled to recognize the other side of the case, and to admit the necessary identity of subject and object *in knowledge*. But, having none but purely sensible categories of thought at its command, it is unable to think this identity as any thing other than a baffling mystery. The actual object is held to be a " modification" of the subject itself, and the actual subject is the *same* "modification." Subject and object are thus viewed as abstractly and sensibly, not concretely and organically identical, and so the question, which the experience of immediate and obvious fact forces the sensationalist to raise, namely, how the actual subject, which by hypothesis is itself nothing but a simple conscious state or contingent series of such states, can yet be aware of or know *itself*, whether as past, present, or future,—this question, I say, is not answered, because from the point of view of abstract unity it is unanswerable, but is simply and arbitrarily put aside as insoluble. Such is always the result of the attempt to construct theory independently of experimental fact, instead of making it the faithful transcript of such fact, and nothing else).

Man, as spirit and as intelligence, is thus himself created "in the image" of the triune God. And it will be observed that we find this image, not primarily in any (to first appearance, accidental) triad of psychological faculties or functions, but (thus far) in the form, nature, and conditions of the fundamental

and universal activity of intelligence itself, whereby
man is effectively constituted a living spirit. The
like image of God, the Absolute, is found, secondly,
in all his works, so far as they in any way partake of
Life;—which is not strange, for we have found Scripture and philosophy agreeing in ascribing to the Absolute, life, as an *essential* attribute, and in regarding
life as the energy of Spirit. And so indeed we find
that all life, all *living*, is conditioned upon a triune
process. It, like self-consciousness, involves at once
the distinction and opposition and also the organic
union or identity of apparent opposites. Philosophic
science finds the rudimentary analogon of life—nay,
let us rather say, as we may, that it finds the present power and the remote, but not wholly misleading
image of the Absolute Life—under sensible conditions
in the molecule which at once repels and attracts
its neighbor, its alter ego, and repels, as the very
condition of its attracting. It is only through this
essentially non-temporal process that it maintains
itself, its individuality, in existence._ It is only thus
that it, as alleged molecule, exists. In higher stages
of natural existence, in what is known as peculiarly
the organic realm, the same thing is more conspicuously and fully illustrated. To Goethe, the poet-
naturalist, the process of life was especially manifest
in the metamorphosis of plants. Here one organ apparently transforms itself into, or goes out into and
under the form of, organs other than itself. It goes
out from itself, and yet remains constantly at home
or "by itself." It goes out into its other, and lo, in

this other, or in the completed, complex organism, which includes both it and its "other," it finds nothing but its full and completed self. It loses, but to find. The final result is identical with the beginning, with this difference, that the former contains explicitly, or in developed fulness, what the latter contained only implicitly, or in compressed and undeveloped fulness. The process of life is strictly a process of the potential universal transforming or dispersing itself into the particular, and yet not changing its own nature,—the rather, simply realizing it under the form of time, or of a temporal process. And yet the process just described is, like the process of self-consciousness, *per se* a non-temporal one, and the non-temporal, here, as in the other case, is the condition of the temporal,—a fact which physiological metaphysics overlooks, and so is led to seek for the living among the dead, by attempting to find the root and essence of life in various successions and transformations of sensible motions, *i. e.*, of motions which are purely conditioned by the forms of time and space. It seeks the cause in that which is in reality only a product. Absolute Life is triune, and temporal life furnishes a *serial image* of this triune nature. But the life of absolute Spirit, which, as such, is the creative condition of time, is, also as such, not in time or subject to its form. It is not serial. It has not to await the full development of its nature from the hands of time. It is only eternal, non-temporal, life. In other words, it is real and genuine life, without limitation or qualification. The absolute process of life and the absolute process of intelligence are in form and nature one. Each is in form triune and each is eternal. (It is "eternal," *i. e.*, absolute life, and, thus, a participation in absolute *being*—a "partaking of the divine nature"—which accrues to them who receive "power to become the sons of God"; being "born, not of blood, nor of the will of the flesh, nor of the will of man, but of God.")

Finally, the same logical and substantial description, which belongs to intelligence and to life, considered absolutely, belongs also to love. If intelligence and life are, not merely accidental and phenomenal modes of existence, but genuine ontological principles—principles of absolute being, or of the being of the Absolute,—the same is true of love. As such philosophy, both in ancient and in modern times (but philosophy, as such, knows no distinction of time!), has recognized it, and as such the Scriptures declare it. Of God it is said, not simply that he loves, or that he is loving or capable of loving, but that he is Love. By as much as God is, he acts. His being is doing, is activity. And by as much as the law and the reality of absolute activity are the law and the reality of intelligence and life, by so much are they also the law and reality of love. Like intelligence and life, so love loses itself in an object other than itself, with the result of "finding," and so first becoming and being, its true, completed, and real self. Like them, it "scattereth, and yet increaseth" (Prov. xi. 24). More than they it seems to express the fundamental energy of being, so that, from this point of view, we may say that it is in love that intelligence and life find their completion. Like them, again, it is organic. It is a whole, an universal, that realizes itself in and through its objects, which are as its organic members. And so, like them, it is an ideal-spiritual process, nontemporal—superior to time,—and triune.

Now all these processes, or this one process under three different names, we have described in accordance with the demonstrative analyses which philosophic science furnishes of the deepest, yet ever-present, foundations and conditions of human experience. Human experience is dependent, partial, incomplete. At its best, it is only a fragment. "Now," says the Apostle, "I know in part" (1 Cor. xiii. 12). But the divine experience, if I may employ this phrase, is not thus limited. It is independent, complete, absolute. But it is not thus rendered wholly foreign and alien in its nature to human experience, so that no inference may legitimately be made from the latter to the former. On the contrary, just because our experience is a "fragment," and a fragment of a living, organic whole, we may read in it the law and the nature of the whole.[5] What human experience, therefore, is dependently and incompletely, that the divine "experience" is independently, completely, and without limiting qualification. What we now "see through a glass darkly," that same God sees and is in the eternal radiance of absolute truth and absolute reality, and that same we—we, our identical selves,

with an intelligence not changed in nature, but
only perfected and completed in kind—may, and
the Apostle declares that we shall, "see face to
face." That which we now perceive to be the ideal
and essential nature—however hampered by finite
conditions—of intelligence, life, and love in us, that
God, the Absolute, is in unqualified reality. If each
of these so-called "functions" is, demonstrably,
within the limits of our immediate, as well as of our
widest, human experience, a process which involves
a triad of terms, the same holds true of these same
functions in God. If, further, in each case the three
terms are not simply so many sensibly discrete individuals, separated by time and space; if, even in
the case of us men and of our intelligent experience
they do not and cannot simply follow each other as
wholly independent terms in a temporal process,
but are also, in another and more essential aspect,
coetaneous or joined together in a relation with
which time has specifically nothing to do (on which,
the rather, time derivately depends); if they are inseparably united, and that in such a way that either,
taken without the others, is a dead and unreal abstraction; if each, while ideally and really (not sensibly) distinct from the others, is no less livingly
and really identical with the others; if the identity
of each depends on its organic identity or union
with the others, so that each *is* the other (this paradox of sense being thus the essential truth of spirit); if, I say, all these things are true, as they demonstrably are, within the sphere of our dependent

experience, not less, but all the more, are they true within the sphere of the absolute experience of God, in intelligence, life, and love. In this diviner sphere all these things are true without limiting qualification. That Trinity, of which man and all created existence bear, not the sensible, but the spiritual, *image*, is with God, the Absolute One, the everlasting and unqualified fact.

Human consciousness or intelligence is, as we have seen, more perfect, the more perfectly it finds itself in, or one with, its object. But human intelligence does not at once thus find itself. On the contrary, its object appears to it at first rather as an unknown and alien limit. The temporal growth or development of intelligence in the individual or the race (and it is only this, namely, the temporal history of intelligence, that empirical psychology contemplates), consists thus, of necessity, in the process of overcoming or breaking down this limit and reducing the object of intelligence into organic unity or oneness with itself, the subject. The "growth of intelligence" is thus but a process of the realization of intelligence,—a demonstration or unfolding, in the dependent order of time, of that which intelligence *per se*, or independently of this order and in its absolute and non-temporal nature, *is*. But in God, who is, precisely, absolute intelligence, this process of growth or development in time both need not and can not be. Consequently that which we have just seen to be the condition of the process—viz., the finding, or seeming to find, in the object of intelligence a pure

limit, or something absolutely alien in nature and
in being to the subject of intelligence—can not here
exist. We have seen, indeed, that the limit is for
us not an absolute one. Of this truth the whole
progress of human intelligence, whether in the individual or in the race, is a constant demonstration.
The limit simply appears to us as an absolute one,
or the object of intelligence appears to us at the
outset as if it were purely and only alien from the
subject, because our intelligence, subjected to the
form of time, is thereby rendered necessarily subject
to the law of growth or development. From an
initial state in which it exists only in implicit or
potential form, it has to await the explicit demonstration, unfolding, or manifestation of its own nature, and thereby of the real nature of its apparently
limiting object, as the result of a temporal process
of evolution. But with the divine or absolute intelligence of God, this is not so. Here the limit indeed exists, but not as an absolute one. From the
first moment—if I may thus speak, in reference to a
relation which is strictly non-temporal—from the
first moment of its existence, the limit exists only
as a limit which has been overcome. By the very
act by which the divine intelligence is aware of its
object, that object, while still remaining true object,
ideally other than the subject and differentiated
from it, is nevertheless recognized, in agreement
with what we experimentally see to be the perfect
nature of intelligence, as not foreign to, but con
cretely one with, the subject.

The collective object of human intelligence is, in the first instance, that which we term "the world," a universe whose substance, as we first conceive it, consists of brute, unintelligible, and absolutely non-spiritual matter. But with the progress of philosophic or real intelligence, the world assumes for us another nature, or, rather, is revealed for us in its truer nature, as a divine language, the mechanical expression of the divine Word, which was in the beginning, was with God, and was indeed God. The world, according to its first intention for us, the world as a mechanico-physical object, the physical universe, known as pure physical science knows or aims to know it, is not the world as it exists for absolute intelligence. Physical science knows the appearance of the world. It knows it as a sum total of sensible phenomena. Absolute intelligence, on the contrary, knows the truth of the world. It knows the world as existing purely and only by, through, and for the divine Word. And this "Word," again, cannot, in agreement with the philosophic and experimental science of intelligence, be a mere abstraction. The science of intelligence requires the perfect object of intelligence to be connatural with the subject. But the true subject of intelligence is not an abstraction, but a living spirit, a person. The true object must therefore be also personal and spiritual. The contrast between human and divine intelligence is then this: the former has for its first or immediate object the physical universe, as a language, the true reading of which brings it to the present knowledge of the divine Word, as the truth, or absolute causal reality of the universe; the latter, on the contrary, has for its first object, the absolute object, the Word, and only —if we may thus express it—in the second instance, or through the Word, by and through whom alone the physical worlds subsist, has it these latter for its object. God knows the world only according to its truth, viz., as the phenomenal expression and work of his own " other." And this other, in the concreter language of the Bible, is spiritual, is personal, and is called his only and eternally begotten Son.

But with the recognition of the distinction of Father and Son, the nature of the Absolute, or of God as absolute Spirit, under the attribute of intelligence, life, or love, is not exhausted. In any proper trinity, or image thereof, such as intelligence, life, or love in man,[6] we know that the living, actual whole, the concrete unity, does not consist in any mere collective union or summation of the first two terms that philosophic science discovers therein. The third term, the " synthesis," as it is called, of the other two, were not, it is true, without the latter, but it does not result from their mechanical composition. It were not without them, but it is not abstractly identical with them. It has reality only in and through them, but its reality is not absorbed in them. On the other hand, it is just as true that the first two, taken either singly or together, in separation from the third, are dead, unreal, inexperimental abstractions. They, too, on their part, have their reality only in and through the third, while yet their reality is not absorbed in the latter. Translating that which is strictly non-temporal into the language of a temporal process, and doing this, as we are aware, at great risk of misrepresentation, we are compelled to speak of what we call the third term as that in which, peculiarly, any spiritual process or reality is completed. Intelligence is, for example, peculiarly the name of the " third term," or active " synthesis," in which subject and object become, not mere abstractions— such as they necessarily remain when separated from this *tertium*—but real. The third term concretely exhibits what may be called the substantial truth, both of subject and object, and also of itself. It thus comes, in consequence of the temporal order of our apprehension, to stand not only for itself (as " third term " or " synthesis "), but also peculiarly for the synthetic, concrete, actual, and living whole, in which both it and what we term its antecedents or component factors are included in organic identity. The like is to be said respecting the third term in the sacred formula, by which the Christian Church expresses the nature of the triune God. The Holy Spirit is the name of the " third person " of the divine Trinity, as distinguished from the other two. And it is also the name by which the concrete reality, or the whole nature, of all the " persons " is peculiarly and explicitly expressed. Man, in respect of his intelligence, is a spirit and an image of the divine Trinity, not as mere "subject," nor as "object," but as the living synthesis of the two. And so there is a sense, in which it is peculiarly true to say that the Holy Spirit is the completing bond of the divine perfection. It is the spirit and bond of "holiness," which, among other things, means the bond of *wholeness*, of "the fulness of God" (Eph. iii. 19; cf. John i. 16); it is the bond of knowledge, of life, and peculiarly of love, which latter is itself called the "bond of perfectness" (Col. iii. 14). "Subject" Father and "object" Son are organically one (John xvii. 21: "thou, Father, art in me, and I in thee") in the—or, as a—Holy, an absolute, a perfect and unqualified, Spirit, or as love.

I am, and can be, only too painfully aware how much remains to be said, in order to render humanly complete the account of the subject that we have been considering. I would fain hope that I have at least said enough to demonstrate that the topic not only demands, but will richly repay, the most studious and faithful attention. I add only one or two observations in justification of the language which the Church adopts, in speaking of "three persons in one God." We men, relying ever too much upon, or giving too absolute a significance or worth to, the sensible analogies, in the midst and by means of which the development of our intelligence necessarily begins, are led to connect with the notion of personality the ideas of differentiation, limitation, contrast, opposition. We forget, if indeed we ever realize, that personality is a spiritual, and not a sensible, category of thought and being, and that in the sphere of spiritual being the very condition of true differentiation and limitation is essential community, communion, or organic oneness. The true citizen of the state, for example,—he who is a citizen by and in the spirit, or as a true and proper man, and not simply as an irresponsible cog in an immense voting-machine,—develops his true personality, in this direction, not by separation from the common life of the state, but by intelligent, voluntary, and hearty identification of himself with it. The spiritual substance of the state becomes and is revealed as his own true substance as a citizen, and that, not to the detriment or diminution, but to the fulfilment and completion, of his own proper political personality.

The state is a spiritual organism "mixed," as Aristotle might say, "with matter"; and this means, simply, subject to the limiting conditions of existence within space and time. The sphere of the state is a sphere of imperfect or conditioned spirituality. It can furnish, therefore, only an imperfect illustration of that which must hold true within the realm of divine or absolute spirituality. Still, we see that in the sphere of the state (as of any other social organism) community of consciousness and life is the fundamental basis, the necessary condition, nay, the essential content of true individual personality. And we see that this is so, just because, and so far as, the substance of the state is a spiritual reality, and in spite of its subjection to the contingencies and limitations of existence within space and time. In other words, just so far as the state is truly a spiritual reality, it illustrates, as in a distant image, what the Church holds to be the truth, in the realm of absolute spirituality, respecting the divine Trinity, viz., that Father, Son and Holy Ghost are three persons, not in spite of their being one God, but because they are one God.

But the image is only distant and imperfect. For instance, the number of persons who may participate in the common life of the state, or of any similar moral organism subject to the conditions of development in space and time, is contingent; it is not limited to three; and, if it were, it would still not be a perfect image of the divine Trinity. For in the cases supposed, the three persons would still remain sensibly individualized and sensibly distinguished from each other, and in this respect would possess, not the concrete unity which is essential trinity, but only the superficial and abstract unity of an accidental mechanical aggregate. It is owing to the like reasons, too, that in the state the complete realization of a single public or common consciousness is and must always remain a problem, an ideal, only partially—and, indeed, very incompletely— realized.

But the Absolute, the Absolute Spirit, we must remember, transcends and is the creative condition of space and time. Here, therefore, the perfect law of spirituality must be perfectly realized. Here no contingency in the number of terms or "persons" involved can exist. The number must be that which is essentially necessary for concrete unity; the number which, for such unity, may rightly be called the "perfect" one; and that, as we have seen, is three. The three terms, further, must be distinct. The ground of distinction, not being sensible individuation, can only be found in personality. This is the only ground of distinction which is known to us in the realm of pure spirituality. (Even among us men sensible individuation is the instrument and vehicle, rather than the true and essential ground, of distinction, which latter is, the rather, truly found only in spiritual personality.) And here, finally, in the realm of absolute spirituality, where no limiting barriers of sensible distinction exist, nought can prevent the ever-complete and perfect actualization of the one life and the one consciousness of the ever-blessed Three in One.

In short, then, it would appear that the absolute personality of a God concretely—*i. e.*, really—one, must and can only be conceived as essential tri-personality.

LECTURE VI.

B Y "the world" we mean, in the first instance, the universe as known to physical science. Or, we mean the whole realm of the finite, so far as finitude consists in subjection to the conditioning forms of space and time. We mean, in short, the universe as the realm of sensible phenomena.

Such, at all events, is the way in which we must at the outset designate the object chosen for our present consideration. For it is as a sensible universe that, in the temporal order of our knowledge, the world is first known to us. This is its first appearance. It is, we may say, according to this its first appearance that we first *know of* the world, and hence we are led to *designate* it accordingly.

And yet it is not with the world according to its first appearance that we have primarily to do to-night. Not the world, as it is simply externally "*known of*," but the world as it is internally *known*, or *knowable*,—not the immediate sensible appearance, but the absolute reality or truth of the world, —this, and the biblical conception thereof, is what we wish now to consider. We want to know what the sensible universe, as a realm of the finite and relative, is *per se* and in its relation to the Infinite and Absolute. This is the question, with which alone, as regards the physical universe, philosophy is directly concerned, and the answer to which is of vital consequence for religion.

At the risk of needless prolixity and repetition, let me say, more precisely, that of the physical universe there are, at least in ideal, two sciences, which may be characterized, with regard to their respective points of view, aims, and subject-matter, as, the one phenomenal, relative, immediate, the other noumenal or substantial, absolute, and final. The former of these may be termed pure physical science; the latter, the philosophy of nature. The former, as I have indicated in a former lecture, is abstract: it abstracts, in considering the universe, from all but its sensible appearance. Its object, if I may so express myself, is to ascertain and demonstrate the sensible or phenomenal What, and the mechanical How, of the physical universe. Its purpose is accomplished, when it has clearly seen, and truthfully reported and registered, all of the immediate or sensibly demonstrable facts or, as they are otherwise termed, phenomena, which alone are presented within its chosen field of observation and which alone constitute the subject-matter of its inquiry. But these facts are knowable and observable only in and through certain relations—not as purely isolated and separate facts. And the relations, in and through which they are known, are all relations of space and time, of co-existence and sequence, or of "configuration and motion." These relations, once determined and expressed, are recognized and described as "rules," "or laws." The relations are mechanical relations; for it belongs to the very essence of a mechanical relation to be a relation of and in time and space. They are, I repeat, relations, rules, or laws of co-existence and sequence. How useful, nay, how necessary, for a prosperous material existence and so, indirectly, for the higher ideal prosperity of mankind, the ascertainment and knowledge of these rules is—this is something on which I need not stop to enlarge. About it there can be no question; but, also, this is not the point now in question for us. Our present need is only to have before us a clear conception of the intrinsic nature and scope of "pure physical science" as such, and then to perceive that with the method by which the results are reached, and with the particular nature of the results themselves, neither philosophy nor religion has any sort of immediate concern. Physical science ascertains what are the precise sensible facts that fall within the realm of her inquiry, and it is not these facts, with their mechanical laws, that concern philosophy and religion, but the interpretation and comprehension of them, with reference to their deeper significance. Their concern is, not with the immediate phenomena, but with the reality which the phenomena denote. The interest of religion in this respect is more indirect, but not less vital and real, than that

of philosophy. For, that other science of the physical universe, of which I made mention above, is
an essential part of philosophy itself, and may be
termed the Philosophy of Nature. This is the
science which inquires respecting the essence and
foundation of natural, or, "physical," existence, and
respecting the real significance, the origin and end,
of nature's laws or "rules."

More especially, nature, or the physical universe,
is never at a standstill. It is involved in ceaseless
and—even where the first appearance seems most
to prove the exact contrary—in absolutely universal
change or motion. Further, the various particular
motions in the universe are not severally isolated
and separate from each other. On the contrary,
they constitute a system, in which each part implies
and depends on every other. They constitute a
whole, and their several movements combine in one
grand collective movement, respecting the law and
significance of which intelligence requires and demands illumination. It is in the attempt to answer
the question thus raised that physical science, on
the side of its widest generalizations, and philosophy approximate most closely to each other, and it
is here that the complementary nature of the relation, which really subsists between physical science
and philosophy (or that part of philosophy which is
termed philosophy of nature) is most conspicuously
illustrated. What, namely, the "law" in question
is, or what is that grand and all-comprehensive law
which, as a visible rule of order among phenomena,

includes all other more special laws and is illustrated
in them all,—this is a question, the answer to which
may and must be sought in accordance with the
method, and without going beyond the peculiar
sphere, of physical science itself. For it is a question relative to the temporal, and indirectly the
spatial, order of phenomena. That is to say, it is
a question concerning something which in kind is
susceptible of sensible, and only of sensible, demonstration. It is a question of historic fact. But beyond the demonstration of the law as an immediate
fact—a rule of temporal order—physical science, as
such, is not competent to advance one step. Here
it is met by the natural ontological limitations,
which bound its peculiar sphere. Just as, in virtue
of these limitations, pure physical science strictly
demonstrates and knows no material substance, but
only, instead, figured space, and no real or substantial force, but only motion, so, in the matter
of the mechanism of spatial and temporal relations
among phenomena, it demonstrates and knows only
the fact of this mechanism, the fact of these special
and general laws of order, but nothing respecting
their ulterior significance. It, as such, cannot say
by what power, from what source, or to what rational end, this moving mechanism exists, or whether
indeed it exists by any power, or from any source,
or to any end whatsoever. It cannot say this, because its eye is methodically turned away from all
such things as power, source, and end, or (in brief)
ultimate and absolute reality. From all these things

pure physical science abstracts, by the very act by which, choosing for its own peculiar sphere and subject-matter the realm of sensible phenomena as such, and choosing its method accordingly, it resolves not, and renders itself positively unable, to attend to or to see any thing else. These limitations—it need hardly be said—are not the fault, but rather the merit, of physical science; they are not to it a mere check or hindrance, but rather (as the history of science has shown) the *conditio sine qua non* of its prosperous existence. But when they are forgotten, and when men, speaking ostensibly in the name of physical science invoke her authority in support of opinions respecting that which lies strictly beyond her purview, then the reign of *mere* opinion, or rather of positive confusion and error, sets in. Nay, I will even say that then it is when that intellectual sin called "anthropomorphism," and which to so many men now-a-days seems to be the only unpardonable one, stands in most danger of being committed, and with most dangerous results. For instance: When, from the circumstance that to pure physical science, as such, with its peculiar and self-imposed limitations, no ultra-phenomenal or sub-phenomenal, *i. e.*, no non-sensible, reality is or can be known, it is inferred and declared that no such reality is in any way known or knowable, then the reign of intellectual confusion—otherwise termed sophistry—begins and, in proportion as the declaration is credulously received by a public destitute of critical information respecting the

constitution of science, extends. Even were such
declaration true it would not be so for the reason alleged in its support. But it is positively
not true, unless human experience is an illusion
and philosophic science, as the interpretation and
exact demonstration of the content of that experience, is all a myth. And no one, to say the
least, can affirm with reason the truth of this last
supposition, who shows himself destitute of the most
elementary knowledge concerning the specific nature, methods, and results of philosophic science and
only alleges, in support of his opinion, reasons which
are in no sense germane to this science or to its peculiar subject-matter.

But again: When, from the circumstance that physical science finds, and so demonstrates, that the *sensible* universe, *as such*, is one vast and unbroken
net-work of mechanical relations—relations (otherwise termed " laws ") of co-existence and sequence—
so that in the one word " Mechanism " all the results
and all the knowledge of pure physical science may
be summed up,—when, I say, from this circumstance
it is ostensibly inferred and is asserted, not only that
mechanism is the highest and ultimate category of
all knowledge and of all existence, but also that it is
identical with a blind, all-compelling and all-comprehending fate, then the intellectual sin of "anthropomorphism " is committed. Physical science
finds in nature, as contemplated by her, no fate,
nor, as we have seen, any other *power*, whether real
or fancied. The man of physical science, as a man,

though not as a physicist—*i. e.*, as one whose whole personal " experience," like that of all other men, never is, as matter of fact, or can be purely and exclusively " physical "—has at least an abundant practical knowledge of " power," and confesses it. Nay, more, in the chosen language of his science he speaks—he finds himself compelled to speak—at every turn of " forces," just as though (so a superficial observer would say) he knew all about them. But such knowledge he, *as physicist*, disclaims, and explains that the word " force," in his scientific vocabulary, is without positive significance for him; it is only a non-significant part of his mechanism of expression, like an algebraic symbol, or, better, like the auxiliary verb employed in conjugation. It is unquestionably true, nevertheless, that in and through the mechanism of the sensible universe power is manifested. And the question as to the true nature of this power has to be taken up and answered by a science less abstract than physical science. It has to be answered by a science which does not, like physical science, abstract from the major and fundamental part of experience, but considers experience on all its sides and in all its concrete fulness, the science which is *par excellence* and without qualification the science of experience as such, or Philosophy. The conception of universal mechanism, therefore, as it comes from the hands of physical science, carries with it no positive notion or knowledge of power, whether as fate or in any other form. The philosophic mechanist who, speaking professedly in the

name of physical science, represents the case in a
different light and declares, in particular, that the
physicist's knowledge of mechanism is tantamount
to the absolute, positive knowledge and demonstration of an universal fate or blind automatism, by which
not only the movements of nature at large, but also
the self-conscious actions of men are determined,—
this one, I say, is guilty, not only of logical fallacy,
but also, in particular, of anthropomorphism. He
views nature, not with the eyes of science, whether
physical or philosophic, but with those of mere human prejudice. He likens her, in effect, to an Orien-
tal despot, whose irresponsible word or decree (*fa-
tum*, "fate") rides on pitilessly and unchangeably to
its execution, in blind disregard, as well of all reason,
as of the fears and entreaties and will of those whom
it may affect.

That which specifically concerns philosophy, then,
is not the determination of nature's particular mechanical laws;—this is the work of the special sciences;—nor of her universal mechanical law,—this is
the task of pure physical science, considered on the
side of its greatest generality;—but the ascertainment of the power, by whose presence and agency
the mechanism of sensible phenomena is to be explained. Philosophy looks for the inner reality, the
controlling reason, and looks for this, not in an inexperimental vacuum of pure abstraction, but within
the present and by no means inaccessible depths of
man's real, concrete experience. And now it is all-
important to note that the interest of religion, in this

regard, is in kind identical with that of philosophy. Accordingly the Bible, as a text-book or manual of religion, is found to be in no sense a text-book or manual of the physical sciences. The special and general results of these sciences are not germane to the nature and purpose of religion. And those who have, in the supposed interest of religion, sought to find pure physical science in the Bible and to use what they have then professed to find for the purpose of controlling or forestalling the methods and results of inquiry in such science, have accordingly always come, and will unquestionably always in the future come, to grief. What religion presupposes with regard to the physical universe, and that, therefore, which, in this regard, must be true if religion is to be true, is not any dogma whatsoever respecting the general or special mechanical laws of nature, but a belief concerning the inner reality of nature, or respecting the absolute ground and end, and the submechanical law, of her existence and of her life. A question of essential interest and importance for religion is, for example, not whether man is allied by evolutionary derivation to the other and so-called lower orders of animals, but whether such sayings as these are true, viz., " The Lord preserveth man and beast," and God "filleth all things."

Hamann, the " Magus of the North," said of nature that it was, to intelligence, like a text written in Hebrew, without vowel-points; the work of intelligence was to find and supply the vowel-points and so render the text intelligible. In par-

ticular, this is the work of philosophic intelligence.
The work which philosophy thus proposes to do, religion supposes to have been already done. How,
and with what general results, the task is undertaken
and accomplished by philosophy, has been indicated
in outline in a previous lecture. We have now to
compare, with philosophy's reading of nature, the
reading which is presupposed and demanded by religion, and especially by Christianity. Only, we first
add, by way of reminder, and as furnishing a fitting
connecting-link between the thoughts that have just
been occupying our attention and the considerations
upon which we are about to enter, that philosophy,
in connection with this conception and fact of universal natural mechanism,—the consonantal " Hebrew text,"—which physical science demonstrates,
does not forget that the word mechanism has an
etymology, and that it is derived from a Greek word
meaning "instrument," " engine," or "contrivance,"
and this meaning of the original, philosophy finds,
is not lost in the derivative. Not only does mechanism *mean* something that is purely instrumental,
but the mechanism of nature *is* purely instrumental.
Its essence is not fate, nor self-directing power,—
though it implies or points to the latter. It is
simply a dependent and inherently passive means.
Mechanism philosophy finds to be but the dress or
garb of organism, its instrument or necessary means,
and also its product. The dead is at once the creature and the servant of the living. And Life is
energy, or self-asserting and self-maintaining reality,

of Spirit. Where mechanism is, there is also organism, there is living power, there is the power
and purpose of Spirit. Mechanism is the sure,
the ever-present sign of organic energy of intelligence. The former is phenomenal; the latter is substantial; and it is only through her recognition and
demonstration of the latter that philosophic science
vindicates for nature her reality and her meaning, and
saves her from vanishing away, for human intelligence,
in that spectral dream of " subjective idealism " which
necessarily results from any and every attempt to in-
terpret nature in the light and with the aid of the
mechanical categories of " pure physical science," and
of these alone. Nature, for philosophy, is real; it
shares dependently in the absolute reality, and only
thus can it be truly and inherently real. It is real
because, and so far as, there is present in it the living
and substantial power of Absolute Spirit. It is indeed
"relative," but that to which it is relative is God.
Of its relation to God we may say,—using the in-
adequate language of sensible analogies,—that the
place of nature is in God, rather than that the place
of God is in nature. The Lord, we may say, with
the confident assurance that no violence is thus
offered to the sense of Scripture,—the Lord has
been her dwelling-place in all generations. Something of the precise meaning which such a statement
has for philosophy's exact thought, you may catch,
if you will recall the demonstration that philosophy
furnishes of what is called the ideality of space itself.
Space and time, which are the essential condition of

all sensible existence and the substance of all mechanical relations, are shown, as you will remember, by the philosophic science of experience to be not themselves sensible objects, but dependent functions of Spirit. The place of space itself—if the use of this expression may be pardoned—is thus in spirit, and, speaking absolutely, in God. What is thus true of space and time, is necessarily true of those so-called sensible objects, whose existence they condition, and of those mechanical relations of the sensible universe, whose essence they constitute. But this is no case of pantheistic "absorption," whether of nature in God, or of God in nature. By as much as the full, fundamental, and concrete conception of experience, both on its subjective and on its objective side, is the organic conception, and by as much as the definition of the relation of the relative to the absolute, or of nature to God, can result only from the philosophic science of experience in its fullest and completest sense, it follows that the pantheistic notion just mentioned has no rightful place in philosophic science. For this notion results only from the attempt to define the relation between God and nature with the use of none but mechanical conceptions, *i. e.*, as we have seen, of conceptions which do not correspond to and represent experience and the object of experience in their concrete fulness and reality, but are formed only through abstraction from all that is fundamental and of absolute significance in the realm of intelligent experience. Applying these conceptions, and these alone, no alternative is left but to regard the whole universe of existence as one vast mechanical aggregate, all of whose parts are—thus to express it—of the same ontological rank, both among themselves, and as compared with the whole of which they are parts. The term "God, or Nature,"—to repeat the phrase which constantly recurs in Spinoza,—is then but the name for the whole aggregate of existence, considered on the side of its wholeness or totality. The ostensible relation between God and nature thus becomes one of abstract or literal, numerical identity. The distinction between them is obliterated. But in this way both God and nature are changed, in our conceptions, from that which they were demonstrated to be into that which they are not. God, who was a Spirit, becomes only a name, and nature, whose reality was demonstrated to be a reality of spiritual power and purpose, is identified with the realm of her mechanico-sensible phenomena; the shell is taken for the kernel—"abstracted" from the kernel. In one word, mechanical distinction or mechanical dependence involves no true ontological distinction. The terms or objects, between which a purely mechanical relation subsists, are, as such, of the same ontological nature, of the same "substance," or, ontologically identical. God, standing in none but a mechanical relation to the world, and known or knowable only in such relation, were identical in nature with the world. But organic distinction and dependence is real, existential distinction and dependence. The relative, in organic dependence on the absolute—nature, in organic dependence on God—exists and lives by and through the present power of the absolute, but is nevermore capable of literal or immediate identification with it. It gets and keeps its true reality through concrete union with the absolute; by mechanical absorption in it—were this abstraction, for the rest, capable of being realized in thought—it would become unreal. Finally, the essence of the world and its relation being of the nature thus indicated, it is seen how and in what sense building men up in true intelligence is, as religion itself claims, the same as building them up in the knowledge of God. The finite bears on its face the evidence of the infinite, which is its active condition. The relative *is* through the indwelling power of the absolute. The true knowledge of the one involves at the same time knowledge of the other. All finite existence is, truly viewed and known, a Theophany.

The Christian Scriptures, now, represent the world as dependent on God for its existence. It is, in its very essence, to God as the dependent to the independent, as the relative to the absolute. There is an Alpha of existence, an absolute order of ontological priority in the whole realm of being; and this Alpha is, not the world, but God. "In the beginning *God* created the heaven and the earth." "Before the mountains were brought forth, or ever thou hadst formed the earth and the world, even from everlasting to everlasting, thou-art God" (Ps.

xc. 2). The world *is*, but its being is not absolute. The world, as distinguished from God, exists, not independently and by itself, or "from everlasting to everlasting," but in dependence on divine power. "He hath made the earth by his power" (Jer. x. 12). So much, then, is certain: the Scriptures regard the world as the dependent work of the divine power. But the more important question is, in what sense is the world the divine work? Is this work instantaneous or continued? Did God, as a mechanical "First Cause," in one instant miraculously "make" the world and then separate himself wholly from it, leaving it to get on henceforth as best it could without him? Could and did he give it power to *be* in independence of him? What did God put into the world? Was it only "brute matter" and "blind forces?" Had he a reason for "creating" it? If so, what was and everlastingly is this reason, and what, consequently, is the absolute law of the world's existence? And, finally, has the world a predestined end, to which it tends; and, if so, in what sense is this true, and what is the end in question[1]?

It is obvious, without argument, that that is a thoughtlessly inaccurate and unjustifiable way of speaking of the divine work of creation, which those adopt, who represent it as resulting, so to speak, from the casual occurrence in the divine mind of a motive similar to the empirical motives, which are the immediate determining ground of most human actions. A man, for example, builds a house, and his motive or reason for so doing may be one of

several. He may build it for his own shelter, or
as a means of profitably investing his money, or,
finally, simply because the *ennui* of idleness is
unendurable and he feels that for his own happiness
he must be busy about something or other. This
last seems to correspond most nearly to the conception respecting God's reason for creating the
world, which is involved in many popular represen-
tations of the subject. The omnipotent Being had
nothing to do, and so, rather than be eternally idle,
concluded to " make " a world. He had all power
and was alone in existence; he was therefore responsible to no one for the use—if any—which he
made of his power. It has even been expressly held
by some theologians that he was not—if we may
thus express it—responsible to himself, or to his own
nature, for the way in which, and the result with
which, his power was used. And so this hitherto
" otiose Deity " resolved to busy himself for an instant, or at most for a few days, with the creation
of a world;—which, accordingly, he did, with results
in which, though there may be " rhyme," (*i. e.*, order,
otherwise termed law or rule), there is no "reason."
The world, it is either practically or expressly held,
is, and is such as it is, because it is. No reason, it
is alleged, can be deduced from the divine nature or
discovered in the nature of the world, for the existence of the latter or for its possession of the character which, as matter of fact, it does possess. If it
is good, it is good because God " made " it, and not
good *per se;* if it is in any sense rational, it is for the

like reason(?), and not because its own nature or the nature of God discloses for it the slightest *raison d'être.* The world and its laws constitute simply one vast though complex fact, and are to be accepted purely as such. Moreover, whatever may be conceded as to their first origin, they are by very many "thinkers" treated as now constituting a fact— or realm of fact—which is independent, in existence as well as nature, of its source. The world, with its assumed blind forces and its so-called inflexible (*i. e.,* automatically self-executing) laws, is practically or expressly conceived as now sufficient unto itself, any active connection with it and its affairs on the part of God, being resented as an impertinent and disturbing intrusion. Nay, more, the mechanical universe comes to be looked upon as that, of whose real and practically independent existence alone a disciplined intelligence can have the fullest assurance; while the admission of God as a *quondam* or so-called "First Cause" is greeted as a great and most edifying concession to the claims, not of religious and philosophical knowledge, but of religious feeling or, as it is even also called, the "religious consciousness" of man (and especially of unscientific men).[2]

All this is a travesty upon philosophic intelligence, as it is also a profanation and degradation of true religious conceptions. This is one of the most depraved and senseless forms of agnostic and pseudo-scientific "anthropomorphism." Philosophic science shows that the very root-conception of being—when this term is understood in its concrete sense—is activity. Absolute being is absolute activity, absolute doing. Whatever absolutely is, and in proportion as it absolutely is, performs a work; or, at all events, a work is performed or goes on in it; so that its existence depends on the work. The activity therefore, ceasing, the reality also ceases. If philosophy knows anything, it knows that the activity of the Absolute is itself absolute. Its activity is perfect. In Aristotelian phrase, we may say that the activity, and, consequently, the being, of the Absolute is perfect, because it never leaves, for an instant, any of its potentialities unrealized; and it is precisely in this that the pure, unqualified, and infinite being of God, the absolute Spirit, differs from the finite being, of his dependent creatures. In short, absolute being is—more concretely expressed than before—absolute Spirit, and absolute Spirit is absolute life, energy, work: the Absolute accomplishes, and only realizes its own being on condition of its accomplishing, an absolute work. And the conception of the divine nature which is presented to us in the Christian Scriptures differs in no respect from this. It was precisely the Hebrew prophet's sense of the ever-wakeful—nay, let us rather say, the absolutely wakeful—activity of the Maker of heaven and earth, which gave their tone of conscious irony to the words with which he "mocked" the prophets of Baal, saying to them, respecting their (anthropomorphic) god, "Peradventure he sleepeth, and must be awaked" (1 Kings xviii. 27). The same thought inspired the Psalmist's comforting declaration: "He that keepeth thee will not slumber" (Ps. cxxi. 3). And so, too, the Christ, whose name is called "Emmanuel, God with us," the Logos, the active and effective Reason, the substance-giver of the world, declared to those contemporaries of his who still retained the word of God only in the form of a dead letter, "My Father worketh hitherto, and I work" (John v. 17). "Hitherto;" not from a certain time in the past, before which he was idle, but "hitherto" without qualification, *i. e.*, eternally. It is as though Christ had defined God as *par excellence* the Worker, and himself as "equal with God" (in the language which his adversaries immediately thereafter proceeded to employ against him), the true Son of God and one with God, just because and only so far as he too worked, sharing in and working the work of the Father. And, finally, man himself, according to the Christian conception, fulfils the requirement to become "perfect"—*i. e.*, to become perfect *man*—and to that end becomes a "partaker of the divine nature," not in idleness, nor simply by working mechanically *for* God, but by being, in living, organic union, a colaborer *with* him.—For the rest, all that was shown in our last lecture concerning the philosophic and scriptural conception of God as Intelligence, Life, and Love, has so obvious and decisive a bearing on the point now in hand, that we need attempt to add nothing more in regard to it.

I need only further remind you, once more, that what is thus true of God, as absolute Being, is also true, *mutatis mutandis*, of all relative or finite being. Of it, as of God, it is true that it *is*, only as it *does*. Its being is conditioned on its doing. Only, its "doing" is dependent, while that of God is independent. But, above all, the being of the relative or, especially, of the so-called physical does not consist in any dead abstraction such as that which is termed "mere matter." Just as mechanism is the dependent product, instrument, and garb of organism, so, too, matter is nothing but the purely phenomenal product—the *manifestation*—of living, organic, spiritual forces. It is incapable of being known as anything else, and as this it is as matter of fact known.

Now, the Scriptures do not deal in abstractions (such as "mere matter" and "blind forces") however natural and, in their proper sphere, legitimate these may be. Still less do they profess to reveal the independent and substantive reality of any such abstractions. The speculative—or, rather, the dogmatic—materialist can find no support for his fanciful doctrine in the Christian's scriptures, any more than in the results of real philosophic inquiry.

Moreover, whatever we may yet find scriptural reason for holding true with reference to the relation of the world to the eternal "work" of God, there can be no doubt that the present relation of God to his work is represented as both active and incessant. It is living and, according to the conception which we have now formed for ourselves of the divine nature, godlike. It is a constant witness to the glori-

ous activity of the divine intelligence, life, and love.
" Thou visitest the earth, and waterest it," says the
Psalmist (Ps. lxv. 9). In language, that is dear and
beautiful to every Christian heart, the Master of
Christians assures them that their Heavenly Father
feeds the fowls of the air and clothes in a glory superior to that of Solomon the lilies of the field. The
processes of organic nature—in other words—do not
go on of themselves alone, but in dependence on
the present power and activity of the Lord of all.
But the processes of organic nature are built up, as
we know, out of processes, or on the basis of the
so-called forces, of that which we are pleased to
term inorganic nature. The power that sustains
the former must therefore bear a like relation to the
latter. And as motion, change, process, activity,
is, according to the testimony of both physical and
philosophic science, an universal category—a category of all finite existence,—it follows that nothing
whatever in physical nature is withdrawn from that
" operation " (=*working*) of the divine "hands," in
giving praise for which the Psalmist declares that
he will rejoice (Ps. xcii. 4. Pr. Bk. version). The
works of nature, no less than those of grace, are,
according to the truly philosophical view of Scripture, not only " begun," but also " continued, and
ended," in God. The "heavens" are not simply the
finished " work " of his " fingers"; they are also, and
far more characteristically, the constant working of
the divine hands. Their "fulness" is not their own,
but 'God's. " Do not *I* fill heaven and earth? saith

the Lord " (Jer. xxiii. 24). Viewed by itself, as pure
physical science views it, the physical universe reveals itself, not as full, but empty, not substantial,
but phenomenal. It can be viewed in its fulness
only as it is viewed in God, the Absolute, who
"filleth all in all." The world is rich, and not
poor; yet not by its own power or in its own right;
it is full of the riches of God (Ps. civ. 24). The world
is a speech, uttered by day unto day, and by night
unto night. And the alphabet of this speech is
adapted to spell out but one name, and that one
not the name of the world, but of God, whose name
alone is, in King David's language, "excellent [*i. e.*,
conspicuous, and full of *substantial* significance] in
all the earth" (Ps. viii. 1). "That thy name [and
here 'name' stands for the person, the being, signified by the name] is near [not in the remote and
inaccessible distance of a mechanical 'First Cause'],
thy wondrous works declare" (Ps. lxxv. 1). And
they that know this name, with all that it signifies,
will put their trust in God (Ps. ix. 10). For this
name stands for a "goodness of the Lord," of which
the earth is declared to be full (Ps. xxxiii. 5). It
stands for universal beauty: "He hath made every
thing beautiful in his time" (Eccl. iii. 11). It stands
for a majesty of divine glory, of which heaven and
earth are full (*Te Deum*, and Ps. lxxii. 19). It stands
for the mercy, of which the earth is full (Ps. cxix.
64), for the power by which the earth is made, the
wisdom by which the world is established, and the
discretion by which the heavens are stretched out

(Jer. x. 12, and Prov. iii. 19). It stands, in short, for the eternal and alone absolutely and independently substantial Spirit, who hath stablished the heavens for ever and ever, and hath made a decree —a system of "laws"—that shall not pass (Ps. cxlviii. 6); from whose presence nought can flee away, except it were into nothingness, since it is in him, who is in all and through all, that all things live, and move, and have their very being; and whom all his works, not only "shall," but *do*, "praise" (Ps. cxlv. 10, and Ps. cxlviii.)

Such being the world, the knowledge of it is not something to be shunned, but to be sought out by all them that take pleasure therein (Ps. cxi. 2). The so-called "atheism of science" is not the atheism of *science*, but only, at most, the non-theism of *partial science;* and that "love of the world," which a Christian Apostle declares to be incompatible with the love of God, is not the love of the world as it is known to complete, *i. e.*, philosophic science and as the Christian scriptures also conceive and describe it; it is not the love of the world in its full and concrete and true reality, but of that abstraction which men have before their minds when they think of the world on the side of its apparent difference or separation from, and independence of, God. And—let me remark again right here—pantheism, too, that peculiar and just horror of the religious mind, consists, not in finding God, the true God, or God as absolute and eternal Spirit, in all things, but in first forming one's conception of the absolute after the analogy of things as they appear when God, as just defined, has been abstracted from, and then calling this false and insubstantial absolute after the reverend name of God.

For indeed—and this now brings us to the distinct recognition of another aspect of the world, which secular science confirms and which is also included in the Christian conception of the world— it is also one of the characteristic things about the world, that it can be looked upon apart from God, abstracting from God. And this possibility is to be regarded as founded, not in any peculiar and accidental infirmity of human intelligence, as distinguished from some real or fancied ideal of absolute intelligence, but in the nature of the world itself. If the world, considered ontologically, or on the side of its absolute reality, is founded in and bears witness only to God,—or, if the world has a side by which it is *pro tanto*, or according to the measure of its *being*, in organic union with God,—yet no less truly, and no less characteristically, it has another side of difference from God and even of opposition to him. It has a side of corruptibility and change. By the world, thus regarded, we understand especially the whole realm of the so-called phenomenal, the relative and finite, as such, and more particularly the whole realm of things which are specifically characterized by their subjection to the forms and conditions of space and time. The universal and inherent destiny of such things is, not to abide for ever, but to pass away. They are a vesture which

shall be changed (Ps. cii. 26). This is, in reference
to the physical universe at large, that "corruption
of the creature," of which the apostle speaks; this
is its "subjection to vanity" (Rom. viii. 20, 21, and
Eccl. i.) "They shall perish, but thou shalt endure" (Ps. cii. 26). Surely, the world is not God.
And, yet, is then all God's work for nought? Is it
indeed to be wholly lost, and not, the rather, saved?
Is there no well-grounded "expectation of the creature?" Does the whole creation groan and travail
in pain (Rom. viii. 22), in the vain hope of a birth
that shall never be?

These questions bring us again face to face with
the broader question concerning the *rationale* of
creation, which we have already propounded, and
the distinctively Christian answer to which we must
now consider. The Christian doctrine of creation
is inseparably connected with the doctrine of the
Trinity or of God as Absolute Spirit and especially
with the doctrine respecting the nature of the Christ,
as the second person therein. The New Testament
scriptures specially connect the existence of the world
with the second person of the Trinity. "The worlds
were framed by the word of God,"—thus we read in
the Epistle to the Hebrews (xi. 3). The initial
words of the Old Testament, "In the beginning
God created the heaven and the earth," are repeated, as we may say, in an amplified and explan-
atory version, in the opening verses of the Gospel
According to St. John. "In the beginning was the
Word." "All things were made by him." "He

was in the world, and the world was made by him, and the world knew him not." And so, in the first verses of the Epistle to the Hebrews, we read again that God "hath in these last days spoken to us by his Son . . . . . by whom also he made the worlds." It is this Son who, in the following verse is represented as "upholding all things by the word of his power." The divine Word, then, or "the eternal Son," is set before us in the distinctively Christian conception of the subject as the direct and especial principle of the world's existence and subsistence. But he is represented as being this in no merely mechanical and external fashion. The notion of mere fabrication is even further removed from the New Testament conception of creation, than from that apparently contained in the Old, by as much as the former is more explicit than the latter. Not only in its origin, but also in its end, and in all its destined historic fortunes, the world is represented as standing in the most constant and intimate relation to the Divine Son. He is its heir: him hath God "appointed heir of all things" (Heb. i. 2). The apparent bankruptcy of the world is no loss; it is the enrichment of Christ, of the Son,—the fulfilment of the divine Word.

The "perishability" of things—their changing, apparently evanescent nature—which to a purely sense-conditioned science seems to constitute their whole nature—is not their whole truth. To mechanical sense the entire universe, with all its significant richness of developed detail, is but so much world-dust, without inherent rationality, life, or purpose. This is but the symbol of existence, not existence itself; or, more truly, it is but the symbol of a potentiality of existence, the active principle of whose realization is not to be found in "world-dust" as such.* Nature is thus viewed in abstraction from that inward process of an ideal, self-realizing life, which, to the more comprehensively and completely experimental eye of reason, or of philosophic intelligence, constitutes her real essence and meaning. For complete science, then, and for religion, whose genuine instinct is the instinct of life and of essential reality, the whole truth about nature is summed up, not in any such conception of a purely phenomenal *product*, or atomically-constituted "element," as is "world-dust," but in the conception of an organic, living and purposeful process, the total significance of which is summed up in the phrase, "realization or fulfilment of the divine Word." In the accomplishment of this process—the writing of this wonderful and all-significant Language of Nature—the atomic world-dust serves but as an insubstantial mechanism of alphabetic symbols. The constitutive source and essence of the process, and its causal principle, are found in the eternal Word, Life, Power, Spirit, among whose "treasures of wisdom and knowledge" are included all the thoughts that Nature strives to utter. In brief, then, and employing the experimentally accurate language of Aristotle, natural existence is a compound of potentiality and actuality; or, more strictly, every natural existence is involved in a process, whereby a definite, typical, ideal potentiality proceeds towards its own realization.[4]   In the Scriptures the living and all-controlling source and end of all such processes is declared to be, not a blind, impersonal, brutely persistent force,—still less, an " unknowable " one,—but the living, personal, spiritual Logos, who is not only knowable, but is also the very principle of intelligence and of all knowledge.   By Him, in organic dependence on Him, the potentialities of nature are realized or, in scriptural language, "redeemed," or " saved."

Thus, then, the true process or history of the universe is not one of bankruptcy, but of rescue, of redemption, of realization.   This is expressed in Scripture as follows: " All things are of God," and " God was in Christ, reconciling the world unto himself" (2 Cor. v. 18, 19).   " Reconciling the world," says the Apostle; and then, as if this statement were not sufficiently explicit, we find him declaring still more roundly and expressly, in another Epistle, that it pleased the Father by Christ "to reconcile all things unto himself; by him, I say, whether they be things in earth, or things in heaven " (Col. i. 20), to the end " that nothing be lost."   The process of the world, I repeat, is a process of redemption. The conception of redemption is a cosmical conception.   That life of the world, for which, in the profound symbolism of Scripture, the Christ is represented as giving up his own, is a life through redemption.   The very reality of the world, its substantial being—and this, as we have seen, is by no means identical with its merely phenomenal, sensible quasi-being—and its substantial significance are a reality, being, and significance in and through redemption alone. Viewed in separation from the Redeemer, by whom alone they "consist" (Col. i. 17), all things are indeed nothing worth, and vanity. Their very essence is, not to be, but to perish. This is that irony of "fate" which rests on all things temporal, so far as they are viewed only as temporal or subject to the form of time. It is from this point of view that, in Goethe's "Faust," Mephistophiles, "the Spirit of Negation," can say with truth,

"Alles, was entsteht,
Ist werth, dass es zu Grunde geht."

(The due of every thing, that originates in time, is that it perish. Or, in other words, the substantive value and significance, nay, the very being of all that has its origin in time and is considered only as it is subject to the law of time, must and can be expressed only in symbols preceded by a minus sign; its very being, thus viewed, is a piece of irony; for it, *as such*, to be, is to cease to be.) And it is because this point of view is not the only one, it is because it is the point of view of relative and partial, and not of complete and absolute, science or knowledge, that the next words of Mephistophiles are wholly false:—

"Drum besser wär's, dass nichts entstünde."

(It were better, therefore, that nought should originate in time.) But philosophy and religion, whose point of view is precisely this larger one of completed knowledge, respectively demonstrate and declare a more excellent truth about the world. The declaration of religion is that "all things were created" not only "by him," but also "for him" (Col. i. 16). All things, therefore, in consisting by the Son (ib. 17), *i. e.*, in having their very being and reality by him, are not merely so many independent and finished products, with which his workmanship has nothing further to do. No, they really "consist," only as they are, through a continuing process, rescued or redeemed from this state of apparent independence and indifference in relation to their creator and are indeed "for him." Nothing is, which does not in some true sense live, and nothing truly lives, which does not "live unto God." The temporal is real, only as far as it bears the form or image of the eternal. "Creation" is not the communication of bare independent existence in time. Such "existence" is a bare and unreal abstraction. Creation is the giving and sustaining of life. In short, "creation" is not merely "creation" *by;* it is also "creation *for.*" It is not instantaneous and transitory, but progressive and continued; it is not a dead and mechanical process, but living and organic; and creative work is, in its very essence, redemptive work.

We have yet only to see how the "reason" for this work, as a work progressing and continuing in time, is founded, according to the Christian conception, not in any casual, empirical impulse or deter-

mination on the part of him, the essential and constitutive process of whose nature, being non-temporal,
is exalted above time and is eternal, but in this very
nature itself. We have to see how creation, as a
temporal process, is grounded in creation as an
eternal process.[5]

In the same breath, in which St. Paul declares
Christ to be "the image of the invisible God," he
also calls him "the first-born of every creature"
(Col. i. 15). Christ, the creator of all things, is
thus himself represented as first or chief of things
created. He is not merely the maker, but also the
head of the creation. Man is accustomed to think
and speak of himself as the head and the quintes-
sence of the created universe; and so, from a certain
point of view, he may do with perfect right. But
the head of man himself, the "Son of Man," the
Man *par excellence*, is the "Son of God." Of man,
considered not simply in his distinction from and
above all other orders of created existence, but as
the microcosm, in whom the essence of all orders
of created existence is summed up, Christ is the
elder brother. Christ is the "only-begotten Son of
God," according to the powerful and significant
symbolism of Scripture. But this generation of
the Son is not represented nor to be conceived as
having occurred "once on a time." It is not a
temporal act, but an eternal one; it is a part of
that eternal *doing*, wherein the eternal *being* of
God, the Absolute Spirit, consists. And its result
is an other than God ("the Father,") and yet an-

other that is God's own Other, in whom God's own fulness is made to dwell; in whom, therefore, God realizes or manifests himself; and on whose part, by a further consequence, it is no robbery that he make himself equal with God. It is an Other, which is rescued or redeemed from the quality and condition of pure otherness (distinction from and opposition to God) in that eternal process of the divine Intelligence and Love, of which, in our imperfect, because sensibly conditioned, way of speaking, we may with equal reason say that it is at once condition and result. It is an Other which, as representing the place of the " object " in the divine intelligence and love, is—as shown by an analysis in a previous lecture—not simply distinguished from the subject of this intelligence and love, but is also, in proportion to the perfection of these functions in God, made inherently one with the " subject " (or with God the " Father ") in the concrete unity of an absolute, triune life. The process of the divine nature, then, which is really signified for us by the word Trinity, is in kind a process of creation and redemption. Only, this process is not a finite process. It is not a process in time. It is not subject to the law and conditions of time. It is not a developmental process, advancing from stage to stage of relative incompleteness and imperfection before it becomes perfect and complete. No, it is the process which is the eternal condition of all time, as it also is of all creation in time. It is an absolute process and is eternally complete. It is, I repeat, the process of the divine and absolute Love, which ceasing, all Being also ceases.

Creation and redemption, then, in the very largest and deepest sense of these terms,—creation and redemption, two names for one fact or process,—express the eternal nature of God in his concrete unity, of God as Intelligence, as Life, or as Love, of God as triune,—in short, of God as Absolute Spirit. They express this nature; their "reason" is this nature. And so Christ is for us "the *image* of the invisible God," not as viewed in abstraction or separation from the world, but only in relation to it, as its Creator and Redeemer. Hence to ask why he should create the world amounts to the same thing as asking why Christ, the eternal Son, should be the image of the invisible God; and this, again, would be the same as requiring us to retrace once more the steps of demonstration which we have already twice trod. The Son, who is "the image," is "with God," and "is God." For him to be, *i. e.*, to be the image of the invisible God, is to create and redeem; and precisely the same truth is expressed in the statement that his being is Love. But, it will be said, in creating the world God in Christ gives contingent, time-conditioned existence to things which in form and apparent substance seem contradictorily opposed to him; nay, more, the men whom he has formed are capable, it will be said, of openly and consciously resisting and denying him. Without stopping to remark on the qualifications, with which alone the statement of these facts by the objector can be accepted, the answer to them (substantially in another's phrase) is simply that it is indeed only God, or Absolute Spirit, who can endure this contradiction against himself, within himself, *i. e.*, within the realm of his own intelligence, love, and power. And he can do it, nay, he must do it, because of the glorious love that constitutes his very being. Of his absolute love the statement is true without qualification that it hath respect unto the lowly. The more it can give, the more perfectly does it demonstrate at once its riches and its unbounded perfection. The lower it can descend, the more perfectly does it realize its own nature and show itself indeed godlike. The absolute love of God must descend to an absolute depth, and there is no grade of existence so poor and mean, but that God, as love, can and must create and redeem it. Think the world out of existence, and you set effectual limits to the Absolute, as Christianity conceives it, —*i. e.*, to the absolute Love.[6]

Is then, it will be asked, the creation and consequent existence of the physical universe without beginning or end? Here a distinction must be made. Ancient and modern theories of "evolution," or of the temporal history of the universe, have made us familiar with the conception of aeons in that history, or of "ages," during each of which the physical universe is held to pass, from an initial state of universal homogeneity, into and through a series of states of, first increasing, and then decreasing, heterogeneity, until at last it returns to its original homogeneous condition,—then to begin anew and repeat the same round as before. If we accept this conception, the account of creation given in the Book of Genesis may be—as it has successfully been—interpreted as an account of the successive steps of development or creation in the present aeon. "In the beginning" may thus mean only in the beginning of this aeon. But when, on the contrary, Christ is said in the New Testament to have been in the beginning with God and as Creator to be "before all things," the sense is certainly different. The relation here expressed is that between the Creator and the created, as such. He who is thus in the beginning of, or "before," all things, is this, not as the temporal, but as the nontemporal or eternal and ideal *prius* of all things. He is prior to them, as the condition is prior to— while at the same time and in the same degree it is contemporaneous with—that which is conditioned. "All things" means whatsoever has for its nature to be within time, to be bounded by time, to be subject to the form of time as such. "All things" are, in technical phrase, the "content of time." Now, just as the content of time, abstracting from time itself, is nought (*i. e.*, is an impossibility), so time, abstracting from its content,—or, time without any content, —is nought. Whenever time is, then "things" are, or the "physical universe," in one state or another, is. If time is without beginning or end, then the same must be said, apparently, of the divine work of world-creation. But time is something which is conditioned, and which has its eternal condition in the eternal, that is, in God himself. There is therefore no reason for setting limits to its extent, whether in the past or in the future, and consequently no reason for setting similar limits to the work of cosmical "creation." In vain do we seek to put a limit of this or any other kind upon the Absolute. Philosophy repudiates the attempt, and the Christian religion, certainly, is not guilty of it.

But, you may again ask, is not the foregoing exposition of the scriptural conception of creation "pantheistic"? I have by implication already answered this question. Here let it suffice to say that it is indeed on the one hand, the scriptural Christian view that God must be "all in all:" but that also, on the other hand, it is only this view —which in so far perfectly coincides with the demonstrations of philosophy—that really and effectively excludes the pantheistic conception. Pantheism, as I have already twice indicated in this lecture, results only from an abstract or partial and essentially mechanical and sense-conditioned view of the world. It results from a view which, not being concrete and hence also complete, abstracts from spirit and its attributes, and reduces the essence of all things to the abstract mechanical unity of an inherently undifferentiated, and absolutely homogeneous substance. Then indeed all things are reduced to unity with a vengeance,—with a vengeance, namely, that wipes out the whole significance of the characteristic differences of things among themselves and, especially, of the difference between the relative and the absolute. Then indeed all is "God," or, more truly spoken, all is nought, is essential vanity. But to the concreter and more complete view of Christianity, as also of true philosophy, while God is "all in all," yet all things are not absorbed in God, as in a numerical unity, nor is God simply merged in and dispersed among the plurality of dependent existences. The recognition of the experimental fact of the organic-spiritual dependence of the world on God puts an effectual barrier in the way of any attempted literal identification of the former with the latter, at the same time that it accords to the latter—to God—the sole occupancy of the throne of absolute being, and denies to the former—to the world—the possibility of possessing any substantial being that is not held in dependence on God.

I only remark in closing that it must now probably be sufficiently obvious both that, and why, the questions raised in purely scientific theories respecting the temporal order or history of the physical universe—theories of physical evolution, and the like—are destitute of substantial interest and importance for the mind whose specific point of view is that either of philosophy or of religion. Such theories are *per se* perfectly legitimate and perfectly harmless; and, so far as they are experimentally verified, they are to be unquestioningly accepted. They become false and justly offensive only when they are stretched—whether on the part of their

authors or of their critics—beyond their true scientific meaning and made to do duty for that, from
which they are specifically and totally different,
namely, for the philosophy of nature. Whenever
this is done, it is done on the basis of a false distinction between what is called "nature and the
supernatural." The natural and the supernatural,
the physical and the metaphysical, brute or soul-
less mechanism and living organism, matter and
spirit, these all are set over against each other in
a "hard and fast" opposition, the one being held,
in each case, to be the contradictory opposite, and
only the contradictory opposite, of the other. The
partisan of "evolution" then becomes, not simply
an "evolutionist"—*i. e.*, a believer in the truth of
the law of evolution as an historic fact,—but a fatal-
ist and mechanist in philosophy, who banishes the
so-called supernatural, metaphysical, living, and
spiritual from all his conceptions of reality. The
unintelligent, but popular, critic of the mechanistic evolutionist, on the other hand, instead of cor-
recting the error of his ostensible adversary, does
really the rather perpetuate it, inasmuch as, while
he nominally sets himself up for the defence of
all that the mechanist denies, he yet also insists
that the "supernatural" is distinct, and *only distinct*, from the "natural"; that the former occupies,
therefore, none but an essentially mechanical relation to the latter, and that, by a still further
consequence, the power of the supernatural over
the natural is only a brute power to "interfere"

and by sheer might to direct, as from without. In this way the "supernatural" is degraded into an equality or identity of rank with the "natural"; and this is next door to pantheism, as above defined.

The mechanist and his opponent alike thus deal only in abstractions. The truth of nature is the true "supernatural." Or, nature, viewed as purely "physical," is an abstraction. That this is so, philosophy demonstrates, and true religion presupposes.

In sum, then, we find Christianity declaring, and philosophy assenting to and confirming the declaration, that all *things* live and move and have their being *in* God; but not that they *constitute* God.

LECTURE VII.

BIBLICAL ONTOLOGY;—MAN.

THE subject of this lecture is strictly continuous, though not identical, with that of the preceding one. Man is, on the one hand, part and parcel of the created universe. If, according to the conceptions reached in the last lecture, the direct result of all creative labor in the universe is not an immediately finished work, existing thenceforth in self-sufficient independence of its source, but rather a divine possibility, which requires evermore to be redeemed from the vanity or emptiness of mere possibility by the incessant and universal actualizing energy of the absolute and divine Spirit, the same is also true of man. The nature of man, like that of the physical universe to which he belongs, is bipolar or two-faced. On the one side, man, like physical nature, is subject to time and to its law of mutability and corruption, and is so represented in the Christian Scriptures. "Man that is born of a woman, is of few days . . . . . He cometh forth like a flower, and is cut down: he fleeth also as a shadow, and continueth not" (Job xiv. 1, 2). "Man being in honor abideth not: he is like

(204)

the beasts that perish" (Ps. xlix. 12). "The first man," *i. e.*, man viewed according to his first or immediate appearance, "is earthy" (1 Cor. xv. 47). He is turned to destruction (Ps. xc. 3), and "goeth to his long home" (Eccl. xii. 5). "He cometh in with vanity, and departeth in darkness" (Eccl. vi. 4). This is the side by which man, like nature, is, so to express it, turned away from God or from absolute reality. This is the side of man's relative emptiness or pure phenomenality;—the side from which alone if we contemplate man, he, like nature, appears as an insubstantial "shadow." But man, as also nature, has another side, which, as we may say, is turned toward God. He is not altogether and only fleeting. He is not wholly swallowed up in the apparently all-devouring "maw of time." He has a side of reality which is exalted above the assaults of time; a side whereby he takes hold of God, the Absolute Reality, or, rather, whereby God takes hold of him, and wherein he, like nature, is sustained only by that creative-redemptive agency of God, which is the universal condition of all truly substantial finite existence. And so man is "part and parcel of the created universe."

But, on the other hand, man has also his side of specific difference from and distinction above the universe that surrounds him. If in all things else a "divine possibility" is lodged, in him there dwells a still diviner one. If nature is, in the hands of her Creator, as the clay to be fashioned by a divine art, in man this art proposes to itself a still more won-

derful work. While nature bears and reveals everywhere the name of God, man is to be made in his
express image. To this end man must be and is
made to bear the image of the divine absoluteness
and independence. Like God, he must be an independent "worker." Like him he must be and is
a self-centred, self-conscious personality, and has
within the sphere of his own being a precinct, in
which his sway resembles by its absoluteness the
sway of God. He must have, and he has indeed, a
power of self-determination and a sphere for the active exercise of this power. And this sphere, as just
intimated, lies close at hand and is identical with the
realm of his own self-conscious personal being. Here
he has a personal, independent work to do. It is a
work which it is impossible that another should do
for him. It is a work, in the performance of which
no one has any power to stay his hand, and to which
also, on the other hand, no one can compel him. It
is a work which bears the image of the creative-redemptive work of God himself. For the work committed to man's hands is none other than the realization, the rescue, the redemption, the salvation of the
divine possibility that is lodged in him and is en-
trusted, as a talent, to his keeping. "Work out your
own salvation with fear and trembling" are the words
that are addressed to him (Phil. ii. 12). In other
words, the true and perfect *being* of man is dependent on his *doing*. He cannot be himself, or, man
cannot indeed be man, by merely and inertly " existing." Thus existing, he is man only in name and

in outward appearance. He is man only in semblance, but not in effective reality. He is as yet only the bare possibility of a man, and in order to be a man in fact, in order to have in him the reality of true human subtance, he must be up and doing. He must act. He, I say, and not another, must act. By his own self-conscious, self-determining, purposeful activity, he must redeem and realize the divine possibility that resides in him. In order to be himself, he must create himself. Thus is man in the image of God and like God. But only like God, not equal with him. The power lodged in earthen vessels, independent and godlike as it is, is not one that can separate itself absolutely from God, except to its own destruction. Its own initiative must be followed up and sustained by the power of God, or all its labor is worse than lost. And so it is that, while man is called on to work out his own salvation, he has also the assured knowledge that God works in him both to will and to do of his good pleasure. The great glory of man, according to the Christian conception of him, is that he is a colaborer with God. In this consists the divinity of man. On the other hand, the pledge of man's possible success in accomplishing the work committed to him, lies in the circumstance that God, the Infinite Love, condescends to be a coworker with him.

Such, stated in general terms, is the Christian conception of man. Such is the Christian idea of man's nature, on the one hand as compared with the nature of the created universe at large and, on the other hand, as related to God and the divine nature. We may say that the greatest immediate practical interest of Christianity centres, and is by the Scriptures made to centre, in its conception, its theory, of man. Christianity is not, in its theory, merely a Theology. It is also, as we have seen, a Cosmology and, as we are about to see, an Anthropology. And my assertion is that, in the order of immediate practical interest, the anthropological element occupies the most prominent place. From this point of view we may say that the theology and cosmology are there for the sake of the anthropology. They are there because no true and complete theory of man is possible without them, or because man cannot truly know himself or be made to know himself without taking into account as well the side of his unity with, as of his distinction from, both God and universal nature.

Or, in still other words, the theory of the Christian religion is (among other things) essentially an ethical one. Ethics is, in the most comprehensive sense of these words, the Science of Man. Its province is to demonstrate and define the essential nature or character of man,—of man so far as he is " true to himself," *i. e.*, so far as he is indeed man and not merely the semblance of man. The province of ethics, I say, is to demonstrate and define this, and also to demonstrate and define the law of practical activity whereby man realizes his true and essential nature or whereby man makes himself to be, and is indeed, man. This is ethical science, and nothing less than this is that theory of the Christian life which is taught both by precept and by amazingly perfect example, in the Christian Scriptures, and most of all in those which are most distinctively Christian. We may say, as we are accustomed to say, with a relative truth that Christian ethics is especially the science of the Christian man or of Christian manhood. But this mode of expression, notwithstanding its unquestioned relative justification and even its practical necessity, is nevertheless likely to mislead us, as indeed we know it does mislead thousands, into the false supposition that after all the so-called Christian man is only one among many possible and really existing kinds of men, the peculiarity by which he is distinguished from other men consisting in certain eccentricities of belief and practice, which are not essential and indeed have no relation to the constitution of intrinsic and perfect manhood; so that the Christian is not more, or more truly, a man than any one else; he is not the perfect man in kind, but only a man of a peculiar sort. And then, as we know, such plausible grounds for maintaining and perpetuating this singular view are furnished by the actual or apparent character borne by a considerable and conspicuous number of those who call themselves "Christians." One could almost wish that the word Christian had never come into common use. Certain it is that this word does not belong to the common vocabulary of Scripture or of the ethics therein contained. There we are bidden to mark, not the "Christian," but the "per-

fect man." The words of Jesus himself are an in-
vitation and an exhortation to us to be, not "Christians," but "perfect" (Matt. v. 48). And the like
description belongs to the ideal set before us by the
Apostles, who drank deeply and immediately of the
spirit of Jesus and all whose labor and instructions
are to the end that those whom they address may
simply be perfect men; that they may "be perfect
and entire, wanting nothing" (James i. 4); and
then—as showing wherein, particularly, the perfection of man consists—that they may "stand perfect
and complete in all the will of God" (Col. iv. 12);
that they may be "perfect in Christ Jesus" (Col. i. 28);
"till we all come," through "the knowledge of the
Son of God, unto a perfect man, unto the measure of
the stature of the fulness of Christ" (Eph. iv. 13).
He, the divine Man, in whom was found no sin, nor
any defect, exemplified, in all its "fulness," the
"measure of the stature" of the "perfect man"; and
to the attainment of this stature the follower of
Christ, in dependence on his "ready help," is called
upon to aspire.

The theory of what we are pleased to call the
Christian life, as contained in the Christian Scriptures, and as constituting the substantial kernel of
"Christian ethics," is then, ostensibly only a theory
of the perfect life and of the perfect man; and the
"laws" which it contains are the laws, in pursuance
of which man is made or becomes, not perfect God,
nor perfect beast, nor even perfect "Christian," but
simply perfect man. Or, otherwise expressed, Chris-

tian ethics offers us the theory of the "Christian" man and of the "Christian" life only because, and so far as,. the term "Christian" is a synonyme for "perfect," and may be and is employed as a more concrete and hence more definite and expressive substitute for the latter.

The Christian Scriptures, now, on the side of their ethical content, or as containing and illustrating the theory of the perfect man, are extremely rich. Heie nothing is conceded to, or advanced under the name of, " mere theory." In other words, the whole theory is strictly experimental and in so far complies perfectly with the requirements of a scientific theory. Its lessons are all taken from life. It teaches no doctrine of human corruption, or of the possible perversion and ruin of the divine possibilities resident in man, for which it is not able to offer in evidence an immediate, actual illustration. And it sets up no ideal of the perfect man, of which it is unable to illustrate the practicability. Its great teacher is also its perfect exemplar and has only to say to his disciples, "Follow thou me." The further evidence of its truth is found in the circumstance that the genius of humanity has recognized itself in the picture drawn in the Christian Scriptures and, thus inspired, has gone about to realize itself in a civilization, which, whatever its deficiencies and how great soever its blemishes, contains in it far more of "man true to himself," or of genuine humanity, than has ever been witnessed in non-Christian centuries or under non-Christian climes. The "measure of the stature of the fulness

of Christ " has in practice been found to be the measure of the stature of the perfect man.   Through the
knowledge of Christ man has come to the best knowledge of himself, and through the imitation of Christ he
has, thus far, most successfully realized himself.   But
not only is this true.   It is also true that, just as
Christian theology—I employ this word here in its
more literal or etymological sense, as denoting only
doctrine of or about *God*—rather corrects and supplements, than contradicts and absolutely overthrows, the theology of the classic Greek philosophy, so Christian ethics, or the Christian theory
of Man, rather completes and is confirmed by, than
opposed to the best of non-Christian conceptions.
God has not left man without the means of knowing
himself, even in times and places not reached by the
words of the Christian Scriptures or by the influence
of specifically Christian ideas.   And the part of wisdom for the Christian teacher is, doubtless, not to
forget this fact, nor to remain in ignorance of the extent of its truth, but the rather to be in full and complete knowledge of it, and to make use of this knowledge, as well he may, for the purpose of demonstrating
the fuller and deeper truth of the Christian conception
of man.

On the other hand, and from another point of
view, there exist in our day peculiar reasons why
the teacher of Christian ethics—and every Christian
minister is called upon, in his peculiar way and
place, to be such a teacher—should have a full
and complete sense of the strictly experimental

and theoretic truth of Christian ethics, considered as Science of Man, and should be prepared, upon occasion, to demonstrate the same. Whether with or without reason, there can be no doubt that, in the minds of a large body of influential men,—men whose sincerity of purpose and conviction is not to be questioned, and who occupy conspicuous positions in the world of science,—the impression prevails that the laws, ideals, and sanctions of Christian morality are not made for man as he actually is, nor dictated by a knowledge of the true and immediate nature of man and his relations. The morality of Christianity is held to be the morality of other-worldliness, *i. e.*, of man as an alleged denizen of an other, non-natural (or so-called "supernatural,") world, in which, as a matter of immediate experimental fact, he does not find himself existing, and of which he can know nothing except on the faith of an arbitrary and wholly unverifiable "revelation." The whole object of Christian morality, it seems to be thought, is to dehumanize man and to make of him, not a perfect man, but an angel,—*i. e.*, something too good for this present world, and about which, for the rest, man must forever remain in substantial ignorance, so long as he continues to inhabit the earth. Christian ethics is thus viewed as a system of arbitrary "moral injunctions," in the form of "divine commandments," whose sanction and authority are derived exclusively from " their supposed sacred origin." I am now citing phrases employed by Mr. Herbert Spencer in the Preface to his " Data of Ethics." In view, now, of the fact that—according to Mr. Spencer's belief, and in his language—"moral injunctions are losing the authority given by their supposed sacred origin," this author holds that the "secularization of morals is becoming imperative." What Mr. Spencer means, and what his followers believe that he has accomplished, by the "secularization of morals," is well expressed by one of his sympathetic Italian expositors, Prof. Traina, of Turin, who, in a recently published work, maintains that "the modern method"—as he calls it, and of which he regards Mr. Spencer as the most illustrious living representative—has "humanized ethics."[1] The "secularization of morals," then, means the same as the "humanizing" of morals, and the demand for such secularization is equivalent to the demand that ethics shall be treated and cultivated as a science grounded in the living, actual, experimentally knowable nature of man. This demand, considered in the abstract, is surely perfectly justifiable, and ought to be quite unnecessary. For, if I have above correctly defined the subject-matter and scope of ethics, it is obvious that there can in no proper sense of the term be any science of ethics, which does not meet the mentioned requirement. But the demand in question is significant, if we may infer from the fact of its being made that the morality of Christianity is or has been currently set forth, by any whose office it is to expound and apply it, in such a manner as to convey to men who are not without intelligence, and who cannot be supposed capable of wilful and perverse intention to misrepresent, the impression that it does not deal with the real, inmost, and experimentally demonstrable nature of man, but is (in Spencer's phrase) "supernatural," *i. e.*, as he understands this word, preternatural, and deals with presuppositions, laws, and ideals that are foreign to man as he really or actually is or can be, and are hopelessly remote from the sphere of human inquiry and demonstration. If this inference is well-founded, there can be no question that the fact to which it relates is a real scandal; that the view indicated respecting the nature of Christian morality is a travesty upon "the truth as it is in Jesus"; and that it is immediately and urgently incumbent on all those, whose special office it is to know and promulgate this truth, that they remove forever this rock of offence. For the rest, I have not here to enter upon a discussion, on the one hand, of the extent to which occasion may really have been given for the forementioned misapprehension of the true nature of Christian ethics, and, on the other hand, of the extent to which the quasi-philosophical presuppositions of Mr. Spencer and his followers may have determined and unconsciously warped their own perceptions. Only, of this I am sure, namely, that whatever may have been, or may still be, the notion of Christian ethics conveyed by any class of professed Christian teachers, the conception of the nature of man and of the law of his perfect being, which is contained in the Christian scriptures and is essential to the Christian religion in its purity, is infinitely deeper, richer, and truer, and hence by so much more truly and genuinely "human," than any which has been reached by the so-called "modern method."² And this I venture to say in the name and with the authority of philosophy, whose "method" knows no distinction of "ancient" (or "antiquated") and "modern," and whose ideal is simply that of the complete recognition and demonstration of the whole content of experience. In distinction from the ethics of philosophy and Christianity, I venture to assert that the self-styled "scientific" ethics, which thus laudably aims and claims to "humanize ethics," abstracts in tendency and, to the greatest extent, in reality, from all that is most essential and substantial about man. Indeed, is it not the well-known and universal contention of the school in question, that only the phenomenal can be known by man, and that the absolutely real is forever unknowable? Does not Mr. Spencer himself seek to persuade us that, not only all other existence, but also, in particular, our own is involved in impenetrable mystery? Is not to him the very belief in "self," though inexpugnable, yet wholly inexplicable and incomprehensible? And so, the ethics, which corresponds to this view and to this "method," contemplates, in fact, rather the simulacrum of man, than man himself, and sets before us rather the phenomenal and contingent than the substantial and eternal law of man's being. It presents us with just such a picture of man, as pure physical science gives us of external nature. Just as the latter does not penetrate into the inner being and spiritual reality of nature, but stops short with the ascertainment of her external phenomena and of their mechanical relations, just so, in theory, does the former proceed with regard to man. I cannot therefore but call it abstract, rather than concrete, ethics, "metaphysical,"³ rather than philosophical, and partially and superficially, rather than completely and deeply, experimental. And I say all this, without wishing to ignore—the rather, desiring fully to recognize and commend—all that, within its peculiar limits, has been solidly accomplished for ethics by the followers of the "modern method."

Let us return, now, to our main theme, and consider more in detail what is the Christian or Biblical conception of man, and of the law and condition of man's perfection. The general nature of this conception I have already indicated, at the beginning of this lecture. I have also indicated, in particular, that, in accordance with the proper and substantial sense of the word being, taken universally, man can be, and is indeed, truly himself only through an activity, whereby he actually realizes himself; that, by necessary consequence, antecedently to such realization man is but a "possibility," though a "divine" one; that the realization or "rescuing" of this possibility depends on an activity, which, in its universal nature, may strictly be termed creative and redemptive; and that to man, by virtue of his self-conscious personality, the direction of this activity is, under God, committed. All this, I say, I have indicated, with the intimation that it is in agreement with the fundamental conceptions of Scripture.

What, now, we must first inquire, is the "possibility" in question? What is the ideal of man, the specific type, or definable "nature," which, according to the view of Scripture, man must actively realize, in order to be man indeed, and not only in name, and in proportion only as he realizes which he is truly himself? The answer is simple and clear. Man is man only as he realizes in himself the image of God. He is perfect man only as his perfection resembles that of his "Father which is in heaven" (Matt. v. 48). But God is a Spirit; the perfection of man will therefore be characteristically a spiritual perfection. Is, now, man, so far as, realizing this perfection, he becomes truly man, an independent rival of God? By no means. Not in separation from God—still less in opposition to or rivalry with God—but in living, organic, effective union with him is man made perfect. The perfect man is a partaker of the divine nature (2 Pet. i. 4), a partaker of the Holy Ghost (Heb. vi. 4), of the everlasting and absolute, divine Spirit. God is his inheritance, receiving which, and so first and effectively becoming a son of God, he first acquires the right to be called in downright and unqualified fact a "son of man." Further, the condition, on which the realization of the perfection described depends, is an activity on man's part,—an activity of the spirit, founded on spiritual knowledge, subject to the will of God (which is but another name for the law of absolute being), supported by the activity of God himself, and manifesting itself in the "fruits of the spirit," the collective and all-comprehensive name for which is love, or "charity." And, finally, the fulcrum, the point of support, for this activity on man's part—the necessary resisting surface, so to express it—and the sphere for its manifestation, is the "flesh" and the "world."

Each of these points we must now consider somewhat in detail, proceeding from the last to the first.

With respect to the negative side of man, or that which I have termed, in effect, the necessary resistant condition and the immediate place or sphere of his spiritual activity, comparatively little needs to be said. It is simply not true, as the critics of Christian ethics often seem to imagine, that Christianity, or true religion, any more than true philosophy, abstracts, in contemplating man, from his surroundings and conditions in time and space, with a view to regarding him solely as the predestined denizen of a realm—a Kingdom of Heaven—which lies wholly beyond the realm of time and space and into which man cannot and must not enter here and now, if at all. The apparently contradictory statements of Scripture on this point are easily reconciled with each other and with the general order of truths demonstrated in these lectures. It is, thus, indeed true that "flesh and blood cannot inherit the kingdom of God:" "corruption" cannot "inherit incorruption" (1 Cor. xv. 50). Yet it is also true that

the body of the true man is, here and now, a "tem-
ple of the Holy Ghost" (1 Cor. vi. 19), of the "living
God" (2 Cor. vi. 16), and is, in "reasonable service,"
presented as "a living sacrifice, holy, acceptable
unto God" (Rom. xii. 1). The state of the case is
simply this: it is not by as much as man is flesh and
blood that he inherits the kingdom of God; it is not
by simple virtue of his physical constitution, as such,
that man is or can be man, *i. e.*, a living spirit; but,
on the other hand, this inheritance is his, and he is
such a spirit, not without the body: the latter is the
necessary mechanical basis and instrumental condition of man's spiritual self-realization and so of his
present and immediate entrance into the kingdom,
at once of God and of man. The relation is precisely analogous to, though in content much richer
than, the one that we have already observed as
existing in nature at large between what may be
termed her outer and her inner sides, or between
the ever-changing (and so inherently "corrupti-
ble"), mechanical, physico-phenomenal garb or
"first appearance" of nature and her permanent
and inward, living, spiritual substance. To the
very conception of nature—to the completely concrete and experimental conception of nature—we
found that the notion, the recognition, of the one
side was just as essential as that of the other.
From neither side was it possible to abstract except
at the cost of rendering our conception of nature
herself abstract, inexperimental, hollow, and dis-
torted. The like is true with regard to man. Only,

man is differentiated from nature in this, that, if I
may thus express myself, his spiritual "filling" is
richer than hers; it is more obvious, explicit, complete, and concrete. It is plainer that there is, in
Job's words, "a spirit in man," than that there is
one in nature. For, in nature, to employ an ancient
figure, the spirit seems to sleep, while in man it is
awake. In the former it seems unconscious, while
in the latter it is self-conscious. In the one case,
it appears as though it were seeking to hide itself,
while in the other it comes clearly forth from its
concealment. In short, that is only implicitly in
nature, which is explicitly in man. The abstraction, therefore, of which I spoke above, customarily
and not unnaturally takes, when indulged, a different form or direction, according as the subject of
consideration is nature or man. On the one hand,
men, looking, through the glasses of pure physical
science, at that side of nature which at first lies
nearest at hand and seems most characteristically
and obviously "natural,"—viz., at the purely mechanical and sensible side,—form a conception of
nature as mere dead and automatic mechanism,
devoid of living, spiritual substance. On the other
hand, others, looking through the glasses of an
equally one-sided and abstract "metaphysics," or
of a misinterpreted "Christianity," at that side of
man's nature which is most characteristically "human"—viz., at its ideal-spiritual side—have formed
the abstract, spectral, and inexperimental conception of man as consisting, properly speaking, of

nothing but a so-called "immaterial soul," out of all intrinsic relation to the body and its physical environment, and to which the body and all physical conditions are rather a clog and burden than at once a necessary and a helpful instrument. Both of these abstractions are equally unphilosophical and irreligious; and, in particular, they are not scriptural. The Christian man — to confine ourselves now to the immediate subject of discussion chosen for this lecture—not only lives in the confident assurance that in his flesh he shall see God, but he also believes that he has seen and evermore sees the Word made flesh, God manifested in the flesh (1 Tim. iii. 16), the invisible in the visible. Instead, therefore, of his regarding "the flesh," or "matter," and, in general, a physical constitution of things, as something inherently corrupt and polluting, something foreign to God and inimical to the perfect being of the spiritual man, he sees in it simply the language in which God speaks to man and the mechanism through which God manifests himself and so really and effectively is or exists for man. And so, too, he is compelled to see in the fact of his own participation, through his bodily organization, in the physical constitution of things, not the evidence of a mistake on the part of his Creator, but rather proof of a gracious intention that man should, here and now, in the flesh, be a coworker with God, that he, too, should in his turn, through his life and activity in the flesh, speak to God (*"Laborare est orare"*) and, as in·a reflected image, reveal him; and, in short, that through the due mastery and use of his "members"—not by ascetic neglect and mortification of them—he should at once develope and demonstrate his own spiritual nature and the true relation of his members to that nature, by rendering the latter "servants to righteousness, unto holiness" (Rom. vi. 19). The Christian rejoices in the leadership of a master, by whom not only the worlds were made, but who, himself incarnate, came, and, by his spirit, evermore comes, into the world, not to condemn, but to finish and redeem and possess, his own work. He rejoices in the saying of that Master, "As I am, so are ye in the world." Not outside the world, not in some fancied, but as yet unrealized (and in fact inconceivable) state of existence in complete separation from a mechanical constitution of things, but "in the world," participating in its life and mastering its uses, does the perfect man, the spiritual man, the partaker of the divine nature, "possess all things." And even the future glory, which he anticipates, is subject to conditions of essentially similar nature. Then, as now, "all things" become his, not through their annihilation, nor by his absolute removal or separation from them, but through his and their "redemption," "salvation," preservation.

The flesh, then, is given to man, in the view of Scripture, not that he may abandon and hate it, nor yet that he may identify himself wholly with it, but that he may, so to speak, the rather identify it, as a necessary instrument, with himself, through the

normal and proper use of it. He, I say, must use
it, and not allow it the rather to use him. It must
be his servant, and not he its servant. To this end
an activity is required on his part, an activity which
proceeds characteristically from the spirit, and not
from the body, and yet which, if I may so express
myself, proceeds, not away from, but toward the
body and, through it, toward that mechanical order
of things, of which the body is as an organic part. It
is an activity which finds in the flesh and the world
the necessary resistant foil and the lever, whereby
it is itself at once rendered possible and definite and
real, so that the agent employing it fights not vainly,
as "one that beateth the air." The further nature
of this activity, with its conditions and its law, are
to be presently examined. Here it is important for
us first to notice that the possibility just suggested,
viz., that the flesh, being more than a mere dead
instrument and endowed as if with a power of its
own, may reduce its rightful master into bondage
to itself and so even prevent his existing in any
other form than that of an unrealized or perverted
potentiality,—that this possibility, I say, is one, to
the recognition of which an important place must
be given in any completely experimental science of
man, and which indeed occupies a position of fundamental importance in the anthropology of the
Christian Scriptures. The Scriptures recognize,
namely, a distinction between the "natural man"
and the "spiritual man,"—a distinction which reappears under such other forms of expression as the

"outward" and the "inward," the "old" and the "new," the "first" and the "second," man, or, briefly, the "flesh" and the "spirit." The former of these comes first in the order of time. It is man as he is first made, man as, independently of his own volition, he is first physically constituted and landed, a helpless stranger, on nature's breast. It is the earthen vessel, as to whose destination, whether for honor or dishonor, nothing is at first determined. It is, considered antecedently to any free and independent activity on the part of the man himself, simply the potential or possible man, the nominal man, sensibly individualized,—defined and located in relations of time and space. It is, thus viewed, the sign of a human possibility, not of a human reality. But it is also, I repeat, something more than this. It is also a power, that resists, and that may enter into successful rivalry with, the true, the spiritual man. Its resistance we have indicated as necessary to the real activity of the spirit. Its successful resistance involves the spirit's ruin. "To be carnally minded is death" (Rom. viii. 6). It is only nominal, not real, manhood and life. The subject of it is, morally and most essentially, a spectre, a corpse, a veritable "body of death." In the flesh there is "no good thing;" and this, in the first instance, simply because the flesh is neither the seat of any good nor of any evil thing; it is morally indifferent. Its action is blind, mechanical, and irresponsible. But when, and so far as, resisting and warring against the spirit, it meets with unchecked success, its work is the abomination of moral desolation. He, whose whole life is absorbed in the service of the flesh, who, not a master, but a real slave, yields submissively to all the motions of the flesh, is not, and cannot be, in the kingdom of God or of Man. Nor does he demean himself as a member of the kingdom of Nature. For then, harmlessly following the normal impulses of nature, and being guided in his course by that universal providence which is to nature as her soul, he would, like the fowls of the air and the lilies of the field, simply fulfil, unreflectingly and spontaneously, the universal law of nature, in a life at harmony with itself and with its surroundings,— a life of relative beauty and service. But this he never does, and the fact that he never does it is one evidence that he cannot do it. He cannot do it, because, though visibly born from the womb of nature, he is not all *of* nature or *for* her. He has another birth, which is of the free self-conscious spirit, and is of God. By this he is specifically differentiated from nature. By virtue of this a specific work is given him to do, a work, the doing of which is essential to the realization of his own proper and complete be-. ing and which nature cannot do for him. The necessary result, therefore, of his seeking to identify himself wholly with the purely natural man and delivering himself over to follow none but carnal impulses, is and can be only the perversion and the ruin, both of the natural and of the spiritual man. It is a human monstrosity, and its works—since no epithet from the realm of God or nature can be found for the purpose of characterizing them—can only be called devilish. They are at enmity, both with nature and with nature's God. In them the image of God is not to be found. And they are also a crying ontological absurdity; for they contradict, as far as is possible, philosophy's universal and experimentally-founded definition of all true and genuine being as grounded in the consistent and regular fulfilment of a definite, typical, and purposeful activity. Hence also, as above noted, the condition which they denote is rightly termed in Scripture one of death rather than life. He who ostensibly " lives " in them, is in reality dead, and not alive. The true man, with the specific marks and substance of genuine manhood, is not there. In fact, he has not yet begun to be; he has not yet been born; and, in order that he may at last really *be*, and not merely counterfeit, or, still worse, present nothing but a wretched travesty upon, the true being of a man, he must, in the expressive language of Jesus, be "born again." He must be "born of the Spirit," and "of God."

The "birth of the Spirit": this, to sense, with its abstract mechanical categories, is that incredible and so-called " supernatural " wonder, in which thought, with its more concrete and completely experimental categories, sees, not the contradiction, but the fulfilment, of nature and of her prophecies. Here the full meaning of creation and redemption—please recall, from the last lecture, how these two conceptions necessarily involve each other—becomes explicit and obvious. Here the work of creation first becomes complete. Herein is fulfilled the word of the Lord, spoken by the mouth of that ancient prophet who, more than all others, seems to have been endowed with the power of "spiritual understanding," saying, "So shall my word be that goeth forth out of my mouth: it shall not return unto me void; but it shall accomplish that which I please, and it shall prosper in the thing whereto I sent it " (Is. lv. 11). That divine word, which, being spoken, goes forth into and creatively constitutes the external universe, and whose sound is heard, even as also its characters are read, throughout the world, returns not to the everlasting speaker " void," or merely as an empty and substanceless echo. It returns indeed, but not until, with the birth of the spirit, all its implicit meaning or content has been explicitly developed, manifested, concretely realized, in the world, and so the thing, whereto it was sent, has been accomplished. It returns in the form of a creation, which, conscious of its true self, can, as nature with her veiled consciousness can not, be conscious of the Absolute Spirit who is imaged therein; a creation which, relatively self-centred in its own personality, can perceive that the absolute centre of all its conscious life and of all its being is there alone where absolute being is to be found; and which, therefore, looking God in the face, can spiritually return to him and say, " Thou art my Father," and be welcomed back to the embrace of the divine life and love.

But we are anticipating our conclusion. The birth

of the spirit is indeed man's true birth, and his only true birth. The spiritual world, in the energetic language of the elder Fichte, is indeed man's " true birth-place." Here first he begins to " have life in himself," and so to have not merely the outward semblance, but also the inward substance, of humanity. From the grave of the flesh, with its dead works, proceeds the resurrection of the spirit " to serve the living God." But the resurrection is not itself the service. The " birth " of the spirit is only its beginning, not its completion. Fresh-born, it is not yet stablished in the image and by the power of the " free Spirit " of God. It is, as yet, only a glorious possibility, the rich content of which has yet to be rescued, redeemed, created, realized, by an appropriate activity. And this activity, I have said, is " an activity on man's part, an activity of the spirit, founded on spiritual knowledge, subject to the will of God (which is but another name for the law of absolute being), and supported by the activity of God himself."

First, it is a spiritual activity on man's part, or proceeding from man himself. A spirit is not made; it is self-made. It realizes itself. Self-determination is the universal form of all spiritual activity. The image of self-determination is presented to us in the processes of nature. With the accomplished accuracy of a scientific expert Aristotle described the process, by which a natural existence is realized, and is maintained in existence, as one which has the form of self-realization: a typical form real-

izes itself in and by means of the material that it
finds lying at hand.[4] The form, I say, of this process
is that of self-determination. But the substance,
which this form necessarily implies, is self-consciousness, or, still better and more explicitly, consciously
self-determining spirit. And it is because of this relation, and because the "substance" mentioned is
not found immediately in nature, that to thought,
the spirit's organ, the form of nature's life proclaims
unmistakably the reality of an omnipresent and ever-
wakeful, divine consciousness,—the self-conscious life
and activity of God. In the case of man, who is a
spirit and destined, so far as he becomes truly himself, to be in the image of God, the Absolute Spirit,
form and substance of self-determination cannot be
separated. The mere form, or image, will not suffice.
By this alone man were in no sense discriminated
from pure nature; he were only "sleeping spirit," no
better than a bare potentiality. No; in man, if he is
to be really man, there must be present the living,
energetic reality of self-determination. He must,
like his Heavenly Father, be spiritually awake; and
this, too, not for a moment only, or from time to
time, but constantly. Not a single act of self-determination only, nor that act spasmodically repeated
at uncertain intervals, but a sustained process is required,—a process that knows neither haste nor rest
and through which the spirit, the real man, finding
means and (so to speak) assimilable material in all
the changing circumstances and opportunities of his
existence, patiently and persistently realizes him-

self in and through the same. "My Father worketh
hitherto, and I work." In these words is sounded
the key-note of the human spirit's supremest obligation and privilege. For in order to be, it must
do,—it must work. It must work out its own "salvation"; it must realize itself.

Secondly, the condition of the self-determining
activity in question is spiritual knowledge. The
object of this knowledge is "the truth," the truth
as such, the universal truth. The knowledge spoken
of is not mere erudition. It does not consist in mere
information, however encyclopedic the latter may
be conceived, respecting the particular facts or phenomena of nature and history and the laws of order—
of co-existence and sequence,—by which these facts
are rendered at once possible and real objects of
human intelligence. It does not indeed exclude,
nor is it necessarily prejudiced by, such "wisdom
of this world"; nay, more, for purposes of practical
application this "wisdom," in greater or lesser measure, furnishes a needful supplement to spiritual knowledge; but the two are not identical, and the latter
of them is the one thing indispensably needful.
The knowledge in question is the knowledge of
that whereby all things consist; it is the knowledge
of Spirit; it is the knowledge of God, the Absolute
Spirit. "The Spirit is truth" (1 John v. 6). This
is "the truth," not only in form, but also in its everlasting substance. This is the truth, the knowledge
of which is to man, the spirit, as "shield and buck-
ler" (Ps. xci. 4). This is the truth, with which he

has his loins girt about (Eph. vi. 14), against which
he can—except at the cost of spiritual self-destruction—do nothing (2 Cor. xiii. 8), and which dwells
in him and shall be with him forever (2 John 2).
It is the truth, in and through the understanding
of which we are to be, and can alone be, "men"
(1 Cor. xiv. 20). And then, more particularly, this
truth is to be known "as it is in Jesus," who, by reason
of his complete organic oneness with "the Father,"
is entitled to call himself "the truth," and whom
truly, *i. e.*, spiritually, to have "seen," is to have
seen the Father. Finally, the immediate result of
his knowledge of the truth is man's freedom. "Ye
shall know the truth, and the truth shall make you
free" (John viii. 32). Positive, substantial freedom,
the freedom of genuine self-possession (truly possessing one's true self) and self-mastery through self-
knowledge, is a part of the completed spirit's very
being; nay, it is identical with its being; and the
Psalmist employs no vain metaphor, when he ascribes this attribute to God and prays, "Uphold me
with thy free Spirit" (Ps. li. 12). Or, again, the result spoken of is "eternal life," a life whose form is
not purely phenomenal, consisting in involuntary
duration, but transcends the form of time and is
absolute, real, substantial. "This is life eternal,
that they might know thee, the only true God, and
Jesus Christ, whom thou hast sent" (John xvii. 3).

I have said that, according to the voice of Scripture, (as also of philosophy,) there is needed, in
order that man may be truly man, a spiritual ac-

tivity on his own part, and an activity founded on spiritual knowledge. And how indeed, if man's being depends on his own doing,—if, in order to be himself, he must, in an essential sense, make himself,—how, I say, shall he accomplish this work, if he know not what he has to do? How shall he make himself a spirit, and the image of God, without knowing what a spirit, and, more especially, what God as a Spirit, is? But the language above employed might lead the superficial observer to imagine that the Scriptures are guilty of that abstraction and exaggeration which are attributed to Socrates, who, rightly recognizing knowledge as the condition of virtue, seemed, in occasional expressions, forthwith to identify the condition with that which it conditions, or with virtue itself. But that knowledge, which is either unto Socratic "virtue" or unto eternal life, by no means ends or is absorbed in "bare cognition." There is a profound truth in the thought that one can deeply and fully know only that which one, by life and action, is and exemplifies. Of spiritual knowledge or the knowledge peculiarly appropriate and necessary for the perfect man, it is even more profoundly true than of any other, that it is founded in and must be confirmed by experience,—taking this latter term in its truest and original sense, as denoting, not a mere passive reception of impressions, but an active "testing," "trying," or "finding out," and that, too, whether with or without the express and conscious aim or intention of "acquiring knowledge." The first condition of a genuine knowledge of the truth is, according to Plato, not mere mechanical intellection, but the active and unquenchable love of the truth. The accomplished mathematician, even, does not become such by merely hearing of and assenting to general mathematical principles, but by working out the problems of mathematics for himself; and this he never does without an enthusiastic and moving interest in his work. And so, too, truths of *life*—the truths of man's perfect being—can only be, in any proper and adequate sense, known, as they are actually *lived;* and they can be lived only as they are loved; for, as Fichte says, "What a man loves, that he lives." Accordingly, what the Scriptures require of the perfect man, and that upon which they represent his freedom as conditioned, is not simply that he possess and give his assent to correct information about the truth in general, but that he *do* it, that he carry it out in practice, in his particular sphere. He is to "walk in the truth," and he that "walketh in the truth," "walketh in love." He must first hear and understand the voice which says, "This is the way," and then obey the command, "Walk ye in it" (Is. xxx. 21). And consequent upon such obedience is to be that fuller, more complete, personal, and experimental knowledge of "the way, the truth, and the life," which shall make him "free." "If any man will do his will, he shall know of the doctrine, whether it be of God" (John vii. 17). A spiritual activity founded on knowledge, or, in other words, a personal working out of the problem of man's true and spiritual being in life, this is at once condition and proof both of one's freedom and of one's spiritual knowledge.

Thirdly, I have said that the activity, whereby man realizes himself, is scripturally viewed as an activity subject to the will of God, and supported by the activity of God himself. Man's being, as we have seen, is only in and through his doing. The law of his perfect doing is identical with the law of his perfect being. And this law is identical with the will of God. The divine will is not arbitrary. God is not a monstrous and unnatural task-master, capable of taking advantage of his own omnipotence to impose upon man the obligation to obey laws which are out of all relation to the nature of man, and which receive at most only a quasi-justification, and one that borders closely upon the blasphemous, when it is alleged that they are instituted exclusively for the "glory" of God. The will of God concerning man is, that man should "stand fast in the liberty" of spiritual manhood; that thus he should be a member of the Kingdom of Heaven; and this law is, accordingly, summed up by its authoritative expounder in the exhortation, "Be ye therefore"—not something other than yourselves, not stocks or stones, not machines, not beasts, nor devils, nor demigods—but "be ye perfect, as your Father in heaven is perfect." The will of God is nothing other than the law of absolute or perfected being. It is the law of the most perfect realization of the spiritual nature. And the activity, I say, by which, as it regards man, this law is carried out, is supported by the activity of God himself.

We approach now the conclusion of the whole matter. Man is not an absolutely independent being. He is not a little God by himself. He belongs to the realm of creation and, consequently, of redemption. He belongs to a realm which does not belong to him as an individual, but belongs to God. And the active sovereignty in this realm is never for an instant abandoned by him from whom it proceeds and to whom it returns. The culminating error of a purely mechanical philosophy consists in the supposition that the world, with all that it contains—including, of course, man,—having been "first caused" or "created" by a divine artificer, is then left to run on, automatically or otherwise, by its own "laws," unaided and unharmed by divine "intervention." But thus, as we have seen, the real relation of things is in conception completely reversed and turned topsy-turvy. The created universe is thus practically put in the place of the Absolute, and God, the true Absolute, is represented as nothing better than a casual outsider, to whom the dubious compliment is paid of admitting that he has the power to "interfere" in the world's affairs, but of whom nothing less can in justice be required than that henceforth he keep his hands off; the world, once existing, is held to be able to take care of iself. This conception, we have already seen, is superficial, being capable of being entertained only by him whose point of view, in contemplating the

universe, is such as to allow him to perceive only
the first surface-facts about the universe. The so-
called automatic regularity of physical phenomena
is but one evidence of the immutable activity of him,
in whom it has its being. The withdrawal of the
divine activity from the world, the cessation of the
divine work, were the contradiction of the divine
nature. And it would also—since the relative or
finite subsists only through the activity of the Absolute and Infinite—be tantamount to the instantaneous annihilation of the world. No, the world
is the incessant divine work, in which indeed no one
"interferes," unless it be man himself. The divine
work in and through the world is, as we saw, a
displaying of the "riches of God," and becomes
complete when, in a finite spirit like man, the image of God himself is realized.

And now we have been considering the responsibility for the realization of this image as resting on
man himself. This we saw to be not only scriptural, but also from the nature of the case necessary,
since man cannot be in the image of God, he cannot
be a spirit, except he really possess and exercise
the power of self-determination. In order really to
be man, he must be responsible. But, I repeat, the
power that he uses is not self-given or self-created.
It is a power of God, lent or committed to him as a
sacred trust. The individual is not absolute. His
highest privilege, and his highest possibility, is to be
a coworker with God. He is to carry out the divine
work. He may indeed neglect or even work against

his divine calling; but, so doing, his work comes
to nought. The result is, not positive, not realization of the true self, but negative, or self-destruction.
"The wages of sin is death." God, the Absolute
Being, the source and foundation of all existence,
is, *per se,* or independently of and antecedently
to any voluntary activity on man's part, man's
"strength." And man makes himself then to be
truly man only as he consciously and with full
knowledge and intent, "makes God his strength."
Beneath him are, without his will, "everlasting
arms." He is, in love and trust and with all the
energy of a fully self-determined will, to lay hold
upon those arms. His own activity becomes genuine, substantial, and effective, only when it is thus
"supported by the activity of God himself."

We have represented that the true object of man's
will is the "true self." It must now be evident that
the true self is something far different from that
which is ordinarily understood by the "purely individual." The type of the purely individual is, as
we have previously pointed out, the mathematical
point, which is without inward difference or complexity and equally without external relation to aught
other than itself; unextended in time or space, and
complete in itself;—complete, the rather, in its absolute incompleteness or substancelessness. It is,
or it is conceived as being, without or independent
of anything else. In general, the individual is the
sensible, that whose relations are, at the most, only
external and superficial. A "thing" is individual.

A person, a spirit, is more than that. Instead of excluding its neighbor, its "other," it includes it. Its essential side is the side of its universality. Thus if we look only at the sphere of man's consciousness, we know that here the self is not to be identified with any one of the myriad different conscious states, through which it passes. The self is rather the universal form and condition of all particular states. But, further, these states are, as such, only the means whereby the self is placed and maintained in relation with a world, which at first confronts man as a stranger—as something wholly and only foreign to him, the conscious subject. With deepening intelligence, however, he comes to see that in this world he is no stranger, but really at home. Nor is it foreign to him, but, in a very strict sense, as it were bone of his bone and flesh of his flesh. On the one hand, he sees in this "world" an organized system, in which he is a member; a system, therefore, which in a very real sense is necessary both to the idea and to the concrete reality of himself; and a system, also, to whose completeness he himself is necessary. On the other hand, he becomes practically so identified with his particular "world," the world of his special, individual environment, that, separated from it, he, as individual, withers and dies. It thus shows itself to be very effectively identified with, or a true part of, his empirical self. But again, man sees in nature, when he looks more deeply and closely, simply the welling up, as it were, and the manifestation under the most varied forms, of a life and substance which he recognizes as one with his own spiritual life and substance. In a deeper sense, therefore, than before, he finds himself in nature, and nature in himself. He finds in nature, not a limitation, but rather a fulfilment, of his own real self, of his personality. And yet not its direct, nor its complete fulfilment. Nature, as such, is not that spirit that man sees in her, but rather its transparent symbol and its constant work.

Man, we have been saying, must will and realize his true self, and we want to know wherein this self consists, or what it is that man wills when he wills and realizes his true self. And we have said, first, that the true self is nothing purely individual, but something universal. Secondly, the point we wish to make now is that while, in a very essential sense, the self of the individual comprehends, rather than excludes, the world of nature, of which it is a part and to which it is immediately related, yet man obviously does not find himself in nature in any such sense or to any such degree that he may say of it, " This is the self that I will and that by my own self-determining activity I realize." He cannot, I say, be said thus to find himself in nature, if you consider her on that side by which she is differentiated from the Spirit which is the source of her life. For, thus considered, Nature herself is also purely individual; nay, hers is the peculiar realm of the individual, the particular, the finite, and hence not of the universal which we seek. The object of our quest is to be found, not in anything that is particular, finite, purely individual, nor in any sum total or mere aggregate of such particulars, but in that which is the source and condition of all that is particular and finite. Not in willing the finite, relative, and dependent does a man will his true self, and not in realizing them, as such, does he realize his true self, but in willing and realizing the infinite, absolute, and independent. In this he finds his real substance. From this, nought can separate him, whether principalities or powers, or things present or things to come. For to this, the everlasting and absolute and ever-present source of his being, he is immediately related. With this he is connected by the inmost springs of his being. It is in this that he immediately lives and moves and has his being. With all else his connection is indirect. With all things finite he is substantially connected only through the common dependence of all things upon the same Absolute, which is the only true foundation of his own being. And this Absolute is God. In him alone man finds his true home, his " dwelling-place." Man finds himself and wills himself, in the truest and most unqualified sense of the terms, when he finds and wills himself in God, and God in him. Then can he say, in the fullest sense, " Lo, I come to do thy will, O my God." And then at last is he, not merely phenomenally and empirically, but substantially, genuinely, and absolutely free. That freedom, which is limited and determined by the empirical necessity of choosing among various finite particulars, or so-called alternatives, but half deserves its name. It is, at most, only an

outward and formal and accidental freedom. It is
not substantial freedom. It is not the "liberty" in
which the perfect man "stands fast." It is not positive and unqualified *self*-determination. On the contrary, when this so-called empirical freedom of choice
among various finite particulars is the only freedom
that one has, one is not really free at all, but only a
slave. Losing sight of the Absolute and of his essential relation to it, and practically identifying himself with that in and about him which is finite, changing, transitory, he is effectively separated from all
genuine, abiding spiritual substance; he is separated
from his true self, and knows it not; and he is the
slave of sin. The life which he ostensibly leads and
which he calls his, is an essential illusion, and on its
"death" depends the salvation, the rescue, the redemption of his true life. To him, therefore, if he
can but understand them, the words of Jesus are full
of a tremendous significance, when he says that he
that saveth his life shall lose it, and he that loseth
his life shall find it. That ostensible life, which is
founded in nothing deeper than the thought and
love and will of the particular and contingent must be
"lost," or one is eternally dead. It is with reference
to this "life" that the Christian Apostle says, "I die
daily." This is that death unto sin, from the grave
of which arises the true and eternal "life unto God."

The will, therefore, which identifies itself with the
will of God,—the will which, primarily or in the first
instance, wills nought but God, and then wills all
else from the point of view of God or of the absolute

and divine will,—possesses that absolute substance
of freedom, wherein consists the perfected reality
of the spirit. This is freedom through knowledge,
love, and practical realization of "the truth." It is
a steadfast freedom, for it is founded on the only
rock that never moves. It is unlimited, for the reason that it is the attribute of a will whose object is
the Absolute,—*i. e.*, that which itself conditions and
so transcends all limits,—and that in so doing,—or
in willing him in whom are the very springs of its
life,—it has willed itself. It is strong, for it makes
God its strength. This is the freedom of those who
can say, "Of his fulness have we received;" of those,
whose bodies are "temples of the Holy Ghost;" of
those who, dwelling in love, dwell in God and God
in them (1 John iv. 16), and who, increasing in
love, "increase with the increase of God" (Col. ii.
19). These are they who, though dead—dead,
namely, to their former, illusory selves, to the "old
man," the "finite, selfish ego"—have yet found and
saved their true selves. Though dead, they are already risen with Christ. Dead unto sin they are
alive unto God, through Jesus Christ (Rom. vi. 11).
They are dead, and yet they still walk the earth.
They are not in the grave. They simply look no
longer on the mere fact of their "walking the
earth," enjoying its transient pleasures, and engag-
ing in its changing occupations as that wherein their
true selves and their absolute life consist. They
are dead, and yet their true life is saved, being "hid
with Christ in God" (Col. iii. 3).

Before leaving this inexhaustible theme—over which we have already lingered too long—there are two points, on which it is indispensable that we say a word, however hurriedly. Of these, one is the connection which the Scriptures ascribe to Jesus Christ with the work of man's substantial redemption and self-realization (or "salvation"); and the other is the absolute remoteness of scriptural ethics and its doctrine of the perfect man from anything like what may be called fanatical, anti-worldly quietism.

(1) We have but to recall from the last lecture the view which we there reached respecting the Incarnate Word, as the Creator and Redeemer of all things, "whether they be things in earth, or things in heaven," and then to extend it to the case of man, at the same time taking into the account the difference by which man has been exhibited as distinguished from and above "nature,"—we have, I say, but to do this, in order to perceive in what special sense Christ is scripturally regarded as the Redeemer and Saviour of mankind. The world, as we saw, is represented to us in Scripture as created and redeemed by the divine Word in no merely mechanical sense. It is created, not simply *by* God in Jesus Christ, but *in* him. The relation involved is not simply eternal and—thus to express it—theatrical, but internal, intrinsic, vital. The divine Word, the Son of God, gives himself,.in order that the world may *be*, and that, being filled with his riches, it may be, not only outwardly and, as it were dramatically

and scenically, but inwardly and really, through the completion of its very life and being, to the praise and demonstration of his glorious and infinite love. In like manner the redemption of man is accomplished, not simply *by*, but *in*, Christ Jesus. Man "works out" his "own salvation," *i. e.*, the rescue and the realization of his true self, in inward, organic union with, and intelligent, voluntary, and loving dependence on, God who "worketh in" him. Thus he becomes a "new creature" or, simply, a "perfect man, in Christ Jesus." The relation is organic, and not merely mechanical; it is ontological and essential, and not merely spectacular and phenomenal. The Master himself has expressed this most clearly and effectively by the well-known comparison of the vine and the branches. "I am the vine, and my Father is the husbandman." "Abide in me, and I in you. As the branch cannot bear fruit of itself, except it abide in the vine; no more can ye, except ye abide in me. I am the vine, and ye are the branches" (John xv. 1, 4, 5). And the perfection of man, the realization, and not the destruction, of his personality,—the rather the fulfilment of his personality through the realization for it and in it of its true, universal, and infinite content,—is represented by the Christ as dependent on the same condition of organic unity. For his prayer is, "that they all may be one; as thou, Father, art in me, and I in thee, that they also may be one in us . . . . I in them, and thou in me, that *they may be made perfect in one*" (John xvii. 21, 23). And in the con-

sciousness of the fulfilment of this prayer the "be-
loved apostle" writes: "We are in him that is true,
even in his Son Jesus Christ. This is the true God,
and eternal life" (1 John v. 20). Again, St. Paul
declares, "He that is joined to the Lord is one
spirit" (1 Cor. vi. 17). This, I must repeat, is the
completion of the spiritual personality,—not its
destruction through a fancied pantheistic absorption
in one abstract, universal, and so-called divine essence or "substance." It is at last having real and
genuine "life in one's self." Besides, this "conclusion" is not merely reached in some far-off and un-
observable future, but also here and now: thus it
has ever been from the foundation of the world and
thus it shall ever be. It is reached and confirmed
and verified in the present experience of mankind,
or else the whole tale is as an empty sound; and
surely no such pantheistic absorption as just mentioned is ever witnessed in man's experience. That
some such relation between the individual and the
Absolute as that which we have been contemplating, must needs be conceived as essential to moral
perfection, is illustrated in all moral theories that
have even in the slightest degree the *form* of philosophic completeness. Thus, in the "philosophy of
evolution," an absolute and universal Power is recognized, the essence and particular nature of which
are held to be unknown and unknowable, but of
which we do know that the universal law of its
operation is the law of evolution. The category of
evolution is thus made the highest category of posi-

tive, substantial human thought. Evolution, so far as our positive knowledge extends, is made to occupy for man the place of the Absolute. But now, it is held, man is only the highest product of evolution. His moral nature is its most perfect work. And man's business, as a moral being, is simply to know this law and consciously to indentify himself with it. It is his strength and his substance; and he is consciously and voluntarily to make it his strength. He, the dependent individual, is to become his true self, by adopting for his own the law and, as it were, the life (if it were permitted in this connection to employ so characteristically spiritual a category as that of life) of the universal (*i. e.*, of evolution). The attempt to build up the science of man on a basis which abstracts from the spiritual nature of man, may well excite regret at useful labor lost; and that the result of it is the "humanization of ethics" may justly be doubted. But the result shows that the philosophic impulse cannot be present and operate, however blindly, in man, as he seeks for self-knowledge, without his seeking, in one form or another, for the Absolute and looking to find in it the spring and the strength and the law of his true life and being. All this philosophy and religion—which, unlike philosophic mechanism, look at concrete wholes and not at parts—find, not in the unknowable, nor in the mechanical law of its sensible activity, but in the Everlasting Spirit, the Father of our spirits, and the very principle and light of all knowledge.

The peculiar nature of the redemptive work ascribed by the Scriptures to Christ in his relation to
man, arises from, or, at all events, corresponds to,
the peculiar nature of man himself, as heretofore set
forth. It has relation to man as, in distinction from
external nature, a self-conscious and responsible
being, capable of error and of sin and of knowing
his error and sin. Man, sinning, feels in himself
the beginning of moral ruin, of moral self-murder;
and thus is sown in him the seed of a despair which,
unless counteracted, must cut the nerve of all his
resolution and all his effort. He has sinned against
himself, and his first feeling is that he can never
either forgive or recover himself. But he has also,
on the other hand, sinned against God, and, thinking of God as of one like unto himself, imagines
that his arm can no longer be stretched out, except
for vengeance and punishment. And now the divine
problem is to bring redemption to such an one. Obviously, this cannot be accomplished by mechanical
might, but only (as saith the Lord) " by my Spirit."
The agency must be a purely moral and spiritual one.
It must be used so as not to destroy, but to restore
freedom. And this is done, not by representing God
as taking pleasure in the sin of man, or interfering
to prevent the moral self-destruction of any who wil-
fully persist in transgression;—this were obviously
impossible;—but by exhibiting him to man in his
absolute nature of love, as one who is able to "endure such contradiction of sinners against himself,"
without contradicting his own nature and falling

forthwith into a state of implacable anger; as one whose arm is always stretched out to save; as one who, instead of coldly waiting to see whether man will "repent" and seek forgiveness, is ever actively seeking to compass the completion of the divine creative-redemptive work in man. With the work of man's redemption the Scriptures represent the life and death of the Incarnate Word on earth as especially connected. And yet the work of Christ on earth, eighteen hundred years ago, is not to be considered as the demonstration of a new disposition on the part of God, or of a new determination on his part with reference to man, but only as a new and most effective demonstration of the everlasting disposition and determination of God with regard both to nature and to man. It is a demonstration, or demonstrative exhibition, of the truth that in the eternal nature of God who is the Alpha and the Omega of existence, the fountain and the goal of all true being, the reconciliation of the world and of man to God has everlastingly its potential and efficient foundation. It brings home to man, in the most impressive and effective way, the truth that the perfection and the supreme privilege of his essential humanity lie in his spiritual union with God, the Father of his spirit, and that the way to this perfection lies in his determined will to become reconciled, through knowledge, love, and obedience, to God (2 Cor. v. 20). He is penitently to abandon, and then to forget and "lose" his former, fancied, individual, finite "self," with all

its moral wounds and putrefying sores, with the end
of finding his true self, in larger and diviner fashion,
in God. "Forgetting those things which are behind, and reaching forth unto those things which
are before," he is to "press toward the mark for
the prize of the high calling of God in Christ Jesus."
And "as many as be perfect" are "thus minded"
(Phil. iii. 13–15).

(2) This doctrine of Christian ethics is no doctrine
of mystic quietism or asceticism. The Christian vic-
tory is not won through an attempted withdrawal
from the world, but by overcoming it;—by remaining in the world and conquering it. The "universal
self" of man is not an abstraction, but, like all true
universals, a power to realize itself in and through
the materials of particular circumstance and oppor-
tunity, in the midst of which the individual may be
placed. Far from being privileged to withdraw himself from the world's work, the "perfect man" realizes that it is only through him that the world's
work can be truly done. Adding to virtue knowledge, he seeks, therefore, to know the world and its
ways and laws by every means, and then takes the
leading part in its work, doing all things to the
glory of God and so turning the world's life and
work into a sacrament. But, above all, he is not
the mere slave of ways and means and laws; he is
rather their master, to learn and know and then
use them. There is therefore in him something
which is higher than, though not opposed to "law."
This is love. Through love—not through ignor-

ance, nor merely through abstract knowledge—
through love he fulfils the law. Teaching the world
this more excellent way, he makes heaven and the
will of God to reign upon earth.

Finally, if the foregoing account is correct, it will
be seen that religion according to the Christian conception, does not simply consist in being informed
of and then formally accepting a "scheme" of rescue
from the damning consequences of sin. It is not
merely *salvation from* something; it is also the *salvation of* something, viz., of the true man. It is the
creative-redemptive realization of the *perfect man*,
in living union with the Absolute, with God. And
if the ethics which it involves is not "*human* ethics,"
then no such ethics ever existed or can, without an
essential change in the nature of *man*, ever exist.

LECTURE VIII.

COMPARATIVE PHILOSOPHIC CONTENT OF CHRISTIANITY.

THE preceding lectures have, I trust, done something to deepen in us the conviction that religion universally, and Christianity in particular, is by its very·nature, a thing which is essentially "of and for intelligence." Other accounts may be, and not infrequently are, also given of religion,—such as that it is an affair of feeling or emotion; or that its realm is identical with that of the poetic imagination, in which realm it strews the flowers that poesy plucks and kindles the fires with which all artistic genius glows, etc., etc. And all these accounts may be, in their way and measure, very true, without overthrowing our initial statement. Nay, rather, whatever of truth is in them may be, and is, conditioned upon the larger truth of our statement. For the being—man—in whose feeling or imagination religion is alleged to have its home, is a being having the attribute of self-consciousness and thought. Religious emotion is the emotion only of thinking beings, just as also it is only the imagination of thinking beings, that is creatively poetic. In reality, all these and other sides of man's active nature are combined within this nature, in a living organic unity, and are consequently all necessary to the whole and complete man; and inasmuch as religion—in the words of another¹—is "an affair of the whole and undivided life of the human spirit," it follows that it will display its life and power in all the directions, or on all the sides, of this life. But of self-conscious intelligence it has to be admitted, that it is not merely one among the several different sides of man's spiritual nature, but that it is also the fundamental one. It is the one common to all and conditioning all. The other sides are as particulars, to which intelligence is as the unifying and self-determining universal. So that religion is, (for example,) an affair of human "emotion," only because human emotion is conditioned by human intelligence.

When we say that religion is of and for intelligence, we say that which, in kind, if not in degree, is equally true of all the other characteristic functions or works of specifically human activity, such, for example, as artistic·creation or the founding and rearing of states. And in each of these cases we mean to affirm, not merely the insignificant truism, that the agents concerned are "intelligent" in the sense of being empirically conscious individuals, but rather the significant truth, that what the genuine artist or statesman does—his activity and the result of his activity—is, partly with, partly and perhaps still more without, his consciousness, determined by and, in its way and measure, a revelation of the absolute

nature and the absolute objective or ontological
conditions of intelligence. What I mean is this: the
genuine artist, engaged in productive work, acts,
not with or from one of the superficial sides of his
nature, abstracting from all the rest; he does not
create his work of art merely by dint of intellectual
reflection, or of pure feeling, or of some special, acquired technical knowledge or skill. Not by any
one of these, nor by all of them, considered as a
mere aggregate of "faculties" or acquired "accomplishments," does he act, but by something that is
deeper than these,—something in which all special
faculties are fused and to which they are subordi-
nated. His action proceeds, not from the outside
of his nature, but from the inside: not from the part,
but from the whole. His whole being—which is
wider than mere reflective consciousness, or pure
feeling, or any and all "accomplishments," though
not exclusive of them—is engaged. He works better
than he knows and better than he feels. His work
is thus a revelation to him, as it is to others. But
it is a revelation of and for intelligence. In the
presence of a work of art one feels, not startled and
bewildered, as if confronted by something wholly
foreign and hostile to, or incommensurate with, one's
self, but supremely at home. Intelligence is not
offended and put to confusion, but satisfied. It finds
its petty, hard-learned laws of technical detail not
violated, but, along with other laws that its reflective consciousness knew not of, respected and
observed in masterly perfection. The artist's whole

being, I say, not only his outward but above all his inward being, has been at work. And as his "whole being" is not a little absolute entity by itself, in effectual mechanical separation from all else that exists, but rests on and is in organic connection with the true and only and universal Absolute, it follows that his work, while it is his, is also the work of that Absolute in which, as artist, he lives and moves and has his being. It is as true in art, as in religion, that "it is not in man that walketh to direct his steps." The "walking," the work, is his, but he feels and knows that it belongs to him, not as a mere finite individual, but as an infinite personality;[2] that is to say, it belongs to him as a spiritual being, whose personal reality and substantial independence are fulfilled, not by pantheistic-mechanical absorption in one universal "substance," but by organic union with an absolute Spirit. The true artist, then, as the common phrase has it, is "inspired." A "divine afflatus" is said to fall upon him, "*Patitur Deum.*" His own genius is at the same time a divine inspiration.

Now what I started out to illustrate was the statement that the true artist's work and activity are "determined by and are a revelation of the absolute nature of intelligence and of the absolute objective or ontological conditions of intelligence." It will now perhaps be sufficiently understood in what sense this statement is intended. It may perhaps be otherwise expressed as follows:—True artistic activity is prompted by the instinct of intelligence, and of intelligence taken in the most comprehensive sense of the term. And by as much as this is true, it is also true—in view of the organic oneness of intelligence and being—that the activity in question is prompted likewise by the instinct of being, or of reality, these terms, in like manner, being considered in their most comprehensive and absolute sense. The work of the artist, considered both as process and as product, becomes therefore an expression at once of the absolute nature of intelligence and of the absolute object of intelligence. It is, so to speak, in its peculiar way an objectified expression or incarnation of the absolute nature and object of intelligence. It may hence be called, in an especial sense, one of the "texts" of philosophy, —a kind of document, which contains implicitly, or expresses in symbolic characters, the sense which it is the whole business of philosophy to render explicit and make manifest for reflective consciousness. It reveals the infinite in the finite and the organic oneness of both these terms. And so it is that a philosophy of art, in the true sense of the term, is possible, or that art is a true text, subject, or datum for philosophy.[3]

What is thus true of the working and the result of artistic genius is also true, *mutatis mutandis*, of the work accomplished by the genius of humanity in all its other directions, as, for example, in the foundation and nurture of states. It is above all true respecting the life and work of man in religion. But the case of religion is distinguished by peculiar dif-

ferences from the other cases, to which we have
referred. In working out and seeking an expression
for his religious ideas, man is more consciously
and distinctly determined by the thought, or by
the dim sense, of the universal problems of existence and by the felt need of discovering their solution, than when working under the influence of
an artistic or politico-social inspiration. Different,
too, is the form in which the results of this religious
activity are finally expressed. For while art—and,
most immediately, literary and poetic art, as in
"sacred writings"—enters naturally, as a means of
formal expression, into the service of religion; and
while the state, too, may and does furnish an objective medium or instrument for the realization
of religious ideas; yet neither the work of art, as
such, nor the state, as such, is the most direct and
characteristic result or expression of what we may
call the working of the religious genius in man.
This "result or expression" is found, the rather,
in what are termed religious ideas—opinions, views,
beliefs, dogmas, expressed and, according to the
belief common to most forms of religion, divinely
communicated to man in the form of myths, stories,
historic narratives, songs, prophecies, proverbs, and
precepts, which are, in form and language, adapted,
as nearly as may be, to the comprehension of the
minds of all classes:—" he who runs may read," and
he who reads will understand, or, at least, will think
and believe that he understands. Further, religious
ideas find symbolic expression in rites and ceremo-

nies, which serve, among other things, as impressive and effective object-lessons in the system of religious instruction.   But it also belongs to the very sense of religious ideas that they are held, not simply as conscious intellectual possessions, and objects of a purely abstract and uninterested intellectual assent, but as a power to mould the heart and direct the life.   They are, in short, not merely theoretical, but also practical.   And so it is that their formative and directive influence reappears, always implicitly, if not also explicitly and to immediate observation, in every sphere of human life and activity, whether private or public.   Still further, the subject-matter of these ideas is, in varying degrees, man and his absolute relations to the universe in which he finds himself placed, the powers of the universe, its origin and destiny,—its meaning, its essential reality, its government, and all of these with special reference to the nature and possibilities, the duties and the privileges, of man.   In brief, religious ideas relate, as, in the particular case of Christianity, we have already seen, both directly and indirectly to the same topics which are the characteristic and final object of philosophical inquiry.   The difference is simply this: religious ideas, speaking universally, express that which has the appearance of being the instinctive judgment of mankind respecting subjects, about which philosophy seeks to reach a reasoned, demonstrative conclusion.   In religion man apprehends or claims to apprehend that which philosophy aims to comprehend.   And, further, religion involves the living and practicing of that which philosophy, as such, only contemplates and endeavors, with cool and unbiassed judgment, to understand.[4]

This being the case, the sense of the expression, "philosophic content of religion," and the propriety of its employment become obvious. We may see what truth there was in the abstract principle enunciated at the beginning of the Scholastic philosophy as a premise justifying the use of "reason" in the attempt to comprehend and demonstrate the substance of "faith,"—the principle, namely, that true religion and true philosophy agree, and are indeed the same. This, of course, was tantamount to a declaration that faith could and must bear to be questioned—examined—by intelligence. And the resolution of the Scholastic Doctors to proceed with the application was a testimony of the highest kind to the sincerity of their conviction that Christianity was "true religion." So, too, one of the early Fathers of the Church, inspired by a like conviction, could declare that faith was abbreviated knowledge, while knowledge was faith in the form of intelligence.[5] It is only, as we have before remarked, because, and so far as, faith and philosophy thus stand on the same ground and deal with the same subject-matter, that the appearance of a conflict between them is possible; while, on the other hand, it is also only for this reason that true religion can and does find in genuine philosophy an appreciative and efficient defender.

If the relation between religion, or faith, and philosophy, or intelligence, is such as has been stated, two or three questions naturally present themselves, which we must briefly notice. First, if faith is abbreviated knowledge, what need—it may be asked—is there of seeking to have it expanded into the forms of explicit and demonstrative intelligence? In what respect—so some one may express himself—is the modest and humble " abbreviation " inferior to the twin-sister, bearing the more pretentious name of knowledge? An other and more serious question is the following: Just us we may say that comprehension depends on prior apprehension, so may and must we not say that, to the very existence of philosophy, the prior existence of religion is indispensable? Can philosophy exist without the data that religion furnishes?

Let us look at the latter question first. Philosophy can certainly not exist without data. Philosophy is science, is knowledge, and a necessary precondition of the existence of science or knowledge is the existence of an object of knowledge. No true science makes any pretence of mechanically creating its own object. In this sense, as we have previously insisted, no science is or can be " a priori." While, in the order of absolute intelligence, there can no more be an " object " prior to a " subject," than vice versa,—both object and subject being, the rather, as has been shown, organically one,—yet, in the order of the development of dependent human intelligence, subject and object have *the form* of separation and mutual independence, and then their union in in-

telligence, or, in other words, the actualization of intelligence, depends in the first instance on what
may be termed the essentially mechanical process
of bringing them together; the subject must find
its object, or the object must be "presented" or
"given," as it were *ab extra*, to the subject. The
peculiar object of philosophy—I repeat now what
has been said in a previous lecture—is the experience
of man, in its whole nature and extent;—not of some
part of experience, considered in abstraction from
the whole;—and, in particular, of experience as a
living whole, a complete and active process, and
not of that abstraction which is conceived and described as purely passive and merely mechanically
receptive experience. Experience, then, is the datum
which philosophy must first have (pardon the apparent paradox) before it can itself exist. If religion is
a necessary part of this datum, or of man's concrete
and complete living experience, considered as it exists prior to and independently of systematic philosophical inquiry, then we must unquestionably say
that its existence prior to philosophy is essentially
necessary for the first existence of the latter.

Now, with regard to the empirical question of fact,
there can be no doubt, which is worth discussing
here, that mankind universally have been distinctively religious, or have had "religions," before they
have proceeded to engage in what is distinctively
termed and known as philosophical inquiry. So
much for the question of historic order. Regarding
the further question, whether religion is a *necessary*

part of the pre-philosophical experience of man,—
i. e., of that experience which, we have admitted,
must be " given," before philosophy can begin,—there
can, obviously, also be no doubt that it must be answered in the affirmative, unless the nature of religion has above been wholly misrepresented. Involuntary apprehension and spontaneous reflection,
grounded in the living experience of man, relating
expressly or implicitly to the ultimate grounds and
ends of that experience, winged with imagination,
reacting on the emotions and the will, and event-
ually moulding and determining conduct and practice,—these primary conditions and first fruits of religion, whether actually contained in any degree in
the " experience " of every individual among the lowest savages or not, do, most assuredly and obviously,
constitute a necessary part of that experience which
must be gone through before men can pass on to
such voluntary reflection, and to such comprehension
through demonstration, as philosophy contemplates
and demands.

But we have not yet touched the point which
doubtless gives to this question its chief interest in
the minds of those who raise it. It is, according to
my observation, not unfrequently declared by Christian preachers that philosophy had, in ancient times,
before the advent of Christianity, reached the utmost limit of achievement which was possible for her
in independence of " supernatural revelation," and
had, through her failure to find the true or complete
solution of the great problems of existence, demon-

strated the essential impotence or limitation of " human reason," and, consequently, the absolute need of light miraculously given from on high, in order to lead man where reason herself is quite unable either to lead or to follow. I suppose, now, the question we are considering to amount to the inquiry, whether the foregoing assertion is not strictly true?

I remark, in reply, that the foregoing assertion contains, by its form, much that is equivocal and misleading. It seems to presuppose, contrary to the words of Scripture itself, as also to the voice of philosophy, a complete and essential mechanical separation between human and divine intelligence, or between "human reason" and the divine mind. It seems to posit an opposition between the finite and the infinite, the natural and the supernatural, and, in each case, a degree of independence on the part of the former with reference to the latter, which, unless all the demonstrations of the foregoing lectures are at fault, both Scripture and "reason" repudiate. The Bible ascribes human understanding to the "Spirit of the Lord"; and "human reason," in the mouth of its worthiest and best-accredited spokesman before the advent of Christ (Aristotle), ascribed its own origin and power to God.[6] Reason claims no power of her own, out of organic dependence on the Absolute Spirit. But she does not, because by her own confession thus dependent for her power, therefore conclude that she has nothing to do except to lie absolutely inert upon the breast of the Absolute and so supinely wait for God to do for her her own proper work of intelligence; any more than according to Christian ethics, because God "worketh in" man, the latter can expect spiritually to prosper unless he also "work out" his own salvation. Reason, now, being the active function of a spirit thus divinely-created and divinely-sustained, did indeed accomplish far more in ancient Greece than is ever understood by those who thus glibly speak of its lamentable "failure." And it did this, not by attempting to soar away into far-off, inexperimental, and hidden mysteries, but by examining and, in its measure, truly knowing the world, as it lies at man's feet and exists in his experience, and man, as he exists for himself in self-consciousness, in intelligence and will and emotion, in society, also, and in religion. And the result was, further, the discovery of the true infinite revealed through the finite, of the Absolute as none other than the absolutely good, as perfect reason, as royal and divine mind, as God; the discovery, also, that the finite or "natural," exists and has its nature through "participation" (according to Plato's expression) in the ideal-absolute or (according to the Aristotelian description) in and by virtue of a process, which is prompted by instinctive "love" of God and tends to reproduce, in the natural product, "so far as possible," the divine likeness; and so, in particular, that the highest duty and privilege of man, his perfection and his virtue, consist in becoming like God,—and "to be like God," says Plato, "is to be holy, and just, and wise." Greek philosophy was not a failure. It was, in its way and measure, a demonstration of the experimental and everlasting truth of spiritualistic idealism,—a demonstration, of which the world can never afford to lose sight, and which Christian theology, to its lasting credit and profit, learned in its early days to turn to its own great advantage. And so it is safe to say that the Christian consciousness, on the side of its intellectual content, or, so to express it, of its intellectual self-consciousness, was richer and more thoroughly and manfully master of itself in those first centuries, when it was defining for itself and the world its grand dogmas, such as Trinity and Incarnation, than in many a subsequent century, when not only the freshness and power of its first inspiration had been largely lost, but philosophy also, swamped in the muddy shallows of pure mechanism and of agnosticism, was no longer able to be to it anything but a thoroughly false guide.

Now, Christian theology was able to use Greek philosophy as it did, only because—if I may thus express my meaning—the subject-matter of the former was continuous or, broadly speaking, of one piece with the subject-mater of the latter. Perhaps I shall presently be able to make my meaning plainer. Let me say, then, that the one great fact, the sense of which seems to me to be blurred in the form above given to the question under consideration, is this, that the revelation of God in Christ and in the Christian consciousness is not the contradiction, but the fulfilment, of the revelation of

God in nature and in the universal or generic consciousness of man.   "Christian experience," in the
genuine sense of this expression, is the experience
of "the perfect man."   Christian knowledge is completed knowledge.   The perfect differs from the imperfect, and the completed from the incomplete,
rather in degree than in kind.   Christian experience
is an experience in which God is, confessedly, immediately concerned.   But the experience of mankind at large before the coming of Christ, and even
to-day in regions where Christ is not known, neither
was nor is an experience wholly without God.
Greek philosophy was an attempt to comprehend,
or to demonstrate the whole ideal content of, pre-
Christian experience.   It dealt with the only positive data at its command; and the substantial result
was to such a remarkable degree in harmony with
the new and fuller consciousness which Christ ush-
ered into the world, that Christian apologists have
justly seen in it a striking "preparation" for Christianity, while natural historians (as they may be
called) of human intelligence have professed to see
in it the root, from which Christianity could be
explained as simply the necessary growth.

It would seem, then, and it is undoubtedly true
that all speculations as to what philosophy might
discover without the aid of Christian experience are
thoroughly idle.   Philosophy, we must again repeat, is nothing independently of experience; it
claims to do nothing but comprehend experience;
and if in Christianity human experience is filled up

and rounded out to a greater degree of perfection and completeness than in any of its non-Christian forms, philosophy is ready and quick to perceive and acknowledge this and gratefully to draw from it the fuller lesson that it teaches. Yes, philosophy did need the light of Christianity, and her only protest can be and is against the notion that she, or that mankind at large,—one of whose noblest functions she is,—ever was, or is, or can be, something wholly profane and undivine, completely separate from and opposed to God, as, according to the shallow conception of a purely mechanical theology, the .finite is said to be separated from and only opposed to the infinite. In short, this whole business of setting religion, on the one hand, and philosophy and science, on the other, over against each other, as if they were *per se* quite independent and rival, or even hostile, functions, should come to a perpetual end; for it all amounts simply—no matter who it is that is guilty of it—to a case of arbitrary, unnatural, and wicked putting asunder, on man's part, of things which God has joined together. These different "functions," as I have termed them, are not simply like so many tools, which a man may take up and lay down at will,—one of which has nothing whatever to do with the other, and all of which have no necessary and essential relation to him that uses them. On the contrary, they are all organically one in, and all equally and essentially necessary to, the completed life and reality of man. The whole man implies them all, and each of them implies, for its ideal completeness, the whole man, in the complete and healthy exercise of all his functions. All of these distinctions of functions are abstractions, necessary, no doubt, in practice, but thoroughly misleading to him who forgets the purely practical necessity, in which they originate, and so treats them as absolute. The Christian Master did not say, "religion" or "philosophy," but "the truth shall make you free." And this truth, as we saw, was to be both lived and known. It was to be present at once in the practical and in the theoretical "experience" of the "perfect man." It was to be the very life and substance of this experience, and of man himself. In the order of time, and especially of the time-conditioned experience of man, we may rightly say that life and practice precede theory, just as sensation precedes intelligence. But the scientific examination of experience, as conducted by philosophy, shows that the absolute or ideal condition of sensation is intelligence itself. And so, universally, the final object and end of "theory," or "knowledge," or "philosophy," with reference to all "life and practice," or with reference to all "experience" whatsoever, is to show how the latter, all contingent as at first it appears to be, is itself conditioned by the non-contingent Absolute and Eternal, which it implicitly contains and reveals. This, as I have previously indicated, is, "spiritual knowledge," for it is the knowledge of the Absolute as Eternal Spirit, and of "all things" as existing through and by Him, —not in the way of mechanico-fatalistic necessity, nor of mechanico-pantheistic identity, but in a spiritual relation like that of the child to the father, where "limitation" is seen to be, not the obstacle, but the condition of substantial independence and freedom. This is knowledge of "the only true God," and "eternal life." And now, that the subject-matter of this knowledge is written in infinitely larger, more legible and unmistakable characters "in the face of Jesus Christ," than anywhere else, I do not hesitate, in the name of Philosophy herself, to assert. That philosophy "needed" this object-lesson, may be asserted with equal confidence. "The life" needed to be "made manifest," in all its fulness, in order that in all its fulness it might be known. Not that it was previously wholly unmanifested, by any means. God never left himself without a witness. He "by whom the worlds were made," the "eternal Son," was never absent from his work. It was not first eighteen hundred years ago that he became "the light of the world." No, from the creation of the world he—"God in the flesh," the infinite in the finite—was ever with the world and in it, as a spiritual, creative-redemptive, sustaining presence. Of the glory of this presence all men were, whether consciously or unconsciously, witnesses, so that those who denied it were "without excuse"; while philosophy loudly and effectively proclaimed it. And yet the light was partly veiled; the life was not made fully manifest; so that, in more than one most important respect, the devotion of the most pious heart and the worship of the clearest head were addressed

to a God "unknown," (*i. e.*, incompletely known).
Then Jesus came and, by *living* "the life," demonstrated that he *was* the Life, as well as the Truth
and the Way; and that he was the true Life, not as
pure *individual*, in separation and distinction from
God, but in organic union and oneness with God; and
not, again, in hostile separation from the world, but
the rather as the One, the everlasting Word, who
eternally gives himself for the life of the world,—the
One who, were he to cease to "give," and to give
himself, the world would cease to be. And how
wonderful was the human consciousness which Christ
awakened, the consciousness of human emptiness
and of divine riches, the hungering and thirsting
after righteousness, fainting for the bread of life;
and how wonderfully did he show himself, and God in
him, to be the "bread of Life," the very "bread of
the world!"   The potentialities of human experience
were all now fulfilled. What had been before only
implicit became explicit. The true and complete
and perfect life of man, the "salvation," nay, the
realization, of his true being, as something to be accomplished by simply taking God for one's strength;
the losing of one's life, in order to find it, or, the
penitent abandonment of the finite self, with all its
load of weaknesses and sins, in order to find the
true self in the spiritual infinite; the reconciliation
of the world and of man to God, and the possibility of such reconciliation as founded on the eternal
mediation of the incarnate Word (of which Christ's
death on the cross was the most signal and the

practically necessary demonstration); all this blessed content of spiritual and of absolute theoretical truth was contained in the perfect object-lesson of the life and death of Jesus of Nazareth. To the world and to man, as the scene and the home of the growing finite,—of the finite, namely, as involved, in human consciousness, in the still unfinished process of realizing to itself its own and the world's infinite content,—this lesson had all the value of an absolutely new revelation. And yet the substance of the truth revealed was, in itself, in no wise new; for it was eternal. The life and death of Christ—as I have once before said—were in no sense the revelation of a new disposition or of a change of nature, whether in the everlasting and unchangeable God or in the nature of things. They were rather a new and complete demonstration of the eternal nature of God and of the eternal "counsel of his will." The demonstration was needed, and "in the fulness of time,"— or, when the time for this wonderful fruitage was fully ripe,—it came. The revelation was made, through forms of sense and in events of space and time, of spiritual truths and realities that transcend and condition and explain space and time, with all that these contain. Then the revelatory demonstration was fulfilled, not only of that which was spoken by the prophets, but also of the creative Word of the Lord, as present in the world itself and in the hearts and thoughts of men. And this revelation still continues. It did not end with the death of Jesus. The rather, it first fully began after his death. His mis-

sion was to show men "the Father." "He that hath
seen me," he declared, "hath seen the Father." And
yet, as he plainly intimated, (and as we have already
noticed in a previous lecture,) the true sight of him
had nothing to do with physical vision, but was the
rather hindered by it. The true sight of him was
spiritual sight. "A little while and [*then*] ye shall
see me; because I go to the Father." When he was
out of their physical sight, the true sight, the sight
through and of the Spirit, was to begin, and to lead
them into all truth. Then would occur the full and
real "revelation." And this revelation, I say, still
continues. For it is, I repeat, something spiritual,
and therefore living. The revelation is a spiritual
light. And it was, and evermore is, "the life"—not
mere words, or physical presence—that is "the light
of men." Far be it from me to detract, or to seem
to detract, by the utterance of a single syllable, from
the unspeakable value and significance of the recorded words of the Master of the Christian world.
But this value and significance will be wholly missed,
if there ever comes a time when the life that they
express is no longer lived. "Ye are the light of the
world," says Christ, to all those in whom the Christian life, the Christian experience, the Christian consciousness, has been kindled and in whom it continues
as a vital flame to glow. When Christianity is no
longer lived, it is no longer capable of being understood. When Christianity is no longer lived, the
"light of the world" is extinguished.

The practical demonstration, then, of the "Chris-

tian religion " is Christianity itself as a living power
in man, illuminating his understanding, purifying his
will, and restoring him, from the lowest depths to
the topmost heights of his living experience, to himself, *i. e.*, to the possession, the mastery, the realization of himself in his true and perfect quality, as a
son or daughter of the Lord God Almighty. This
is called, pre-eminently, "religion," or "having religion." The theoretical demonstration of it is "philosophy"—or call it, if you will, speculative theology
or Christian knowledge. It is the demonstration of
the eternal content and foundation of the Christian
consciousness. And it is the demonstration that
"human reason" is not confounded by the content
of the Christian consciousness, but is strengthened,
illuminated, satisfied, nay, completed by it. It is not
a demonstration that the Christian life, the "Christian consciousness," can now be dispensed with. It
is rather a demonstration of the absolute necessity
of this life and consciousness to the completed reality and perfection of man. And so the life and the
knowledge point to and imply each other; and both
are inseparable in the realized ideal of the "perfect
man," knowing the true God and Jesus Christ whom
he hath sent.

We are now prepared to admit the assertion of our
imaginary questioner in this sense, viz., that the everlasting "light of the world" shone far, far less brightly
in the experience of mankind before the coming of
Christ, than thereafter; and that, as philosophy is
nothing without the light of experience, it needed

the new and added light which Christianity brought. But the assertion must be decidedly repelled, if the meaning of it is that Christianity involves, in any sense, the miraculous supersedure of reason or its disgrace.[1]

On the other hand, I trust that nothing more need be said by way of answer to the first question above raised, respecting the sufficiency of faith, as "abbreviated knowledge," independently of the fuller and more explicit forms of reasoned intelligence. The idea to be inculcated is, of course, by no means that all Christians are to be philosophers; but that the leaders and teachers of the Christian world, by whom the judgment of the world at large with respect to Christianity is most apt to be determined, and from whom the tone of Christian life in the humbler ranks of the Church must, inevitably, to a large extent, take its coloring, should in the fullest sense know in whom they have believed, and be able to render, for the hope that is in them, the demonstrative reason which the nature of the case at once demands and supplies. Who shall overestimate the manly strength and comfort which come to all who seek to love and serve God, when their pastors, being after Jehovah's own heart, are able to feed them "with wisdom and knowledge"?

Richer "food" of this sort than that which the true Christian pastor can offer is not to be conceived, if that is true which the Apostle says of the Christian pastor's divine Master, "In him are hid all the treasures of wisdom and knowledge" (Col.

ii. 3). That this saying of St. Paul is a true one, that Christ is indeed " the Truth," that the spiritual knowledge of him is the key to all absolute intelligence, and that in this knowledge lies the indispensable way to man's perfection, to his true, self-mastering Freedom and to eternal Life,—of all this I am profoundly convinced, and I shall wish that these lectures had never been delivered, if they accomplish nothing toward the propagation of this conviction.

If Christ is indeed the Truth, if in knowing him as the Son of God we know God, the unconditioned and everlasting fount of all being, and in knowing him as the creative principle of all finite existence we are introduced to the knowledge of the essence of all such existence, it is obvious that the " Comparative Philosophic Content of Christianity" is very great;—that, indeed, it is so great that a greater cannot be conceived. And it is obvious that philosophy, finding this to be the case, must admit and approvingly reiterate the claim of Christianity to be called "absolute religion." And this has indeed been done, through the mouth of the deepest, most comprehensive, and most instructive philosopher of modern times;—I refer, of course, to Hegel.[8]

By what standard or principle is the philosophic content of a religion to be measured? By none other, assuredly, than the one by which the content of philosophy itself, universally, is measured. And philosophy's standard is simply Reality, as apprehended in and through spiritual self-consciousness,—the true consciousness or knowledge of the Self, as Spirit.

All consciousness whatsoever, as we have seen, has the form of self-consciousness, and all knowledge, of self-knowledge; and the Real, which knowledge apprehends (or else it is not knowledge), must and can, accordingly, only be, *in form*, self-known. And we have tried to intimate—the present was no time for exhaustive demonstration—how, along with, and conditioned upon, the development in man of his true, substantial self-consciousness, comes the demonstrative consciousness or knowledge of the Absolute as Spirit, as Person, as God, and of the world as a reality, whose true significance, being divinely derived, is also, though dependently, spiritual. And this, of course, is possible only on condition that the self-consciousness of man contain, either explicitly or implicitly, that which some Christian psychologists call the element of "God-consciousness," as a part of itself, and, on the other hand, the universally admitted element of "world-consciousness." And we have sought further to indicate how the self-consciousness of man, as a living spirit, may and does include both these elements—namely, by virtue of what may summarily be termed the organic connection of the individual with the finite universe, on the one hand, and with God, the Absolute, on the other—and how real knowledge of both God and the world may result from the development of the respective "elements," without our being necessarily forced to any such absurd conclusion as that man is mechanically and numerically identical, either with God, or with the sensible universe, from both of which he distinguishes himself. Philosophy is thus the knowledge of God and the world, in and through the knowledge of man. The knowledge in question is living and spiritual knowledge. It is knowledge by a living and spiritual being, and has for its object varying degrees and forms of living and spiritual reality.

Of this knowledge the ideal and the conditions are exemplified, nay, rather, actualized, in the Christ. The Man, whose thought was the divine thought, whose life was divine life, and whose very being consisted in his being " one with " the divine " Father "; the everlasting Word, who, as the principle of the world's existence, was and evermore is the true light and life of the world; how has he not indeed in himself " all the treasures of wisdom and knowledge ? " How shall not he, who has spiritual " knowledge of the Son of God," who, united to him as the branch is united to the vine, participates in his self-consciousness and so comes to the true consciousness of " the perfect man " and " unto the measure of the stature of the fulness of Christ,"— how, I say, shall he, who thus has " the mind of Christ," and is " renewed in knowledge after the image of him that created him," not be adjudged— unless all the principles of knowledge are to be denied—to be in the requisite intellectual position for knowing all things ? Not that he, not that the " philosopher," is to be able all at once, or, perhaps, ever, to be informed about all the detail of the world or (in the same sense) about the unfathomable riches of the divine nature; but that, in Aristotelian phrase, the What of the world and of the divine nature, the principle and conditioning, or spiritual, essence, shall be known to him and shall illuminate all his intelligence,—be the latter rich or poor in the knowledge of particular, empirical facts. The substance of the unlettered Christian's living faith —not of his merely abstract and formal " belief "— touches, though in an other way, the same goal with the philosopher's loftiest demonstrations. And this, I repeat, because both have to do with the whole substance of living reality, and not merely, like the special sciences, with some particular aspect, phase, or department of reality, in abstraction from all else.

The philosophic history of religion, now, notes in the different " religions," as also in the different " philosophies," the symptomatic expression of so many diverse stages reached by man in the endeavor to attain to full and complete self-consciousness, and through this to reach the true knowledge of the world and of God; in this latter respect seeking " after the Lord," as St. Paul says, " if haply they might find him," who is " not far from every one of us " (Acts xvii. 27), and who " said not to the seed of Jacob, Seek ye me in vain " (Is. xlv. 19). In other words, the conceptions of God, or of the Absolute, or of the absolute Power of the universe, and the like, which are contained in and determine the character of the different " religions," depend, ideally, on and correspond to the varying degrees to which the founders and adherents of these religions have, or have not, come in practice to the consciousness of man's true nature and substance as a spiritual personality. The like is true with regard to the different so-called philosophies, if in place of the expression, " in practice," you substitute in the foregoing statement the words, " in theory."

In all of them—religions as well as philosophies —so far as they are imperfect, we may thus see arrested attempts of man seeking to " come to himself," and to be in feeling and in intelligence at peace with himself. Another way of stating the case, as it regards especially the religions of mankind, is to say that in all of them man is exhibited in the process of trying to find his spiritual centre. Not that he always is explicitly aware that he has such a centre, or that while he is seeking it he necessarily knows just what he is seeking. But always there is at least the vague unrest, the sense, variously manifested, of the individual's insufficiency in himself, of his need of supplementing or completing himself by practically identifying with himself, for the supply of his needs and the aversion of his dangers, a power other and greater than, but yet in some way akin to, himself. And at every stage the power in question is conceived after the image of the consciousness which man has of himself. At the lowest stage where the " spirit in man " is scarcely more than an unactualized potentiality and the life of its nominal possessor is as nearly as possible a purely natural one, the power is conceived as a natural ob-

ject or as hiding itself in such an object,—a stone, a
bush, the earth, the sun, or the heavens. At a higher
stage, where man has arrived at the abstract, but,
essentially, only negative, conviction that he is in
in his essence not-natural, he has a corresponding
conception of the absolute Power, by practical or
literal identification with which he must secure present help and final release. "Release," I say; for the
conviction that the "natural," as such, is foreign to
him, carries with it the pessimistic sense of it as
his essential enemy and as the seat of nought but
evil, and subjection to it or association with it is
necessarily looked upon as an evil and a burden.
But as the conviction under consideration is only
negative; since it only consists in the certain belief
that the essential is not the natural, that the soul
is not the body, that the Absolute is not subject to
the forms of space and time, and that the latter,
together with all that they condition, is purely phenomenal and illusory; and since therefore, the positive conception of substantial spiritual personality,
and of the natural as its not unreal matrix, its
friendly foster-mother, and its willing instrument,
is wanting; the conception of the absolute Power
becomes equally negative; it is the everlasting Nay,
Nirvana. The philosophic and the religious conception, it is seen, thus run hand in hand.

I mention the foregoing cases merely by way of
illustration. A complete account of all the cases
possible, and that are illustrated in the history of
religions, would require a volume. That in the

Christian life, and in philosophy, drawing instruction from the Christian consciousness, man truly comes to himself, and so is, with reason, both in mind and heart at peace,—enjoying the freedom which truth, known and practiced, begets, and participating even now in eternal life,—this is a conviction, to the confirmation of which in your minds I heartily wish that the present course of lectures may have contributed. May the God of Love enable us all, by an intelligent confession, to bear witness to the truth that Christ is " the wisdom of God "; and may the Lord of all power and might, who is the author and giver of all good things, graft in our and in all hearts the love of his name, increase in us true religion, nourish us with all goodness, and of his great mercy keep us in the same, to everlasting life, through Jesus Christ our Lord.

APPENDIX

---•◦•---

NOTES TO LECTURE I.

NOTE 1, PAGE 6.

L. Oscar, *Die Religion zurückgeführt auf ihren Ursprung,* Basel, 1874, p. 2.

NOTE 2, PAGE 6.

Hegel, *Vorlesungen über die Philosophie der Religion, Werke,* Bd. XI, Berlin, 1840, p. 3.

NOTE 3, PAGE 9.

H. Spencer, *Synthetic Philosophy, First Principles,* p.

NOTE 4, PAGE 10.

I am, of course, not unaware that Mr. Spencer, as chief spokesman of Agnosticism in our day, is so far from seeing, or desiring to see, anything hostile to religion in his doctrine, that he, the rather, professes to find in the latter the impregnable bulwark of "true religion." That "our own and all other existence is a mystery absolutely and forever beyond our comprehension, contains more of true religion than all the dogmatic theology ever written," (*First Principles,* p. 112). "True religion" consists, namely, in the recognition of the fore-mentioned absolute "mystery." Its "subject-matter is that which passes the sphere of experience" and so "transcends knowledge" (*ib.* p. 17), *i. e.*, the "Unknowable." So far, therefore, as religion professes really to know the object

(283)

of its belief, so far as its "subject-matter" is definitely and positively formulated as an object of ostensible knowledge, and so far, in particular, as it declares and claims to know the Absolute, or God, as Spirit, and the root and goal of "our own and all other existence" as themselves also spiritual, just so far must religion be pronounced the victim—or propagator—of illusion.

Now Mr. Spencer is not to be charged with the slightest insincerity, or with any other impurity of motive. The negativism of his religious philosophy follows of necessity from a certain theory of knowledge, which he holds in common with a long line of predecessors in the history of British speculation, extending from the Middle Ages down to the present day. According to this theory, all knowledge proper, whatsoever, is limited by sensible conditions. The conditions are not merely instrumental to knowledge, but are themselves held to be the final objective limit of knowledge. In other words, all real knowledge is held to be, in nature and method, mathematico-physical, and to have, for its only object, the sensibly "phenomenal."

Now, admitting this theory of knowledge, it follows, with truismatic evidence, that the "subject-matter" of religion— provided that the latter be not wholly an illusion—must be the "Unknowable." But the true conclusion from this theory is, the rather, that religion is, indeed an illusion. For, as has often been pointed out, (compare, among others, John Caird's *Introduction to the Philosophy of Religion,* chap. i.,) from the acceptance of the theory in question as an exhaustively true and complete account of the whole nature of knowledge it follows that the assertion of the existence of the Absolute Unknowable is impossible and absurd. And religion, so far as this is regarded as its true and only "subject-matter," is a pure hallucination.

There have been many, among those theologians who have ostensibly stood for the defence of religion during the last few centuries, who have been inclined to coquette with the agnostic doctrine and some who have completely adopted it. The result, naturally, has never been a reinvigoration of "faith" or of the religious life. It is one of the happier signs of our times that the nominal "gift," which the Agnostic "Greek" brings to religion in our day, is looked upon with well-nigh universal suspicion.

Note 5, Page 15.

At the beginning, in the seventeenth century, of the modern period in philosophy, the modern mind, in the persons of its most conspicuous intellectual leaders, sought, so to speak, to insulate itself, and, in particular, to cut itself off, as much as possible, from all connection with that historic past, from which it was in fact itself but an historic growth. The attempt was made to effectuate a solution of intellectual continuity, by placing the past under a ban of disgrace. This solution, breaking-up, or analysis, had its relative justification; but only its relative and temporary justification; and that as a step in a process which could become complete only in a final synthesis, enriched, indeed, by all the acquisitions of modern science, but not excluding the riches of the past; the rather, uniting past and present, or the synthetic and the analytic sides of human experience, in the concrete unity of one unimpaired and all-significant whole. To the achievement of this final synthesis the greatest and most significant contributions have, thus far, been made in German philosophy. British thought has to the greatest extent, until recently, remained in that "irretrievably analytic" frame of mind, which J. S. Mill recognized as having, in his own case, all the quality of a disease. It has remained practically insulated, with respect not only to Greek but also to German philosophy. And this insulation has been result, as much as cause, of that more radical separation or estrangement of the inquiring mind from the eternal problems of philosophy—which are also the perennial problems of life—that is necessarily connected with excessive devotion to the methods of mechanical analysis. Thus it is that in our day one of the most urgent of intellectual and spiritual needs is the revival, in philosophy, of the historic sense, and that as one of the most direct means for restoring the philosophic sense and so leading, ultimately, to the renewed and convincing demonstration of that solid objective basis for the vital interests,—and realities—of human life, the very existence of which seems, nowadays, to be, for many men of serious and, in other respects, cultivated minds, a matter of grave doubt.

NOTES TO LECTURE II.

NOTE 1, PAGE 26.

To J. S. Mill the personally identical self is an "impenetrable, inner covering," an "inexplicable tie" or "bond of some sort," which, says he, "to me, constitutes my Ego." See note to J. S. Mill's new edition of James Mill's *Analysis of the Phenomena of the Human Mind*, Vol. II., p. 175. From the belief in this "bond" or "tie" it is, according to J. S. Mill, impossible to escape. But of it no rational account is said to be possible. It remains as a "final inexplicability." See J. S. Mill's *Examination of the Philosophy of Sir William Hamilton*, chap. vii.

Herbert Spencer declares that the belief in self is one that "no hypothesis enables us to escape." See Spencer's *First*

Principles, p. 64. On the following page Spencer affirms that this belief is one which finds "no justification in reason." This simply means that the search for a fundamental, spiritual, living, and absolute reality, like that of Self, by psychological inquiries pursued under the limitations, and determined by the presuppositions, of the method of purely physical science, must necessarily be fruitless. The very fact that the search, thus prosecuted, is hopelessly unavailing, while yet the "belief in self" persists in the mind of the inquirer as one which "no hypothesis enables us to escape," should, apparently, be of itself sufficient to convince him and the whole cohort of his followers that the method in which he and they put all their trust, and which they style "experimental," is—not, indeed, in its proper sphere, inexperimental, but—abstract, partial, incomplete, and not commensurate with the whole nature and content of experience; requiring, therefore, to be supplemented by a larger and more liberal, but not less strictly scientific, method, which is not unknown to philosophy and which, not being arbitrarily conceived and forcibly imposed on experience, but simply founded in and dictated by the recognition of experience in its whole nature, is alone entitled to be termed fully and without qualification "experimental." I may add, pertinently, that Mr. Spencer's confession of the inevitable necessity of the belief in self is, on his own part, purely theoretical, and without further or ulterior consequence for the development of his psychological and ethical views. His psychology remains a *"psychologie sans âme"* and his ethics is made to conform as much as possible to the psychology. Take, for illustration, his treatment of the question of the "freedom of the will." If "free will" is a phrase having any positive, substantial meaning whatever, it means, or points to, a function of the true self, or "Ego." The true self, now, being, according to Mr. Spencer's confession, something which we must believe to be existent, but which is for him "unknowable," he is in strict reason debarred from all right to discuss the question of freedom. He does ostensibly discuss it, nevertheless, and in so doing forgets all about the true, but "unknowable" self, proceeding as though the whole and true self or Ego were completely and only identical with the mechanical aggregate of "knowable" internal states, or "feelings," which at any given instant make up the sum total of the content of our empirical, sense-conditioned consciousness. The view of the conscious self thus obtained is only static, not dynamic, and it is not strange that the will, considered in relation to this "self," seems purely phenomenal, a substanceless, mechanically determined state or "point of view," and freedom an "illusion." The free-will "illusion," says Mr. Spencer, consists in supposing that "at each moment the ego is something more than the aggregate of feelings or ideas, actual and nascent, which then exists" (*Psychology*, Vol. I., p. 500). But this supposition, as we have above seen, is precisely one that "no hypothesis enables us to escape."

The members of the Scotch or Intuitional school, on the contrary, have the peculiarity and merit of insisting that the confession of objects of "necessary belief" shall not remain merely verbal, but shall bear fruit in the further determination of psychological and ethical notions. And so—to remain by the case in hand—they insist upon freedom, as an attribute of the true self. But inasmuch as to them, just as much as to their opponents of the "necessitarian" school, there is wanting the full and substantial conception of the true self as a spiritual reality, whose essence is activity, and whose activity is organic (*i. e.*, takes the form and has indeed the nature of self-realization;—see further above, Lecture VII.), it results that they, too, are unable to vindicate for the word freedom a substantial meaning. The whole discussion is carried on by them in the terms and with the categories of pure mechanism. The resulting conception of "freedom" is purely formal, negative, contentless, and falls a too easy prey to necessitarian argument. (See again Lecture VII, above, and F. H. Bradley's *Ethical Studies*, Essay I, London, 1876).

NOTE 2, PAGE 27.

See Hume's *Treatise of Human Nature*, Book I, Part III, Sections 7, 8, and 10; and Part IV, Sec. 6. No scholar needs to be reminded of the existence of the edition of Hume's *Philosophical Works*, edited by the late Prof. T. H. Green and T. H. Grose (London: Longmans, Green, & Co.) and of the very special value and importance of Prof. Green's General Introduction to the same; but it is peculiarly needful that the attention of the beginner in philosophic studies should early be directed to it. In his Introduction Prof. Green examines the whole ground-work of the psychological philosophy of Locke and his successors, exhibiting the ground of its weakness as a theory of knowledge. Here, says Prof. J. Croome Robertson (in *Mind*, Jan., 1883, p. 7), "Locke and the others are charged with assuming for the explanation of mental experience that which is itself unintelligible except as the result of a mental function." This statement covers also the ground of the objection made in our text to any attempt to find in empirical, or purely sensational, psychology, a substitute for the philosophic theory of knowledge. Prof. Robertson adds that "so far as it bears against Locke in particular, the criticism, it must be allowed, is not to be repelled." Nor, he continues, "did Berkeley and Hume define their ground with sufficient care, nor proceed far enough in the way of systematic construction, to evade the criticism as it was to be levelled also against them." It seems significant that Mr. Huxley, in his volume on Hume in the "English Men of Letters" series, makes no mention of Messrs. Green and Grose's edition of the philosophical works of Hume.

NOTE 3, PAGE 27.

In all that I have to say in the text concerning psychology it will be understood that I think of psychology not as including all that, in possible agreement with the etymology of the term, may conceivably be comprehended under it. Thus, for example, Aristotle brings into his treatise "Concerning the Soul" his most important contributions to the philosophic theory of knowledge. I employ the word psychology according to the now prevalent usage, as denoting the analytic and inductive science of mental phenomena. As such science, psychology simply takes cognizance of the phenomena which it finds, noting their order of co-existence and sequence, and so determining their "laws" or rules of order. The ostensible "processes" which it thus observes and analyzes,—sequences and other changes among given mental states—are modal, and not causal; they are mechanical, and not organic. But as the modal and mechanical always depends on, and is but the symbol of, the organic and, if I may thus express myself, creatively causal, it appears that the apparent processes observed by psychology are, for pure intelligence, its own product. They are not the organic-causal process of intelligence itself. On this whole subject compare the Article by Prof. J. Croome Robertson, on "Psychology and Philosophy," in *Mind*, Jan., 1883.

NOTE 4, PAGE 29.

Mr. Spencer himself also has the notion of the final identity of the facts of physiology and the facts of psychology—or, in his language, of "matter and mind"—in the "unknowable" Absolute. But the identity which he conceives is abstract, mechanical, and exclusive of difference, and not concrete, organic, and inclusive of difference.

NOTE 5, PAGE 31.

See Kant's *Critique of Pure Reason, passim.*

NOTE 6, PAGE 36.

It is but a few years ago that Mr. J. S. Mill was entertaining and astonishing the reflecting world in Great Britain and America with the attempt to show how the matter-of-fact belief in the existence of both object and subject—respectively identified by him with "external world" and "mind"—could be justified, on the basis of a theory which reduces the whole substance and range of knowledge to a mechanical "series of conscious states." See Mill's *Examination of the Philosophy of Sir William Hamilton*, chaps. xi. xii.

NOTE 7, PAGE 37.

See Leibnitz's *Nouveaux Essais sur l'entendement humain.* In this work, which is composed in the form of a dialogue, Leibnitz follows, Book by Book, chapter by chapter, and paragraph by paragraph, the course of Locke's discussion in his *Essay on Human Understanding;* commenting, in a tone of utmost liberality, on the successive positions adopted by Locke; warmly applauding the many views of Locke, which meet with his own approval, but also laying bear the weaknesses of Locke's theories with equal unreserve; and performing, too, in this latter connection, not merely the negative task of the purely destructive critic, but also the positive, constructive one, which he only can perform, who is deeply familiar with the past history and the perennial nature of the problems of

philosophy.   Leibnitz used to say of the "monads," which
played a fundamental *rôle* in his philosophy, that each of them
was "big with the future." Of the mind and doctrine of
Leibnitz it may be said that they were equally fructified through
absorption and comprehension of the best wisdom of the past
and the minutest and most varied knowledge of his own times,
and that they are big with germs that have borne abundant
fruit in the subsequent progress of philosophy in Germany.
It suggests no favorable comment on the philosophic interest
of the countrymen of Locke that the above-mentioned reply
of Leibnitz to Locke has never (so far as I can ascertain) been
translated into English.

NOTE 8, PAGE 40.

See, in Kant's *Critique of Pure Reason*, the first parts, under
the head of "Transcendental Æsthetic" and "Transcendental
Analytic." I think that I may properly and usefully refer any
learner, who may be interested in the subject of this Lecture,
to my critical version of the argument of Kant's *Critique*, published in *Griggs's Philosophical Classics*, Chicago, 1883.

NOTE 9, PAGE 40.

For, as I have already intimated, following the strict requirements of the method in question, no such form or
faculty of synthesis as memory can be either posited or recognized as existing; and without memory no synthesis whatever
of sequent "impressions" or "ideas" is possible.

NOTE 10, PAGE 41.

In the first, or constructive, half of his *Critique of Pure
Reason* Kant proceeds as if the supposition mentioned in the
text were, not only relatively, but absolutely and unqualifiedly, true.

Note 11, Page 43.

Such as the theory of a realm of "things in themselves," assumed by Kant in accordance with the wholly arbitrary procedure referred to in the foregoing note. The "things in themselves" are "objects" conceived in complete mechanical separation from the subject of knowledge, hence as wholly foreign to and inaccessible for it, and hence, again, as wholly "unknowable." The ground of this gratuitous and, strictly taken, unthinkable hypothesis lies, as I trust the further progress of our discussions will make sufficiently evident to the reflecting, in Kant's naïve but wholly inexperimental conception of the subject-agent of knowledge as, like its supposed object, a *thing*, and not as a *person;* as essentially limited, like the body or the brain, by and to a definite locality in space and time, and not as a spirit which, by its intelligence, shares in a nature that transcends and conditions space and time and is in potential organic unity with all things, as well as with their absolute creative source and condition.

Note 12, Page 43.

Toward the recognition and full appreciation of this experimental truth, in all its broad significance, Kant appears, in his several "Critiques," as one who is blindly, yet energetically, pushing forward; *blindly*, because clouds cast by the philosophical formalism and sensationalism of his age obscured and limited his intellectual horizon; yet *energetically*, because moved by the strong and faithful impulses of an unusually deep and vigorous living experience. The same struggle is significantly continued in Fichte; while, with Hegel, the truth in question obtains complete recognition. The same truth was clearly perceived and expressed by Aristotle. See in particular Aristotle's *De Anima*, Book III.

Note 13, Page 45.

Existence means only *being objective*, and to *be objective* means to *be in organic correlation with a subjective, i. e.* to *be knowable.*

Note 14, Page 47.

The case referred to in the text is one in which sensible imagination abstracts, or seeks to abstract, from all its own forms and contents, and still fancies, or tries to fancy, that it has a remainder or product, which, if germane to any faculty of intelligence and so capable of being apprehended or known by any, is germane to *it* (*i. e.*, to sensible imagination). The remainder, naturally, is indeed nought (0), = *Ding-an-sich,* the "Unknowable."

A case in illustration, where something does *appear* to remain after abstraction, and which is therefore more easily seized, is that of the ordinary, popular conception of time and space as real containers or receptacles, and nothing else; —"baskets," as it were, in which a world unrelated to them is contained.

Note 15, Page 49.

See above, p. 38 *et seq.*

Note 16, Page 50.

This means simply that the self-conscious intelligence of the individual is finite, or conditionally—not essentially— subject to limiting relations of space and time; or, again, that it has a developmental history. Eternal in its nature— as we have occasion more fully to notice in Lecture V. —it is temporal in its fortunes. There is, in other words, a particular time and place, when and where it first becomes aware of its *particular* objects. It is in this way, only, that it is subject to mechanical contingency. But the temporal history of intelligence has nothing to do with its essential nature. Locke, however, and many others, who have followed him, seek (ostensibly) the absolute science of knowledge in its contingent (human) history.

NOTE 17, PAGE 52.

According to Hegel's truthful and beautiful definition of philosophy:—" *Die Philosophie ist nur diess, sich überall zu Hause finden.*"

NOTE 18, PAGE 54.

And yet Kant considers the faculty of human intelligence as something which is wholly conditioned upon the particular and contingent constitution of the human race, the latter being regarded, in agreement with our observation above, under note 11, as an aggregate of particular things or individuals, who are the special " subjects " of this intelligence. It is this which Schelling has in view, when he says (in his *Philosophische Briefe über Dogmatismus und Kriticismus, Werke, Bd.* I, p. 295) that " in the Critique of Pure Reason the faculty of intelligence is regarded as something peculiar, but not necessary, to the subject." In other words, it is held that in an absolute subject of intelligence, such as God, intelligence is something wholly and absolutely different in kind and essential nature from what it is in man; so that no positive inference can be made from the latter to the former. The fact is, the rather—and the total tendency of Kant's own demonstrations is wholly in the direction of this fact—that to completely experimental inquiry human intelligence presents itself as possessing, in spite of the contingency of much of its special subject-matter and even as the condition of its having any subject-matter whatsoever, implicitly and really an universal and I may even say an absolute nature; a nature which must be presupposed and understood, in order to understand the specific differences—such as they are—of "human intelligence"; a nature, therefore, which transcends the peculiarities of the particular individual or race, and by his participation in which the individual transcends himself (as individual) and is truly an intelligent person, a spiritual being, in living connection with the Absolute Being, and so himself potentially infinite.

NOTES TO LECTURE III.

NOTE 1, PAGE 57.

Droyssen, *Grundriss der Historik*, 3d ed., p. 54.

NOTE 2, PAGE 59.

Matthew Arnold, *Contemporary Review*, xxiv. 988, cited by F. H. Bradley, *Ethical Studies*, London, 1876, p. 282. Mr. Arnold's original use of the expression cited in the text is innocent enough. His own subsequent treatment of the "question" is that of the philosophical "tyro" indeed.

NOTE 3, PAGE 63.

"Matter" and "force" are the names which physical science, as such, gives to the essence of physical existence only provisionally or, rather, symbolically. A "philosophy," which allows no authority but that of physical science and no conceptions but physical conceptions, is either materialistic, and dogmatically asserts the unconditional and all-conditioning validity of the conceptions of brute, inert matter and blind force; or else, it is, more warily and justly, agnostic, and declares the absolute essence or foundation of existence to be unknowable. The next step is to proceed by a short cut to the identification of the unknowable, but materialistically conceived, essence of physical existence with "God." This is a doubtful compliment to the divine being.

Note 4, Page 64.

See A. Bolliger, *Anti-Kant, Bd.* I., Strassburg, 1882, p. 223 *et seq.*

Note 5, Page 67.

Kant, in his *Critique of Pure Reason,* currently and legitimately employs the expression, "pure physical science" (*reine Naturwissenschaft*), to denote the science of nature as a sensible object, or, all knowledge which is conditioned and determined, as to its content, by "sensible affection." Compare *Kant's Critique, of Pure Reason: a Critical Exposition,* in *Griggs's Philosophical Classics,* chapter v, *init.*

Note 6, Page 71.

Compare above, Lecture VI.

Note 7, Page 73.

In demonstration and development of this truth the philosophical works of Aristotle and, more notably, of the German philosophers from Kant to Hegel, are rich.

Note 8, Page 73.

See, for example, Leibnitz, *Op. Philos.*, ed. Erdmann, p. 202; *et passim.* How, further, for Leibnitz, activity is not motion in space, but is an ideal-spiritual function, no student of him requires to have pointed out.

Note 9, Page 74.

Aristotle, *Metaphysics*, B. XII, chap. vii. : ἡ γὰρ νοῦ ἐνέργεια ζωή.

Note 10, Page 75.

This distinction is often adverted to by Hegel. See, for example, *Werke, Bd.* XVII. p. 250. In his lectures on the History of Philosophy, the criticism which Hegel passes on Fichte is, that the final result of his demonstrations is something "certain"; but what philosophy is after, adds Hegel, is not the certain, but the true.

Note 11, Page 76.

To the early demonstration, in modern times, of the ontological limitations of physical science such philosophers as Berkeley, Leibnitz, and Kant contributed most effectively. The recognition of these limitations is to-day a commonplace with pure physicists.

Note 12, Page 76.

Compare, further, *British Thought and Thinkers*, Chicago, 1881, p. 296.

Note 13, Page 77.

"Absolute matter" is conceived as, in its essence, absolutely and irretrievably opposed to the essence of "soul" or "mind." So, for example, by Descartes.

Note 14, Page 78.

Compare subsequent Lectures, and especially Lecture VI.

Note 15, Page 79.

This, in the correspondence of Leibnitz with Dr. Sam. Clarke, was the burden of the complaint of the former against the latter, and against Newton.

NOTE 16, PAGE 80.

They live, move and have their being "in Him," *i. e.*, in *living* dependence on God, the Absolute Spirit. Compare Kant's *Crit. of Pure Reason*, in *Griggs's Philos. Classics*, chap. ii.

NOTE 17, PAGE 80.

Of course, the acknowledgment of spiritual existence by the theoretical or practical materialist cannot, without self-contradiction, be otherwise than merely verbally made. But cases of such self-contradiction very often occur, especially in popular "thinking."

NOTE 18, PAGE 82.

See Aristotle's *Physics*, ii. 8: A natural existence is "one which, receiving continuous motion from a principle within itself, attains to a definite end." The inward principle of motion is here nothing other than the "end" itself, which latter is to the natural object as its "soul," its essence, its self-realizing life, and is the true force, of which all the "motion" of the object is but the insubstantial and fleeting phenomenon. Thus "final causation," or causation as a living and ideal process, whose form is the form of self-realization, is exhibited by Aristotle as the precondition, in natural existences, of that serial "causation" (*i. e.*, rule or law of sequence among phenomena), which alone purely sensible knowledge, or "pure physical science," is able to recognize. Leibnitz, among other modern philosophers, is rich in demonstrations to the same effect.

NOTE 19, PAGE 83.

Aristotle, *De Anima*, iii. 7: ἡ γὰρ κίνησίς τοῦ ἀτελοῦς ἐνέργεια.

NOTE 20, PAGE 85.

See, further, Lecture VII.

NOTE 21, PAGE 85.

Compare note 8 to Lecture IV, below.

NOTE 22, PAGE 86.

Compare p. 73, above, and Lecture V.

NOTE 23, PAGE 87.

Compare Lecture VII.

NOTES TO LECTURE IV.

NOTE 1, PAGE 95.

One of the pregnant sayings attributed to Buddha is, "All that we are is the result of that which we have thought."

NOTE 2, PAGE 111.

Full of significance, in this connection, are the words of the Psalmist (Ps. xlvi. 10), "Be still and know that I am God." Is it not as though the royal speaker were saying to us, "Put a quietus on your individual selves, in the matter of knowledge; learn that the individual factor in human knowledge is strictly subservient and instrumental to, and is conditioned by, an universal factor; so that all true knowledge is, by direct implication, the knowledge of Him who is the condition of all knowledge, that is, of God, the 'free Spirit.'" It goes, of course, without saying, that what the Psalmist here requires is in no sense the negation or stagnation of thought, but rather, in reality, the highest, purest, and truest activity of thought: sham thinking, "free" thinking, thinking that has, so far as in it lies, separated itself from the absolute and universal conditions of thought,—this it is, to which the Psalmist addresses the just and imperial direction, "Be still."

So Hegel (*Philosophie der Religion, Bd.* II, p. 227), discussing the knowledge of God as Love, and as Triune, says: "God exists here only for the thinking man, who holds himself back and is still (*der sich still für sich zurückhält*). The ancients called this Enthusiasm; to apprehend and be conscious of the pure Idea of God,—this is pure theoretical contemplation, the highest repose of thought, yet at the same time the highest activity."

The purest and most perfect expression of the Christian consciousness, that is to be found outside the covers of the New Testament, is contained, to my mind, in the historic prayers of the Church. They are as a cup, full to overflowing with the richest vintage of the Christian life and with the soundest thought of the Christian heart. In one of them, which is nearly as old as Christendom, the relation, in true thought, between man and God, comes to expression in the following supplication: "Grant to us thy humble servants, that *by thy holy inspiration we may think* those things that are good." See *Book of Common Prayer*, Fifth Sunday after Easter.

NOTE 3, PAGE 111.

But most of all to them that seek. No wisdom, no knowledge, in the genuine sense, is had without an active and sustained search. In this respect, as in others, the well-verified promise is, "Seek, and ye shall find."

NOTE 4, PAGE 118.

Those whose view of the scriptural revelation is of this mechanical nature are inclined and accustomed to lay stress on

the fact that the revelation is *from* God, but do not apprehend it as a real, living, and effective revelation *of* God.

Note 5, Page 119.

And the notion of self, like that of personality, is a potentially infinite or all-comprehending notion.

Note 6, Page 120.

Just as, for philosophy, all final or absolute truth is truth
of life—the Absolute Reality is an Absolute Life—so all genuine revelation is the revelation of a life; it "brings life . . . .
to light"; and it must therefore itself, in order to be effective,
be clad in or, rather, instinct with the life which it reveals.
The true Christian revelation is the Christ himself. In him
was the life made manifest, and this life was the "light of the
world." Misunderstood or, even, verbally denied this light
might be, and yet it—the light of the divine life—was there,
in the minds and hearts of all men, as the very "light of the
world." Those who, by dint of magnifying, whether theoretically or practically, the finite, individual self, and ignoring
the universal Self, in which they really lived, and moved, and
had their being (and this is the abstract description of all *sin*),
did not consciously have "God in all their thoughts"—*i. e.*,
saw not, or even denied, the light that was in them—these
found this light reflected and focused in the spiritual person
of a perfect Man, and of one who, just because he was perfect
Man, was God-man, Jesus, the Christ. And so the revelation
was effected, not of something previously remote, far-off, inaccessible to human "faculties," and so (in particular) for
ever and hopelessly beyond the grasp of human intelligence,
but rather of a light divine, which was and is the ever-present
and indispensable condition of all intelligence and is intrinsically more "knowable," in the Aristotelian—and just—

sense of this term, than aught else.—The living Christ, I say, is the true revelation; and the recorded words of Christ, and, in general, the words of Scripture, are primarily and most truly a revelation, only so far as they, being "words of life," awaken in man the sense of a life which is the true light of the world, is divine, and is "eternal."

I cannot forbear, in this connection, to bear witness to the pregnant significance of the chapters on "Revelation" in Mr. Elisha Mulford's work, *The Republic of God* (Boston, 1881). The studious perusal of them is, in my judgment, to be heartily commended to all who possess a thoughtful interest in the subject.

Note 7, Page 120.

How love, in organic identity with intelligence, is of the very essence of spirituality, we shall have occasion to see in the next lecture. Here I mention only that for St. John, "dwelling in the truth" and "dwelling in love" are one and the same thing. "We know that the Son of God is come, and hath given us an understanding, that we may know him that is true; and we are in him that is true, even in his Son Jesus Christ. This is the true God, and eternal life" (1 John v. 20). "God is love; and he that dwelleth in love dwelleth in God, and God in him" (1 John iv. 16).

A man of thought, approaching the consideration of this subject by the way of Philosophy, considered as Science of Knowledge—*i. e.*, by way of the *very science of the nature and fundamental conditions of intelligent, living experience*—says, "Love, in the most comprehensive sense, is a desisting from the limitation of the heart to its own particular point [to the purely individual self], and the reception of the love of God into the heart is the reception of the unfolding of his Spirit, in which all true and objective content of intelligence and of

love is contained, and which, thus received, eats away all of
the heart's [vainly self-centred] particularity" (Hegel, *Philos.
der Religion*, ii., 390]. By the flame of true, objective love
(in distinction from merely subjective sentimentality), as by the
flame of true, objective intelligence (as distinguished from the
pure phenomenalism of mere "Subjective Idealism," or "In-
dividualism"), the "gnats of subjectivity" are singed. Truly,
"Spirit itself, named in the language of feeling, is eternal love.
The Holy Spirit is eternal Love" (*ib.*, 227).

NOTE 8, PAGE 121.

"Now," says the Apostle, "I know in part" (1 Cor. xiii.
12). St. Paul, obviously, does not mean that his present
knowledge is to such degree partial knowledge that it is essentially false; and still less that it is as good as no knowledge
at all. The difference between his present knowledge and
the knowledge which is to come is one of degree, and not of
kind. It is a difference, as we may say, not in respect of universal principle, but only of special detail. From this point of
view one may easily estimate the value of such not uncommon
utterances as the following: "The truth can always be known
only by the few" (E. von Hagen, *Kritische Betrachtung der
wichtigsten Grundlehren des Christenthums*, p. 119). *Per contra*,
the "truth," and nothing else, is of a nature to be known by
all, if not necessarily in adequate expression, yet at all events
in its practical power, significance, and reality. The more
universal (in the true sense) it is, so much the more "knowable" is it, and so much the more is it adapted to simple expression and to universal apprehension. Its complexity of
detail in application is the "unsearchable" (inexhaustible)
and difficult element in it.

I must add that, in the phrase immediately following the
one above cited from St. Paul's wonderful hymn to "Charity,"

there is contained, by obvious implication, a striking agreement with the final results of our ontological analyses, as founded on the science of knowledge. The Apostle says, "Then shall I know even as also I am known." The argument which we may easily read into, or from, the writer's words is:—The first and immediate fact is that "I know," though only "in part." And the correlative truth is that, in the final and absolute "object" of my knowledge, I am confronted, not with a mere impersonal, dead and brute, unintelligible and "unknowable" Somewhat, but (agreeably, as we must say, to the philosophic demonstration of the organic unity of subject and object in knowledge) with an object which is, like myself, a subject, a Spirit, and by whom "also I am known." The very condition of my knowing any thing is thus that I also be known; and he, by whom I am known, the absolute Object of my knowledge, is himself absolute in knowledge. When my union with him becomes perfect, being henceforth wholly mistress of the conditions of space and time, and no longer materially limited by them, "then shall I know even as also I am known." Then shall I have, not a new kind, but a new degree of knowledge: the imperfect will give place to the perfect; and whereas I now "see through a glass, darkly," I shall then see "face to face."

NOTES TO LECTURE V.

NOTE 1, PAGE 138.

The identity in essential kind and in generic description between the process of love and the process of intelligence—as also the process of life—is indicated further on in this Lecture (V). The express recognition of the truth that Love is, so to say, the energizing principle of the Absolute Intelligence and the Absolute Life, is due, in philosophy, historically to that practical explication of the implicit content of human consciousness or human intelligence, which was introduced in Christianity. In ancient philosophy this truth, in all its amplitude of significance, was not fully perceived and expressed, but it was not "belied." The rather it was positively, even if also only faintly and for the most part unconsciously, adumbrated. So, for example, in the Platonic conception of God as absolutely "the Good" and "without envy";—it is in the unenvious goodness of God that Plato finds the reason of the world's existence. Aristotle finds the ascription to God of a positive, outgoing, and conscious relation to the world— such as love implies—to be inconsistent with the conception he has formed of the divine perfection. But he finds a *nisus* toward the divine to be the inherent principle of movement in all natural existences. " God," he says, "moves the world in the same way in which an object loved moves its lover." An instinctive love of God leads all things to realize in themselves, "as far as possible," the divine likeness.

I need not attempt to follow the fortunes of the truth in question, in the history of philosophic thought during the Christian era. I mention only that in the essentially superficial, mock-reverential, mechanico-deistical theology, which has monopolized—or, rather, strangled—so much of the nominally Christian thought of the last five centuries, God is at most only verbally recognized as love. A loving God means an Absolute, which does not separate and withhold itself from the relative and finite, but attests, manifests, demonstrates its own absolute and infinite quality by its constant creative and redemptive presence in and upon the relative and finite. But to a mechanical theology, where the relative is, there God is not. The relative is an impenetrable vail, behind which God is completely hidden. God is thus not Love; he is the Unknown and the Unknowable.

NOTE 2, PAGE 145.

Formal logic, considered as the simple application of the principle of abstract identity and contradiction, furnishes at most only the anatomy of thought. It grasps the skeleton, and not the pulsating life, of existence. It deals with the mechanical relations of parts, and not with the organic articulation of a living whole. Formal logic lays its hand on a single part of an organism—and in the present particular case, I am thinking of the organism of intelligence—and calls it "A," and then on another, which it calls "B," and so on; and then views and demonstrates their mechanical relations. But the sense of "A" and "B" and of their relations, as instrumental to and members in a "life of the whole"—or as "particulars," through which a living, "concrete universal" realizes itself—is missed. The results reached are "correct" or "certain," as far as they go; but the concrete, vital truth of the case in hand is not reached.

> ". . . . . the parts in his hand he may hold and class,
> But the spiritual link is lost, alas!"
> —GOETHE'S *Faust*, Part i, Sc. 4.

NOTE 3, PAGE 147.

"We cannot naturalize the 'human mind' without presupposing that which is neither nature nor natural, though apart from it nature would not be—that of which the designation as 'mind,' as 'human,' as 'personal,' is of secondary importance, but which is eternal, self-determined, and thinks." Prof. T. H. Green, *Hume's Treatise on Human Nature*, Introduction, Vol. I. p. 299, London, 1874.

Note 4, Page 148.

This "trinity"—or, the concrete unity of human intelligence—is, nevertheless, and obviously, not absolute, because subject to the law of time and of temporal development. The mechanical relations of subject and object in human intelligence are, as we have seen, not only instrumental to such intelligence, but also constitute for it a (moving) limit; whence, also, as indicated in Lect. II., man, through his intelligence, only imitates, but does not fill, the *rôle* of the head of the universe. Or, as indicated in our text, man, through his intelligence, images, but does not reproduce, the divine trinity; he is "in the image" of God, but he is not God.

Note 5, Page 153.

We have seen that God, as Absolute Spirit, is the *absolute* correlative object to the relative human subject. By the principle of the necessary organic unity of subject and object in knowledge, it follows that the absolute nature of the latter must be reflected in the former. Grant that seeing God in this reflection alone is seeing him in a glass darkly. The doctrine of the divine Trinity, as founded on objective facts, illuminates human intelligence by setting before it an object which is seen to meet the ideal and essential requirements of the subject.

Note 6, Page 158.

It is very necessary never to forget that intelligence, life, and love are names of processes, activities, whose form is that of self-realization. They are not "products," except so long as the conditioning and creative processes are maintained.

NOTES TO LECTURE VI.

NOTE 1, PAGE 179.

An important part of the answer to the last question in the text falls, for treatment, under the subject of the next Lecture (VII).

NOTE 2, PAGE 181.

The text indicates the way in which theological mechanism and agnosticism plays into the hands of "scientific" agnosticism. For illustration, see H. Spencer's *First Principles,* Part I.

NOTE 3, PAGE 191.

When sense has abstracted from all but that which it can perceive or imagine, the residue is pure, brute world-dust, or "bare matter." But as the conception of this residue is the result of a work of abstraction, and not of a process of concrete comprehension and demonstration, it follows that the content or putative object of the conception is, taken by itself, unreal. What is taken for "bare matter" is but the phenomenon of the presence of an Absolute Life; and it is no wonder if the experimental "philosopher" sees in it something more than "mere matter," viz., the "potentiality of life."

NOTE 4, PAGE 192.

The *form* of the natural process is, I say, the form of self-realization. The potentiality, which stands at the beginning of the process, and the actuality, which crowns its end, have both the same definition. The movement of the process is thus, as it were, a movement from self to self.—On the connection between the New Testament Logos-doctrine and the cognate conceptions of earlier Greek philosophy, compare, among others, G. Teichmüller, *Geschichte des Begriffs der Parusie*, being vol. iii. of the author's *Aristotelische Forschungen*, Halle, 1873.

NOTE 5, PAGE 195.

In popular conceptions creation means the origination or sequence of the world in time, or, so-called "mechanical causation." The absurdities of this view I have not now to point out, nor have I to show how the essence of no truly causal or "creative" process is to be found in any temporal relation of sequence, whether "regular" and "invariable," or only "unique" or single. The fundamental element in the Christian conception of creation or causation is "redemption," as, in the philosophic conception, it is (with change of term, but not of meaning) "realization."

NOTE 6, PAGE 198.

And also as philosophy must and does conceive it. It is only an abstract, sense-conditioned "metaphysics," knowing none but physico-mechanical categories, that can see in the existence of the world a possible limit to the divine absoluteness and infinitude.

NOTES TO LECTURE VII.

NOTE 1, PAGE 214.

Tommaso Traina, *La morale di Herbert Spencer*, Torino, 1881, p. 11.

Note 2, Page 216.

The generic identity of what is here termed the "modern method," with the method which in ancient times was applied by Epicurus to the determination of moral questions, is expressly recognized by Prof. Traina, as indeed it is by all those who employ it.

Note 3, Page 217.

The epithet "metaphysical," as employed in the text, is applicable to any ostensibly philosophical inquiry, which is carried on with the use of uncriticised and uncomprehended categories.

Note 4, Page 230.

Compare note 4 to Lecture VI.

NOTES TO LECTURE VIII.

Note 1, Page 253.

O. Pfleiderer, *Religionsphilosophie auf geschichtlicher Grund-lage*, Berlin, 1878, p. 255: Religion is "*Sache des ganzen ungetheilten Geisteslebens.*"

Note 2, Page 255.

Take the first book on the nature of art, or the first biography of a great artist, which may come to hand, and, if the work be executed with the slightest touch of philosophic insight, you will meet with recognition or illustration of the truth implied in the phrase, "infinite personality of the artist." So, for instance, in one of the days when this course of lectures was in progress of delivery, I took up, by way of diversion, in an hour of leisure, a pamphlet entitled "*Das Musikalisch-Schöne: Vortrag von S. Bagge*, Basel, 1882 "; and there I found (p. 20) the truth expressed that the "original- ity" of the artist does not always date from the beginning of his physical existence, or individual consciousness, "but is developed in proportion as the artist becomes more firmly self-centred and conscious," *i. e.*, just in proportion as he de- velops his true personality, and becomes conscious of the same. And then I found the cases of the great masters of musical composition cited in a way to show that by the development of their personality they were not separated from the "spirit of their times," but were, the rather, identified with it;`it be- came their own spiritual substance and their works expressed it; and yet more, I found that the greater these artists were, so much the more was their "genius," their "inspiration," or the spiritual substance of their personality found to be uni- versal, or identical, not merely with the "spirit of their times," but with the "spirit of the world."—It is but a special ap- plication of the same truth that Ruskin has in mind, when he writes, "And so, finally, I now positively aver to you that no- body, in the graphic arts, can be quite rightly a master of anything, who is not master of everything!"(*Ariadne Florentina*, § 56).

Note 3, Page 256.

It is well known that Schelling found at one time in the philosophy of art the key, and the goal, for all philosophy.

See Schelling's *Akademisches Studium*, last Lecture; and *Transcendental Idealism*, by Prof. John Watson, in *Griggs's Philosophical Classics*, Chicago, 1882, chap. vii.

Note 4, Page 259.

From this judge the truth of such a statement as the follow ing:—" A religion is the philosophy of many; a philosophy is the religion of a few "; see F. Schultze, *Philosophie der Natur-wissenschaft.* 2. Theil, p. 418, Leipzig, 1882.

NOTE 5, PAGE 259.

Clemens Alexandr.: Faith = σύντομος γνῶσις; knowl-edge = πίστις ἐπιστημονική.

NOTE 6, PAGE 263.

And Aristotle may be taken as spokesman, not only for himself, but also for his spiritual progenitors, Plato and Soc-rates.

NOTE 7, PAGE 274.

There is indeed a so-called "reason," the "supersedure" of which is an indispensable condition, not only of spiritual salvation, or of the entrance into the heart of true religion, but also of the very existence of a truly positive and substan-tial philosophy itself. To this truth the whole history and the intrinsic nature, both of religion and philosophy, bear di-rect and abundant witness. The "reason" in question is one whose whole industry is absorbed in the detection of abstract contradictions and identities. Its spirit and its weapons are only mechanical and dead, not organic and living. It is ab-stract, and not concrete. All its logic is formal (see above, note 2, to Lect. V.), and not substantial. It is "metaphys-ical," dealing with "uncriticised categories" (see, again, note 3, to Lect. VII.), and not philosophical. Its "dialectic" is subjective, artificial, and superficial, not objective, contentful, and dictated by the essential nature of whatever may happen to be the subject of its inquiry. In short, and in fact, it is sense-conditioned *reason-ing*, and not sense-conditioning *rea-son*. The Germans distinguish these two under different names, calling the former *Verstand*, or "understanding,"—as though its characteristic work were best described as consisting in arresting, or bringing to a *standstill*, the living, moving process of reality, with a view to the separate, analytical examination of its parts and of the mode of their mechanical combination.   To the pure understanding, reason proper and all its objects—all living, organic wholes, and all vitally synthetic processes—are a mystery and incredible.   What reason, as a faculty whose seat is at the very centre of human experience, perceives, is imperceptible for the understanding.   Reason is the faculty of *insight, i. e.*, of essential, thoroughly and completely objective, or *experimental intelligence;* understanding is the faculty—if I may so express myself—of *outsight*, or of superficial, *empirical*, contingent *information* respecting external particulars, viewed in abstraction and separation from their essential and vital ground.

To men of the eighteenth century "reason" meant "understanding"; and the self-styled "Age of Reason" was, accordingly, not the age of true, concrete, vital *reason*—which, *in operation*, is simply equivalent to *experience taking true and complete and unprejudiced account of herself*—but rather the age of "*reasons*," of *argument* or alleging of "reasons" *pro and con*, and of consequent "doubt," respecting all that can be made a subject of argument—as everything can.—Let us not, then, confound the "reason" of Thomas Paine with the reason of Aristotle or of philosophy.   And, finally, let us not forget that, while any true revelation may be expected to transcend and confound the "reasonings" of an unvitalized "understanding," the very condition of its reception is the existence of reason, as also the condition of its effectiveness is that by it reason finds itself truly illuminated.

As matter of fact, philosophy has received illumination from the Christian consciousness in regard to its three fundamental conceptions, of the Absolute, of Nature, and of Man.

And let it be remembered that when I say "philosophy," I do not mean any mere jargon of words, nor any arbitrary collection of dogmatic opinions, but philosophic science—the science, in the strictest sense, of experience, and of experience taken in the deepest, most comprehensive, truest and richest sense of the term. Under the influence of the Christian consciousness, then, philosophy has come to a more definite and complete conception of the concrete, living unity of the Absolute, as Spirit. It has, secondly, been enabled to conceive and comprehend more distinctly the personal, living relation of the divine Logos to the world. It need hardly be said that, in proportion as this relation is distinctly conceived and its truth perceived, the possibility of a lapse into pure naturalism or pure pantheism is taken away. And, thirdly, Christianity has contributed to philosophy a fuller sense, and demonstration, of the truth that man is made perfect man, not through mere "imitation" of God, or "resemblance" to him, but "in one" with him, by an organic union which, so far from interfering with his freedom, is the very condition of his true—*i. e.,* his spiritual—freedom and of his true spiritual personality.

NOTE 8, PAGE 275.

Hegel, *Philosophie der Religion,* Part III.